Advance Rea

"This is a fascinating history the bygone world in which he operated so well. It is splendid, a tour de force. I loved it and couldn't put it down. The author's turns of phrase are compelling; for example, referring to the early 1900's: 'Women were less expressive then, more furled, better hushed.' It's not surprising that David Paton received Princeton's writing prize when he was an undergraduate."

Morton F. Goldberg, MD
Director Emeritus, Wilmer Eye Institute,
The Johns Hopkins Hospital

"Townley Paton was a great man and a very major asset for our discipline. I believe he did not realize how large a role he actually played in terms of surgical progress for the cornea blind of the world- currently at the level of around 180,000 transplants a year worldwide The book is superbly written, making the subject so much more appealing and approachable."

Claes H. Dohlman, MD PhD
Professor & Chairman, Department of Ophthalmology, Emeritus;
Harvard Medical School, Massachusetts Eye & Ear Infirmary

"This annotated biography of Dr. Townley Paton's behind-the-scene life broadens understanding of his characteristics and personality. The testament to his collaborative work with the inimitable Aida De Acosta Breckinridge is both informative and insightful. Be prepared for never-before published surprises, both amusing and poignant. In the end, providing the gift of sight through eye banking is elevated to a much deserved higher level of societal significance, and that cannot fail to increase public participation in its cause."

Patricia Dahl, Executive Director/CEO
The Eye-Bank for Sight Restoration

"David Paton has provided us with a panoramic account of the development of American eye banking. It is also an insightful look at American medicine and the context in which contemporary ophthalmology emerged."

Mark J. Mannis, MD FACS, Professor and Chair
Department of Ophthalmology & Vision Science,
University of California Davis Eye Center, Sacramento, CA

"The saga of creating the world's first true tissue bank required the right combination of human strengths for a difficult challenge and a successful outcome. Dr. Townley Paton's weaknesses are not avoided in this frank portrayal of a partially gifted, yet partially impaired man of clinical science. The insight of the author provides off-beat explanations of the peculiarities of Townley and his father and the justification for the under-recognition of their important contributions — which did not bother either doctor in the slightest. Their wives were less forgiving. The importance of innovation, perseverance and modesty in professional and personal accomplishments were strong traits in Townley, but by far his most important contribution was the gift of eye-banking to an eventually grateful surgical specialty. The background of the early Johns Hopkins Hospital is an added bonus."

Bruce E. Spivey, MD MS M.Ed.
Immediate Past President, International Council of Ophthalmology
Founding CEO, American Academy of Ophthalmology,
Chairman, Pacific Vision Foundation

"The text is the perfect balance between medical and the non-medical reading public, reflecting a creative mind and the gift of story-telling– a biography accomplished with aplomb."

Larry Schwab, M Associate
Professor of Ophthalmology,
West Virginia University

"The world now takes tissue transplantation for granted as a medical event occurring many times each day. David Paton bestows the insider's view of a real medical saga—the interplay of personal, societal, medical, and ethical forces that led to the world's first modern eye bank. This innovation in turn facilitated a revolution in our approach to corneal blindness. And he does so not through a dry recitation of science and facts, but weaving into the story's fabric the history, society, and personalities of the time. We learn of Townley Paton's late night drives to electrocutions in Sing Sing prison and journeys to visit the Shah of Iran. And we come to realize the global impact on millions of individual lives of one man's stoic determination and courage."

David W. Parke II, MD
CEO American Academy of Ophthalmology

"It's a marvelous story which draws the reader in, so personal, reflective and warm. The description of setting up the formal mechanism of an eye bank, both from the administrative and the medical perspective, is riveting and daunting."

Patricia Aiken O'Neill, EBAA Former President/CEO

"David Paton, himself a leader and innovator in eye surgery, reminisces about the medical Brahmins of American ophthalmology. Through insider anecdotes, and a few family secrets, he tells how eye banking began with the humility and humanity of a clinical hero who made a lasting difference to corneal transplantation."

Kirk R. Wilhelmus,, MD PhD
Professor Emeritus, Baylor College of Medicine; co-producer with
D. Townley Paton, 1999 documentary:
"Pathos and Nobility: The Birth of Eye Banks."

"Dr. Townley Paton transformed the lives of millions of cornea-blind individuals in the United States and around the world. He also established standards and practices that have helped shape organ and tissue donation, touching the lives of millions more. David Paton's intimate access to this ophthalmic trailblazer, as his son and his protégé, offers an unparalleled perspective on the man and his work."

Kevin P. Corcoran, President/CEO EBAA

"I owe a great deal to my close personal and professional association with Townley Paton who was twelve years senior to me and one of my most valued mentors. In the 1940s I became an instructor in his weekly clinics for ophthalmologists seeking to learn keratoplasty. Finally, in 1961 I was able to return the teaching favor by helping Townley to adapt to microsurgery. His Eye-Bank represents a huge step in the history of keratoplasty for which ophthalmology and the world owe him so much. Congratulations for this great accomplishment and tribute to Townley."

Richard C. Troutman, MD FACS DSc (hon.),
Former Professor and Head of Ophthalmology at SUNY Downstate

*Feb 14, 2017
To my dear
Cousin Betty
with love from
David*

INSIGHT

Richard Townley Paton MD
and the
World's First Eye Bank

An Annotated Biography by His Son
David Paton, MD

Joan told me I had NOT sent you this book and you would like to read it — I hope it has some memorable bits.

INSIGHT. R. Townley Paton and the World's First Eye Bank
Copyright © 2016 by David Paton MD. Printed in the United States of America.
Create Space Publishing Services, c/o Amazon, Inc.
Cover Painting: William Draper, ca. 1961, owned by the Paton Family
Cover Design: conceived by David Townley Paton; completed by Pierce Rosen-Keith
Editor: Nancy Hardin for the primary text
Editorial coordination: Tom Clavin
Biographical design: Phil Keith
ISBN-13: 978-1530364534
ISBN-10: 1530364531
First Edition: July 2016

This book is dedicated to the memory of Aida de Acosta Root Breckinridge whose indispensible participation in founding the first eye bank helped assure its survival as the primary model for countless eye banks thereafter.

What better introduction to the story than a poem written by Patricia Aiken O'Neill, former President and CEO of the Eye Bank Association of America:

SIGHTS UNSEEN

Recorded thoughts and images
preserve our immortality,
defining fashion and movements
as feckless as the people
who inhabited them:
A fixed smile, a starched collar,
a stiff upper lip
bespeak a moment only,
not that life and time.
The next generation holds onto them
finding a familiar bosom
from which to draw succor.
But memories weaken,
leaving only one dimension
on which to draw,
wondering what's on the other side,
the one away from the lens,
the words left unspoken.
Stories from people I never knew,
but faintly recognize
touch me.
Lost to any other touch
they form a picture of people
as a remnant of time.
Their photos paint stories
to explain events and times
I never witnessed
But are my responsibility to pass on.

CONTENTS

Preface..	i
Prologue: Last Rights..	1
Chapter 1: The Essence...	9
Chapter 2: Old Blue Genes..	18
Chapter 3: Townley and His People................................	33
Chapter 4: Malignant Malaise.....................................	52
Chapter 5: Roster of Revolution..................................	68
Chapter 6: Copacetic Minds.......................................	87
Chapter 7: Career Crux...	104
Chapter 8: Duo of Do-ers...	125
Chapter 9: A Wilmer Eye Man......................................	146
Chapter 10: The Transformative City..............................	164
Chapter 11: Private Lives..	184
Chapter 12: The Quartermaster....................................	197
Chapter 13: The Hyphenated Bank..................................	215
Chapter 14: Happiness Gets Complicated...........................	237
Chapter 15: Years of Thanksgiving................................	252
Chapter 16: Denouement...	268
Epilogue: Eyes of the World......................................	281
Appendix I...	293
Appendix II..	299
Acknowledgments..	302
Index..	314

PREFACE

While the author of this delightfully contrapuntal book insisted that he is not to be acknowledged in this preface, it is impossible for me not to do so. The scion of a medically (and otherwise) illustrious family, he is like many of his family's ancestors, accomplished, innovative, and thoroughly thoughtful, tying together concepts and institutions rarely linked in the same breath.

This ode to David Paton's father goes well beyond filial duty, and brings together the workings (good and bad) of family influences (nature and nurture), luck, need and circumstance. In this particular instance, and against formidable odds, the result was the founding of one of the most influential institutions in modern medicine, the "eye bank," and an appreciation of how one of the most individualized, patient-centric curative procedures in all of medicine, corneal (and organ) transplantation, depends in large part on selfless community action more commonly associated with public health.

Townley Paton was one of the earliest corneal surgery enthusiasts in the United States. Because one actually uses only the clear, minimally vascularized cornea in the front of the eye, it was possible to transplant the cornea with much less risk of immunologic rejection than initially confounded the transplantation of more heavily vascularized organs. On a large scale, the cornea is probably the first human tissue ever successfully transplanted from one individual to another, and therefore the forerunner of modern day transplantation of many living human tissues and certain body parts

PREFACE

with their requirements for tissue matching, and suppression of the inevitable rejection mounted by the recipient's immune system.

But the early promise of corneal transplantation faced a major obstacle (and, to some degree, still does): the availability of donor corneas. Successful corneal transplantation was exquisitely choreographed: the patient had to be both known and readily available as soon as an eye was freshly obtained for its cornea; and the eye had to be obtained as soon after death as possible, as its viability rapidly declined. But while eye banks nowadays have expanded to include other tissues and to provide corneas efficiently, they accommodate large segments of society by advance directives or by the deceased nearest of kin at the time of death. Modern eye banks can now sustain such tissues long enough to transport them worldwide. While now common, Paton established the first such "eye bank," in New York, in 1944, despite negative public and professional opinions. Indeed, he was personally hampered by the AMA Code of Ethics from publicly advocating for its support; therefore much of the promotional responsibility fell upon his collaborator, Aida Breckinridge, who had been instrumental in the founding of Johns Hopkins' Wilmer Eye Institute.

The transplant situation has changed radically in large part because of Dr. Paton's passionate pioneering work, and the work of those he enlisted in his efforts. So much so that we now take organ transplantation for granted, when it was a little over half a century ago anything but. Even more profoundly a change, as David Paton points out, is the way in which most people both accept, and many donate, their own corneas and their organs to be used upon their death, helping people they have never known but whose lives will be immensely benefited. In many countries, and in many states in the

PREFACE

U.S., all one need do to contribute one's components is to acknowledge this intended generosity on the back of a driver's license. People of all faiths and creeds have made this generous donation. In an irony the author takes pains to explain, Townley Paton the apostle of tissue donation, refused to donate the eyes of a beloved daughter who died in a tragic accident, but did donate his own. That strange fact is eventually accounted for with a diagnostic solution that surely only a physician and well-read reader might discover.

As David Paton insightfully notes, "public health," in which communities organize efforts to benefit everyone at large without consideration of wealth or standing, is about as remote from the surgical use of individually donated and transplanted human corneas as any two medical approaches could be. Yet the latter, at its core, is the beneficiary of exactly the same participatory societal impulse to "community effort." Without the selfless donation of one's corneas (and often one's organs as well) for the great benefit of unknown others, modern transplant surgery, with all its technical wizardry, could not exist. Tens of thousands of individuals benefit every year from sight-restoring corneal transplantation, and many more from the donation of other organs.

How far we've come since Townley Paton's efforts is told with pride, helpfully embroidered with fascinating anecdotes, as written by his accomplished son.

Alfred Sommer MD MHS
Dean Emeritus, Johns Hopkins Bloomberg School of Public Health;
Distinguished Professor and Gilman Scholar; Professor of Ophthalmology,
Professor of Epidemiology and International Health, Johns Hopkins University

PROLOGUE: LAST RIGHTS

More horrible than the curse in a dead man's eye.
"The Rime of the Ancient Mariner," Samuel Taylor Coleridge, 1772-1834

Early in 1944 in Manhattan and in the dead of night, a lone man finds his parked car in a crowded lot and backs onto an empty street. He drives west to the highway that goes north, parallel to the Hudson River. From here to his destination, his imagination envisions the regional land as a memorial to human death. Not far across the river is where a duel led to the death of Alexander Hamilton. The man for whom the river was named either froze to death in a small boat up the river or was murdered in cold blood by a mutinous crew. Now he is crossing a bridge from Manhattan to Queens where a town crier drowned trying to warn of an approaching enemy army. Further along comes White Plains where that same army in another year shot to death several hundred Americans. Death has been everywhere—and all too meaningless.

At last the driver finishes the final mile to Ossining, a small town on the river's eastern shore. It harbors Sing Sing prison, a correctional penitentiary of small-windowed brick monstrosities crowded within a 30-foot-high circumferential concrete wall dotted with guard towers. Almost two thousand prisoners live in those buildings, each having been taken "up the river" to serve "hard time" generally measured in years. Some will "sing," in hope of improving their lot by "spilling the beans" on fellow criminals still "on the outside." Death has been a part of their game on the outside, and on the inside over the years hundreds have been executed–legal human killing–with another coming up tonight.

INSIGHT

The driver arrives at the prison wall, and sits in the car waiting for the gate to be opened. He is a 43-year-old doctor, an eye surgeon, who has come to Sing Sing because he received a message that a death is scheduled at the usual time. Again he wonders why they don't do this in daylight instead of Thursday nights at eleven. Grotesque as it may sound, Dr. Townley Paton is here to remove the eyes from a prisoner who has consented to post-mortem surgery.

The gate opens. A guard waves the eye doctor into the prison compound. The gate closes with a creaky noise of steel. He parks near the smallest cell block, the Death House. He grabs a small handbag from the rider's seat and walks to the nearest building, now joined by an interior guard who leads him through the secure entry and down an empty corridor to a lighted "waiting room." Others have assembled in its small space, state witnesses. There is an interior window where these observers have a close-up look at "The Chair"— the final resting place for hundreds of prisoners over the years. Paton's private guard is nonchalant, fat and smiley.

The warden arrives, remembers the eye doctor, shakes hands, "Hello, again." They sit as the guard and the others sit, some stand. The doctor small-talks knowing the answer to his question, "Do these fellows get their favorite dinner the evening before …?" The warden nods benevolently, "Sure do."

The criminal is "entered" in handcuffs and leg irons. He has three guards of his own — you never know. The official observers exchange muffled words. Small talk. Two of the guards bind the fellow to The Chair with nine broad leather bands, neck to ankles.

LAST RIGHTS

"He killed three people," the warden says—an off-hand comment meant for the doctor to hear. Now more directed to that principal visitor: "It's the law of the jungle, Doc. An eye-for-an-eye, you might say." He shakes his head, satisfied with his cleverness. Paton wonders if he planned to say that when driving back to the prison tonight for this evening's grim performance.

The fact is, this event is more significant than the warden's calming humor suggests. Paton feels better with that thought. This is to be a generous event but unworldly! That's the word he wanted, "unworldly."

The prisoner looks in his 20s. One hand is not fastened. The third guard hands him a cup for a last drink in the moments before final readiness.

"A drug?" The warden shakes his head, "Water." The doctor thinks there should have been a goodbye slug in the stirrup cup. But this is no horseback ride, nor a hospital discharge. This guy is not a deserving patient.

The murderer swigs, then spits out the single gulp. A final defiance. An awful smile. Now there's a hush. The observers are leaning forward, frozen. Respectfulness? The fellow's arm is secured.

A priest enters. He drones last rites. Latin. Now he stands aside. What if the prisoner were to ask, "Speak so I can understand. Go slow." No sign of appreciation for the priest's ministrations. Two guards drench the fellow's head with wet sponges. A wired helmet is strapped to the fellow's head. The fat guard next to Paton's seat is standing, slouched—the body language of déjà vu. He rolls a tooth pick and picks his teeth. Nonchalance.

INSIGHT

Flickers, testings. Someone is still fiddling with the lights. Paton sits straighter. Lights stay dim. Paton knows that's to soften reality--good murder manners. The man's expression is obscured by shadow and helmet straps. A dead space of time.

Something clicks. A disconnect? More dead space. Then, faintly: zzzzzzzzzzzzz, ZZZZZZZZZZZZ.[1] Maybe three seconds each. The prisoner is grossly tensed, like he's holding a pose. Then he goes limp.

It's over.

The full lighting returns. A last act without applause. Paton is thinking that it's the ultimate retaliation for abominable sin. But saying "abominable" to himself turns into "abdominal." Amusingly enough, the good doctor has a stumbling tongue even without saying the word. Someone among the witnesses heaves a sigh. A thought pause. Paton recalls the warden's lecture-sentence at his first Sing Sing visit, "Electrocution is a warning to others that justice calls for drastic measures."

The doctor follows in the wake of the prisoner's body now on a gurney being rolled to the autopsy room, pushed by an aide. His obese private guard takes the liberty to express his opinion: "Good riddance!" Paton nods to be polite — his prison manners — hoping to be asked for the next time.

The body is ashen, lashed again, this time to the gurney to keep it from rolling off. Both hands are tied to keep from dangling. The small room wreaks with disinfectant, but a fly is alive and buzzing, sounding almost electric. Paton opens his small bag, removes and opens a kit of hand instruments, turns to the prisoner's body and deftly removes the dead man's eyes. It takes a few minutes. The guard is no longer nonchalant, now as ashen as the deceased, visibly nauseated.

Dr. Paton puts the eyes into small bottles and screws on the tops. He places the bottles in the black bag. To the queasy guard: "You'll feel better soon. These eye-outs take some getting used to."

Paton finds his car in the darkness near the concrete wall. Off he goes with his small bag and bottled eyes. He feels philosophically disposed, as often happens on the road home. As he drives away, he speaks soundlessly to himself in souvenirs of thought from a new batch of visual images—call it his "darkness enlightenment." It's for a cause. But it's not pleasant being thought a body marauder. His variant act of "retrieving eyes" goes beyond the indecent to meet a human need.

In a few minutes, passing Tarrytown, he notices a roadside sign with an arrow pointing to the village of Sleepy Hollow. The sign reminds that a character named Ichabod Crane[2] was thrown from his horse when struck in the face with a severed head thrown at him by a galloping headless horseman — a 19th century horror story. Paton thinks about legal murder and now about Irving's horrifying decapitation tale. He wonders, could that street sign be a bad omen? Could he be facing an Ichabod disaster from removing prisoners' eyeballs? Threats come to mind. Someone says, "He deals in human trophies." Someone else: "He does what no religion would permit." And then, "Taking out two eyes are two wrongs that don't make a right." At this late night spooky hour there is no distinction between what he has been told and what he imagines, but the disquieting mood is entirely real. "That doctor should lose his medical license!"

INSIGHT

Back in Manhattan after parking the car and walking to his apartment building, he feels more upbeat, "Sticks and stones..." but he interrupts himself with the classic platitude, "No good deed goes unpunished." He takes the elevator to the eighth floor.

As previously, he puts the bottled eyes in the kitchen refrigerator to keep them fresh for surgery later this morning, then takes the few remaining hours for sleep. The alarm wakes him. On surgery days, he is always first in the kitchen. This was not a typical morning. Edna, the family's Finnish cook, opens the refrigerator, sees two human eyes staring at her from their bottles. She muffles a cry. Her revulsion is intolerable. She decides to quit this barbaric household.

Paton's wife, Helen perennial defender of her husband, tries talking Edna from quitting. She certainly has no understanding of why this eye surgeon has brought home such trophies and what he will do with them. Dr. Paton starts an explanation, but it is not learning time for Edna. Ultimately Helen may have prevailed. (Here the family story meets with mixed outcomes from Edna's threat to leave.)

The surgeon puts the two bottles in his black bag and takes a taxi to the Manhattan Eye, Ear and Throat Hospital on 64th Street near 2nd Avenue. Despite his fatigue, he is upbeat. Townley Paton generally keeps his own counsel. It is enough to think that today, two more blind people, each almost totally blind, will have the possibility

LAST RIGHTS

of their eyesight being restored, thanks to the contribution of a prisoner's pledge that the doctor himself had instigated at Sing Sing.[3]

NOTES TO PROLOGUE

1. On June 3, 1944, a 24-year-old New Yorker by the name of Louis Parisi was executed at Sing Sing.
2. Washington Irving authored "The Legend of Sleepy Hollow," published in 1820.
3. The story of Sing Sing's prisoner collaboration is true and important in portraying the challenge Paton faced in obtaining human donor eyes for corneal transplantation, but today--as will be covered in later chapters--only the corneas are removed from donor eyes, leaving the eyes quite as normal in appearance as

INSIGHT

they would be had a pair of soft contact lenses been removed by the eye bank technician. Therefore, the intent of the factual Prologue sets the scene in the 1940s when eye banking — in the minds of some — was worse than grave-robbing. For further prison information see Teeters, NK: *Sing Sing Prison Electrocutions, 1881-1963*. Pamphlet Ossining Historical Society, Ossining, 1989.

CHAPTER 1: THE ESSENCE

An eye full of gentle salutations-and soft responses.
"Shandy," Laurence Sterne

A modest and self-effacing man, Richard Townley Paton was nonetheless a pivotal figure in 20th century medicine, for in 1944 he founded the world's first eye bank. It was the predecessor and model for a host of other eye banks, thus establishing the way for tens of thousands of sight-restoring surgeries worldwide each year. With eye banks solving the supply-side dilemma, corneal surgery could eventually become the leading cure for global blindness. In turn, that use of living donor tissue has helped to inspire numerous other human donor tissue uses in virtually all variants of surgery. No previous book has been written for the public to provide an extended account of how eye banking evolved and what it has become as a result of the global invigoration of corneal surgery.

Over the ensuing decades, as his leadership in eye banking developed nationally and internationally and as its social and technical aspects were assimilated and progressively refined, R. Townley Paton became recognized as the "Father of Eye Banking."[1] His companion in that undertaking, Aida Breckinridge, is highly acclaimed in the pages that follow, for she had rare talents in organizational and fundraising skills essential to the goal. The doctor with the dream and the responsibility for creating the system that has been emulated globally remains almost unknown beyond the world of ophthalmology—a fact that did not disturb him in the slightest but did not escape the notice of his watchful wife, Helen, and she had a point.

INSIGHT

The doctor and his wife had a love affair that never lost its bloom. There are no tales of juicy entanglements nor of any struggle to "find oneself" in this world fraught with temptation and self-reproach. Theirs were endlessly devoted years of mutual support and family contentment with few problems over the decades they were together. What a crashing bore that doctor must have been!

But he wasn't. And a novelist's deprivation can be a biographer's picnic in probing beneath a smooth surface into depths- with facts as food and truth for easy digestion. Two previously undiagnosed pathologies are associated with the bio-protagonist, and an observation about the potential identity of eye banking constitute a total of three new adjuncts to Dr. Paton's story, both personal and social. These come individually much later in the book.

However, the temptation that exists for all biographers is the introduction of relevant fiction to help dramatize or deny certain realities, and to form a good story out of some seemingly disparate happenings by means of the Pinocchio paradox dropped upon the reader. To put it clearly, this writer will have no elongating nose from the only very occasional small bridge that ties together hard facts. Such interpretation will be expressed not as fact but as logical deduction. Admittedly, however, this writer tends to write too densely for speed-readers, and the intended meaning of the text is better understood if the reader were to use his paired eyes like a single forefinger to guide his glance over the anomalies of composition.
Townley Paton had a similar wording complexity even with formal notes, but it would always be wrapped in friendly schmoozing. Finally, be it said to undertake a serious book of this nature, there has to be the occasional banter of straight-faced fun to break the monotony of old history.

THE ESSENCE

A large cache of old records, letters, photographs and family tree notations have been carefully reviewed. In some the handwriting was prohibitory but fortunately not for the key ancestors. About seventy old books from Paton's personal and medical trove of memorabilia have proven helpful in assembling family stories that bear upon his history. This accounting will turn quite often to peripheral topics to capture what American social writer and philosopher Eric Hoffer[2] refers to as "the temper of our time," here to reflect the mores, societal environment and sciences that characterized the period in which Paton lived, for these contextual realities help explain his path and his choices.

An annotated biography of the nature intended consists of a factual account fully dressed in related historical paraphernalia that in itself seems to the writer important to share. Part of the challenge in writing Townley Paton's biography is the fact that he neither wrote nor said much about himself other than in family chatter and patient-care correspondence. He had his reasons, but they were difficult to discover. He had no diary and he must not have perceived any need for documenting his thoughts beyond those in the dialect of medicine. One of his books is a medical text on the subject of corneal surgery in which he reviews 347 of his own transplant cases.[3] In that 280-page book he used the pronoun "I" once and then only in the Preface. Such restraint testifies to a well-buried ego and suggests someone quite immune to the seductions of the limelight.

INSIGHT

Moreover, his avoidance of references to himself holds a clue to an inviolate sense of privacy. His career dedication became an indisputable passion, a word usually confined to emotional types with determinations of iron. He does not seem to fit that description of abundant emotional drive until one learns that it is there but insulated from public observation by a stiff upper lip tradition linked to a family tenet that Paton men never cry.

The reason for these tedious explanations is the perceived need for more precision than required of most biographers because the subject of this biography was this author's father, a detail that should not muddy the water but is necessary to point out. In fact, several times before, this writer has published sketchy biographical information about his father. There was no one else with the facts of his professional life to do him justice, as this book will clarify. It was not right for his identity to be left as frozen as the smile on his portrait, though it now means uncovering complexities that bore upon his life and hid a significant degree of his intellectual ambition.

Additionally, he had conflicts he kept within himself which are brought to the surface for the first time in this book. These reveal the frustrations of a stoic and uncomplaining man, metaphorically in fencing matches with a masked opponent. He would forgive these revelations today, for they are not transgressions but character-shaping endurances. What he accomplished needs no apologies, only appropriate praise. He was a happy warrior, as that expression is applied to a fighter of his own unspoken issues, and he was a gentleman of inordinate kindness.

Townley Paton was this author's homebody-hero, and due to a copycat career (cornea surgeon) it should be easier for the son

THE ESSENCE

to recount the medical as well as the social and personal components of his father's story. From this point on, Dr. Townley Paton will be referred to as "Townley," a privilege denied his children but now, strangely enough, providing a healthy sense of distance by its unaccustomed familiarity. To a degree beyond that found in most other biographies, this one is unusually dependent upon family history influences as well as numerous close-by people who created an environment of medical contagion. It infused him from an early age. Townley lived his entire life in a hotbed of Medicine in revolution. It lit a fire within that was never extinguished. Much attention will be given to the environment and the faculty that created — arguably — the greatest medical trams-formation ever to arise at a known location and by a small group of activists within a short period of years. That famous eruption occurred in the family's backyard and to an extent he had a share of its precipitating genes and nurturing environment. The nature and nurture of Townley were key to accomplishments he later achieved against the odds and in conflict with the views of laymen and even of medical people, some of whom were colleagues who foresaw no need for an eye bank and did not hesitate to say so.

The best way to introduce eye banking *per se* is to tell a typical story about how it serves those who are blind from corneas with permanently lost transparency by providing a donor cornea and thereby restoring the lost eyesight. What follows is a fictional, yet typical, patient history presented as it might be found in any eye bank brochure across the country and used as a means of humanizing eye bank purposes:

In the spring of 1940 in Brooklyn, New York, a 30-year-old woman was on a morning walk that led her beneath scaffolding at the exact moment when a worker aloft knocked over a container of tar-containing sealant which

INSIGHT

poured down upon her head, covering hair, face and eyes with a mordent black sludge. She received prompt medical care, which helped limit further eye damage, but when the other consequences of this disaster were healed, her eyesight was all but gone.

There was almost no chance she would be contradicted. Under the usual circumstances in mid-20th century medicine, that conclusion was statistically correct and emotionally devastating. She soon learned there were thousands of others in New York and millions of others worldwide whose futures were equally curtailed from a wide assortment of blindness causes. Having such "virtual company" did not diminish her misery; it merely confirmed the reality of an horrendous predicament. Somehow, with support from friends and family she managed to cope—as a blind dependent stripped of a once-promising future. Even her children had become strangers at her home, for they now lived with her ex-husband.

On a memorable day in 1946, a full six years after the accident, her ophthalmologist referred her to the Manhattan Eye, Ear & Throat Hospital, where she was seen by a corneal transplant surgeon. He told her that an eye operation might restore vision to the left eye, the right eye being too damaged for a comparable hope. Dr. Paton explained what a corneal transplant operation entailed, and although he cautioned that it might not be successful, he was nevertheless optimistic about a chance for vision improvement. He said it would be necessary to put her name on a waiting list for availability of tissue for transplantation thanks to an eye that had been donated to the New York Eye-Bank.

After a few weeks of apprehension on her part, a call came that a donor eye was available. She would never know anything about the cornea donor, but here it can be told that the donor was a Haitian-born New York policeman killed the previous day. He had been on motorcycle patrol when a

THE ESSENCE

speeding car crossing 125th Street against a yellow light forced his bike to crash into a solid balustrade used for restricting traffic to a single lane before an entryway to the Triborough Bridge. His motorcycle was totaled as momentum thrust his body forward into the kinetics of the collision. Death was immediate.

Knowing the risks of life as a police officer, the deceased had once told his wife about a briefing his squad had been given regarding the use of eyes for surgery donated by individuals who had recently died of almost any cause. Permission was to be obtained from the nearest of kin. His wife, though beside herself with grief, was an intelligent and community-oriented person who realized her husband's eyes could be the last but the greatest contributions any person could make to someone else, even a complete stranger. She signed the permission form. The police officer's eyes were obtained by an eye doctor participating in the work of the Eye-Bank, and her ophthalmologist was given priority scheduling to perform the operation.

The operation was performed the following morning. As a result and following over several months of post-operative care, the 36-year-old lawyer's left eye was restored to almost perfect vision. This was a gift of science and society that she would always regard as a miraculous example of human caring–not a solo act but a collaborative one on the part of numerous participants and most especially the thoughtfulness of an anonymous donor. In addition, thanks to that donor, the same benefit also went to the fortunate recipient of the other donor eye. Another fortunate person obtained what in 1946 was an almost unprecedented gift as the tragedy of an unnecessary death was turned into a magical outcome for two blind individuals brought back into the sighted world.

Turning now to the instigator of eye banking, if anyone were to say admiringly to Townley that his contribution to world blindness

INSIGHT

was a work deserving the ultimate in praise, he would have simply dodged the politesse of thanks with a constructive response such as saying with a smile, "Good, then you are ready to make the pledge, and I'll read it over to be sure you have agreed to willing us both eyes. That way, you only have to make the pledge once." It never mattered if his humor was too banal. His own eyes and his pleasant smile told his truth and his sincerity.

Now that the book has begun with two so-called "eyeball anecdotes," it is time to start the first of many steps in the process of teasing out an answer to the question of "Who exactly was Richard Townley Paton?" by examining some of Townley's forebears.

THE ESSENCE

NOTES TO CHAPTER 1:

1. Title asserted by Dr. A. E. Maumenee in: Paton, R.T.: "History of Corneal Transplantation. From Advances in Keratoplasty." *Internat. Ophthal. Clinic.*, Summer 1970, Vol. 10, No. 2, p.186, Little, Brown and Company, Boston.
2. Hoffer, E.: *The Temper of Our Time*. Buccaneer Books, 1967.
3. Paton, R.T.: *Keratoplasty*. McGraw-Hill, New York, 1955.

CHAPTER 2: OLD BLUE GENES

It seems to me that man with all his noble qualities still bears in his bodily frame the indelible stamp of his lowly origin. "The Descent of Man," Charles R. Darwin, 1809-1882

Townley was a third-generation blue-eyed male who spoke less about himself than what came from his expressive eyes that offered megabytes of unscripted message substituting for the articulate wording that some might have expected of a true trailblazer. The clues to his character and personality may have better hints from his genetic background than from his ocular sign language. At least, one can hope so.

It is common knowledge that the basic creature that each of us is comes from the silence of our genes that we share semi-anonymously. The "semi" reminds that every individual has a gene pool with a gene content that has statistical possibilities but no certainties other than the inheritance of obvious features such as an aquiline nose, an under-slung jaw, or a widow's peak that have appeared in former family members. Further, the same genes passed to one person may be used to different effect by someone else who has other modifying genes. By no means does a would-be medical doctor inherit a ready-made package of genes for doctoring, but they can become very useful or very troubling.

It remains for the future to better exploit the individual's genealogy, but even today research scientists are using visual details of the faces in young children to predict their adult appearance.[1] Similarly, but with much more complexity, in the future genetic inheritance will become more predictable of future manifestations. For now the best one can do with family histories recorded with scant individual specificity is to identify likelihoods by focusing upon the observation of common traits. Overestimation of gene effect probability is easily adapted to boast of one's worthy background, for surely too little is known of the forgotten scoundrels.

Everyone has an inheritance worthy of examination — a personal pedigree — and those who may appear to be the least advantaged in the society in which they live could have had the most admirable forebears who were heroes within their own environmental confines. Therefore, the best that can be done by observation of one's family tree is to find heritable characteristics in some degree of abundance, especially in the bloodline of the person in question. As to Townley's family tree, he was an untargeted person in two long gene chains containing all known forebears. They were compiled over many years as the intermittent homework of dutiful and intellectually responsible family women whose records are adroit, but free of ancillary information except for those who made names for themselves.[2]

In the early 20th century, these discerning women worked from handwritten lists and notes sometimes matched with tintype photographs. As time passed, the records and the photos improved with technique and technology, thanks eventually to the Brownie camera. By the latter part of the 20th century, the men and women pictured actually began to smile at the camera. Thankfully, the work of two women in the family was eventually typed and re-filed in boxes, ultimately ending up in moldy suitcases. That mass of often unarranged information has not been dealt with as a whole, only used superficially now and then to settle bets or disprove wild theories, such as when baldness actually began in someone usually photographed with a hat on his head. This Townley biography has offered a chance to benefit from those charts and papers to find family tree threads that may have structured the fabric of his mind and — -in the romantic vernacular of a former century — the ambitions of his heart. If that has a poetic sound, it is to dodge the dry and unavailable science that need not be required to characterize Townley's backlog of favorable tendencies in the context of his social expectations.

Townley's tree is largely rooted in southeast Scotland and northwest England, in the origins of the Patons and the Towneleys (as it was then spelled), respectively. Both of those locations were populated in the Stone Age, but the family pathways were not recorded until somewhere between the 10th to 12th centuries, depending on the side of the family being studied. Family sequences were not well specified for some listed names until the 13th century. Specific genetic traits have been traced over as many as six preceding generations[3] but are thought to continue their power indefinitely unless some genetic disabilities were to arise.

To generalize, both Patons and Towneleys produced scrappy men with warrior intents, some with known rank in clans that led to rewards from landowners and/or a monarch or two. The Patons were evidently the more unruly, but over several centuries and up to the current one in Edinburgh, the name Paton became almost as common there as self-deprecating humor, tartan kilts and tight wallets. At the same time the name Towneley, generally the more devout of the two family lines, was being bandied about among other townsfolk in Burnley, England. Neither group seems likely to have included people who sat still and kept quiet. They were Type A in abilities, although some were B in conduct, to use a grade system of the 1950s.

Eventually, the rowdies calmed down as wars yielded to government rule and the Towneley bloodline shifted to an assortment of farmers and merchants, upon a few of whom were bestowed titles, for having pleased the king. The Paton line was less well identified but remained centered in Scotland until Townley Paton's ancestors left for America in the 19th century.

Fortunately, the Towneley ancestors were especially well documented. [4] Accountable from the days of William the Conqueror, there was a long bloodline of English males with the last name of Towneley, later spelled Townley. The early Towneleys were staunch Roman Catholics whose women not infrequently "took the veil." [5] At least one offspring became ordained as a priest in 1636 at Valladolid, Spain, then returned two years later to his family home at Towneley Hall. He refused to renounce the foreign version of his Christian

Towneley Hall.

faith, and thus was imprisoned for three years by unsympathetic Anglican authorities who finally put him to death for the crime of being ordained "beyond seas." Over the ensuing centuries, Towneleys were belligerent Catholic fighters for their causes that usually were those of their royal leaders—at least until the 19th century when Townley became the family's typical middle name, appended to various surnames such as Halsey, Haines, and Wilder.

An example of a religious but brash gene-donor ancestor is Sampson Vryling Stoddard Wilder, born in 1781.[6] Townley's maternal great-great-grandfather and well within the known stretch of genetic influences. Because of family misfortunes and the death of his father when the boy was only ten, Wilder had an early life that shaped him into a self-made man using his boundless initiative in acquiring considerable wealth. As an adult, he was an ardent evangelical Christian while still able to enjoy what today might be called the elegant life of an industrious businessman, and a man of considerable moxie, manners and ingenuity.

Among various services he performed during the presidency of James Madison, Wilder had the honor of representing his country at the second marriage of Emperor Napoleon Bonaparte.[7] The pugnacious dictator had "divorced himself" from Josephine for her inability to bear him sons. A few months thereafter, when his army had driven the Austrian Emperor Francis from Schonbrunn Castle, his home, Napoleon took over the castle and selected for himself the bedroom of the Emperor's daughter, the comely Maria Louise Hapsburg, whose portrait still hung over the fireplace. Napoleon (according to Wilder) was attracted to her beauty. She was from a proper enough family, thus he sent word to her father that he wished his daughter to become his second wife, a picture bride he would accept without even meeting her, which was at the very least a fine compliment to the portrait painter.

At first, her father noted that the blood of forebears of emperors and queens from several generations flowed in his daughter's veins, whereas the blood of Napoleon did not contain, as Wilder pointed out, the same "ancient and distinguished" lineage. Even in those days a bloodline of commendable inheritance was given much credence, and the fact that Napoleon was the Austrians' primary enemy was of less importance than the blood from which he had sprung. Emperor Francis rejected Napoleon's first offer but a political deal was then made, leading to a short-term improvement in the relationship of Austria with France and to immediate wedding preparations.

Because of the sudden illness of the American ambassador, Wilder was asked by the Napoleon-sized[8] but not Napoleon-tempered President James Madison to represent him and the United States at the Emperor's wedding scheduled to take place in Paris on April 2, 1810. Wilder, who happened to enjoy formal dress, was delighted to attend as the official representative of his country. In fact, he made his appearance in full court costume, from "golden shoe buckles" to "the immense cocked hat," relics of previous royal ceremonies to which he added his own bespoke clothing for the most formal events. Sampson Wilder was won over by the Emperor, his new wife and the diversions of government as conducted in such elegance. Were those the genes whose intermixing would allow Townley to be at ease with people of all classes and to reach a helping hand to the halt and the lame? And were those the same genes that amused him by dressing in drag for his wife's 50th birthday?

INSIGHT

Wilder describes in his book a day when he was in Sweden and decided on the spur of the moment that it would be rather enjoyable to meet the country's king. Wilder went to the king's castle and, without pre-arrangement but with the help of a house guard who spoke a few words of English, managed to be received by a somewhat nonplussed monarch. The king spoke no English but held out his hand, palm down, for the hand to be kissed. Wilder wrote that he misunderstood the king's expectation and shook the hand in a friendly manner. They had a short but pleasant mutual visit. The next day when Wilder was walking with a friend, the king drove by and waved the hand in question, happily confirming in Wilder's mind that he had indeed made a favorable impression on the country's person of most importance.

Five years later another French revolution was at high pitch, Paris was in chaos as citizens poured into the city; civil war became inevitable, and the abdicated Napoleon Bonaparte was at risk of assassination by the government. Sampson Wilder contacted the beleaguered Emperor, proposing that he escape France in disguise as Wilder's "valet" since he "already had a passport" for such a position in his household. Once "on board an American ship" that Wilder would have "a hogshead" (large cask) prepared, in which Napoleon would be "concealed until beyond the limit of danger." That was quite a proposition for a man who at his peak ruled an estimated seventy million people and who by present day estimate was to have 300,000 books written about him. [9]

The formidable Frenchman received the invitation and thought it over. In the words of Wilder, Napoleon "finally declined- to his honor, be it said — because he would not desert friends who had been faithful to him through prosperity and adversity." One may also surmise that being treated as a valet and stuffed in a barrel on Wilder's ship was unimaginable to Napoleon. In reaching for genetic characteristics, Townley's gene pool might have included a couple of Wilder's genes to account for a naïve friendliness, pure intents, and ease in relating to pompous philanthropists, frightened patients and commanding civic leaders of all stripes. It may be a stretch but it is entertaining to consider the origin of his social concerns.

Early in the 19th century the Paton family tree gave rise to a successful businessman, William Paton, who was born in Scotland in 1818, immigrated to America and married Anne Staveley Agnew.[10] Of their three children, the eldest was William Agnew Paton (b. 1848), a successful businessman, like his father. He was also a magazine editor, book publisher and philanthropist who traveled widely with his family and could well afford such luxury. The next oldest of the three was David (no middle name) Paton (b. 1854), a lawyer by training who changed fields to become a prominent Egyptologist and Princeton professor, described in a published Princeton obituary as "likely the world's leader in that field;" and in the university's Alumni Weekly his work was named "a monument of industry and original scholarship."[11] The third Paton child arrived eleven years later, the year that President Lincoln died: Stewart (also no middle name) Paton (b. 1865). He was to become a "neuropsychobiologist," best known at the time by the inelegant title of "alienist" and finally renamed "psychiatrist."

Stewart married Frances Margaret Halsey (Paton) in 1882 and they had three children: Frances Evelyn (Powell) (b. 1894), William (no middle name) Paton (b. 1897) and this book's protagonist, Richard Townley

INSIGHT

Paton (b. 1901).[12] Townley's wish to become a doctor from an early age was largely inspired by his father, whose gentle persuasiveness and a mind bursting with the enthusiasm of medical preoccupation provided the boy with a yearning to find similar satisfaction.

But he also had an ancestor, who from his energies and role as an ophthalmologist was inspiring, and that was his great-granduncle Cornelius Rea Agnew. For Townley, the accomplished Dr. Agnew was a George Washington-like ancestor, idealized in part by the grandeur bestowed by distance. He was the first fulltime ophthalmologist in the State of New York and that was just the least of his achievements.[13]

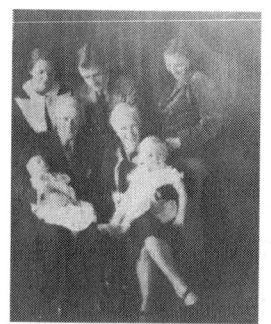

His mother's 50% share of her son's gene pool linked Townley to even more genes from pro-medical carriers. Margaret's two brothers were physicians in New Orleans, where they and Margaret were brought up.[14] In addition, Margaret's sister, Lilian Halsey, was to marry Johns Hopkins' Professor Lewellys F. Barker MD PhD, the research and clinical physician who succeeded William Osler as Professor of Medicine at Johns Hopkins.[15] In addition, also in Baltimore throughout Townley's childhood was Margaret's first cousin and the first Professor of Surgery, William S. Halsted MD,[16] whose career — despite severe personal difficulties — became highly influential by revising clinical procedures based upon his own laboratory research and deriving instruments and operations yielding much improved **clinical outcomes**.

That smorgasbord of medical expertise among relatives provided a family tree of genetic possibilities and theoretical enticements that might favorably support Townley's inclination toward a medical career if he were to have the right stuff in mental machinery to become the physician he soon yearned to be. He had the earnest disposition, the warming smile and the straight gaze that signified an alert and eager learner.

Today, it is clear that genes plus individualized neurological modifications[17] not only form the basis of character but also are important elements in determining career success, while providing the ability to overcome failure.[18] Was his endowment of pooled genes strong enough to overcome a moderate deficiency in scholarship? Based on his apparent character as a boarding school student, he seemed to have the "compulsion to strive and the talent to prosper."[19] That phrase is taken from a research report that favors nature (genes) as being the main element in determining career success, but who knows? There yet may be a few genes hiding sub-rosa that could torpedo his ambition, inflict damage to his appealing character and impair competitive academic performance. Townley's actions suggest he worried about not being competitive enough. He needed some kind of reassurance that he could be successful. With adolescence, he began to focus on athletics where he had no difficulty in excelling.

In decades ahead, with greater knowledge of how better to identify the raw empowerment of genes, biographies are likely to be much more enriched by updated analysis of the subject's nature and nurture at an early time in life before career decisions are made. A longstanding current conundrum is whether nature or nurture is more powerful in determining the pathway of lives. It is typically American to believe that all men are created equal, and—if necessary, with Creator aside—that each otherwise achieves or fails as his own independent operator rather than being guided by uncontrollable genetic forces. Not so! Genes are very powerful. Happily, in every life a variable amount of luck plays a role in career choice and in the career's long-term stability.[20]

Townley from sometime in childhood felt an irresistible urge to consider a career in Medicine. He scarcely knew of other options. In truth, his family tree and parental influences gave him the "on paper" probability of being a good bet for doctoring. If he were to revise his adolescent choice, this same fellow could become an abject failure. For instance, if he were to select architecture, law, religion, education, or engineering, a portion of his nature and much of his available nurture might become quite irrelevant. If he decided to become a stage actor, like his non-sanguineous but compelling cousin, Margaret Barker, or even an Egyptologist, like his lawyer-professor-uncle David Paton, he would have to possess very different memory and language skills. Even worse, if Townley were to choose music because of his love of its melodies, his tone deafness would surely have led to disappointment and disillusionment. Similarly, were he to decide to be a businessman, like his wealthy Uncle William A. Paton, he would need to consider carefully the mathematical requirements, for numbers were not without challenges for him.

Moreover, as is the usual circumstance, he would be well into young adulthood before his genetic inheritance became fully evident. Genes tend to take their time. Blue eyes at birth may require a decade before their final coloring has settled in. Genes affecting character, ambition, intelligence and determination may not be evident until adolescence or long thereafter. Sometimes, due to a life's requirements, a change in career choice is no longer an easy option. In a study of infants adopted at birth and therefore totally isolated from their biological parents, some were found to exhibit quite abrupt personality changes as young adults—and those changes caused by inherited genes previously unexpressed were traits clearly identifiable in their biological parents.

Every person is the raw product of his gene pool, and the determination of gene pool distribution remains a wait-and-see process. No matter how good his situation with respect to the medical profession looked on paper, Townley's choice of Medicine at age sixteen could well have been a mistake if genetic traits badly matched to a medical career were to emerge.

With such an introduction of the protagonist, the biographer will turn to the facts of Townley's upbringing, with the reader now in possession of the knowledge that the baggage he carried was not all of Vuitton quality.

INSIGHT

NOTES TO CHAPTER 2:

1. J. Suo, S. C. Zhu, S. Shan, and X. Chen: "A Compositional and Dynamic Model for Face Aging," *PAMI*, 2010.
2. The two women were Noel B. Williams and Rosalie V. Halsey, the latter being a sister of Townley's mother, Margaret H. Paton. Independently, they collected many names, dates, relationships and facts about the lives of the Paton and Townley bloodlines. Several autobiographical books are the source of numerous stories, a few of which are cited in this text. The two family scribes recorded heavily branched family trees which, despite some pruning (whether intentional or otherwise), constitute a list of 903 names, most of whom are not directly related to Townley Paton. None of his direct bloodline over several centuries is passed over, whether or not the history is worth mentioning. Scottish, English and some French blood were the only geographic and linguistic variants. What is known is that an unnamed independent Towneley "lord" (sic) before the Norman Conquest of 1066 used a stone house at Burnley, Lancashire, as a stag and fox hunting lodge for entertaining visiting acquaintances. The building was named Villa de Tunlay, the origin of today's Townley. The family's bloodline history begins in 1235 with a Richard de Towneley, who became the owner of that building when it was used for defense against marauders. Under his management it was converted from a sports lodge into a lofty hall as tons more stones were added, turning it into a formidable structure used for township meetings and public meals. Finally, the structure was called Towneley Hall, and it eventually became the museum and art gallery that it remains to this day, a tourist site for those interested in ancient English art and history of the region. The Towneley family owned the Hall for 500 years, finally taking their leave in 1902. Over that period of time there were numerous Richard Towneleys.
3. Clark, G.: "The Son Also Rises." *Princeton University Press*, Princeton, 2014.
4. The information about the Towneleys is taken from "The Official Guide to Townley Hall" by John Allen, issued by the *Art Gallery & Museum* subcommittee of 1909 and reprinted in 1926 by Burnley: John Dixon, Ltd, Printers, Manchester Road.
5. Ibid.
6. Records From "The Life of S. V. S. Wilder," published in 1865 by the *American Tract Society*.
7. Ibid.

8. Madison stood at five feet, four inches, about the same height as Napoleon.
9. Roberts, A.: "Napoleon's Last Charge," Smithsonian.com, June 2015.
10. Through her, the Paton family also had a family relationship to Philadelphia's most prominent general surgeon-cum-ophthalmologist, the aforementioned D. Hayes Agnew.
11. *Princeton Alumni Weekly* 23:489-497, 1923.
12. A reader, put off by the possible overreach of family boasts, might inquire as to why these traveling ancestors did not take the crossing to the New World with bunks on the Mayflower? In fact, Townley's great-great-grandmother, Rebecca Townley was a direct descendent of John Alden and Pricilla Mullins, who arrived on that ship's only America-destined voyage on November 11, 1620. Several of the jammed-in passengers died while at sea and most of those remaining succumbed to exposure and starvation during the bitterly cold winter that followed. The Aldens lived initially in constant fear of crew insurgencies and "Indian" attacks, but over time they had ten children and John became the virtual leader of those Pilgrims, reaching 89 years of age after having started as a carpenter and ended as a retired government official.
13. C. R. Agnew will come into this history at a later time. Suffice to say here that his older first cousin, David Hayes Agnew MD LLD, was a distinguished academic Professor of Clinical Surgery at the University of Pennsylvania who included eye surgery in his patient care, having trained at the Wills Eye Hospital starting in 1863. As a leading surgeon, he was called in consultation to assist in the management of the fatally injured President Garfield when he was dying from a retained assassin's bullet. He examined the dying president in the same house in which Aida de Acosta Root Breckinridge would soon thereafter be born. Small world. This Dr. Agnew was a part-time specialist in ophthalmology as one of his several fields of surgical interest, whereas his cousin became a full-time ophthalmologist.
14. Margaret's older brother, Richard Townley Haines Halsey, was an expert in American antiques and instrumental in founding the American Wing of the Metropolitan Museum. Her sister, Lilian, married Dr. Lewellys Barker, as noted earlier.
15. He became Sir William Osler, knighted in England upon being recruited from Johns Hopkins seven years after he began his work in Baltimore.
16. Townley's important exposure to the Johns Hopkins medical faculty and its crusade to transform the medical profession will be the subject of Chapter 5.
17. With apology for dodging an eplanation, that phrase refers to the influence of epigenetics that is beyond the reach of this chapter.

INSIGHT

18. An excellent example of this inherent drive is found in Georgescu, P. with Dorsey, D., *The Constant Choice: An Everyday Journey From Evil Toward Good*, Greenleaf Book Group Press, 2013.

19. Clark, G.: "The Great Divide," cited in a New York Times article, "Your Ancestors, Your Fate," February 2, 2014.

20. Clark, G.: *The Son Also Rises*, p. 264.

CHAPTER 3: TOWNLEY AND HIS PEOPLE

Be curious, not judgmental.
"Leaves of Grass," Walt Whitman, 1819-1892

On April 7, 1901, within a typical Baltimore row house at 213 West Washington Street, a spunky infant, apparently in quite a hurry, was born before his mother could leave for the hospital. Normally, there would be nothing much to be said about the arrival of this third child, except that both parents delighted in having what each had silently yearned for: a second son. In Baltimore, where a new breed of medical doctor was one of the most venerated goals of its medical academia, a boy arriving to Johns Hopkins medical parentage was about the hottest thing in diapers — a chance amid that group of enthusiasts for a sync with genetic destiny. It was almost as elementary as that.

So it was indeed happy news for Stewart and Margaret Paton when this infant arrived with the right gender for doctoring. He looked just as he should, with the usual accouterments and behaviors of the just-arrived, including eyes that reputably were bluer than most in that early time of life, but that probably was a parental whimsy.

Their first child, Frances Evelyn Paton was a daughter with determined mind and independent purpose. Four years later William Paton arrived, a splendid male child. Bill was irresistibly lovable but in need of considerable attending, for he had food intolerances, allergies, lung issues that led to asthma, and a long period of infantile coma of unknown origin. Nevertheless, he had gumption and spirit that spoke for a good life ahead if he could get beyond childhood as unscathed as possible.

INSIGHT

It was four years later when this third baby was welcomed by experienced parents increasingly involved in the father's obsession with Medicine. Members of the Johns Hopkins medical faculty were the family's highest valued friends and neighbors. Few other groups of medical people elsewhere could feel as united by the institutional purpose that had brought them together from across America.

The new baby was given the ancestry bedecked name of Richard Townley Paton Surely that meant he would be called "Richard" or "R-T" or "Dick." No one would want to be called "Townley." But neither would anyone really want to be called Rudyard, another middle name whose best-known owner was born the same year as Townley's father. Both of those middle names were from an era when adults were not too hurried to speak both syllables, short nicknames being codes to familiarity that for strangers was unwarranted.

Yet, according to an amused remark that Evelyn made when brother #2 was born, when he was still in his swaddling clothes lying in a bassinet, giggling nurses on the obstetrics staff referred to him as "Little Dickie." A stop was put to that, but he was indeed called "Dick" throughout school and college, never at home. "Townley was a one-of-a-kind personal label that his mother insisted upon and it probably made him more memorable to others over the years ahead.

As for Townley's father, he was of paramount importance to the son's career and his interests will be extensively covered hereafter. As a man with traditional Scottish characteristics, he was inordinately reticent about his financial assets, but it would not take a tax collector to figure out he had an ample source of unearned income. Although no information about his own father's wealth is available, upon the death of Stewart's mother, Anne Stavely, the Surrogate Court of New York in a full statement to his mother's executors reported that each of her three sons was to receive approximately the same bequest, Stewart's share being exactly $219,845.01, which in today's money would exceed three million dollars.[1]

Except for the cost of family travel and lodging, Stewart raised his family like any sensible parsimonious academic with Scottish forebears–his fists opened slowly and locked easily. Still, he had the financial wherewithal for the family to travel quite freely and they were unencumbered by debt in the early part of his adulthood. He avoided institutional restrictions that might require long-range commitments and administrative obligations, making his academic standing more that of a consultant than an in-house fixture. Over the first decade of the 20th century, he was as peripatetic as his unquenchable intellectual curiosity called for, choosing to pay his own flights of intellectual fancy to satisfy his insatiable pursuit of European medical knowledge.[2]

It would be likely that Townley's father could pay the cost should the boy wish to pursue a medical career. Family financing was a requirement for almost every medical student in the 19th and early 20th centuries. They came from advantaged backgrounds, which meant that medical doctors enjoyed the culture of opportunity, in turn tending to support a traditional medical noblesse that could easily develop into a somewhat patronizing attitude. That was not a Stewart Paton problem. There was never a chance that anyone would consider Stewart or his wife elitists, in the sense of hubris and snobbery. They were willing and able to support their children as long as it was necessary for positive purposes. That would always be the rule. There were no frivolous trips to any equivalent of Disneyland, if anything of that sort had existed. The Paton children were captives of purposeful parents in a period when the behavior of children was more often used as a measure of their parents' character.

Townley's mother, Frances Margaret Halsey (Paton), was three years younger than her husband, born in 1868 on Mardi Gras in New Orleans. She and her two sisters married doctors and both of her brothers were doctors; one of them, Dr. John ("Jack") Taylor Halsey (1870-1951), became prominent as an academic physician and researcher, best known in the profession as Professor of Pharmacology at Tulane Medical School from 1904 until his retirement in 1937.

Margaret had a mind fortified by a very good education at several private schools, at least one of which, the acclaimed Miss Porter's School in Farmington, Connecticut, was limited entirely—by the very statements contained in published admissions requirement—to "very intelligent girls." It, too, provided a top-quality education inclusive of what was termed "a finishing school" that kept its young ladies beautifully kempt and highly informed about what women were supposed to know, and more than the school intended of what they were not supposed to know. (Margaret let on about that when her niece was attending the same school a generation later.) With three years of what in those days was decidedly rounded and advanced schooling for precocious women—

although not college *per se*—she became the American equivalent of a fine British lady, with formal manners and verbal independence.

Mrs. Stewart Paton would become to some eyes a "grand dame." She was willful, smart, stylish, proper and always up-to-date with current world news and campus observation. She and the companionable Stewart were sophisticated Americans, familiar with foreign expression and intellectual conversing. After marriage and several years of living here and there in Europe while Stewart pursued his post-graduate medical studies, Margaret became adept at speaking in the tongues of household servants or nurses, whether they were French, German or Italian. The consecutive governesses, in turn, were expected to converse with the children in their native language, never mind that it was also the Scottish way for one's children to speak "foreign" wherever they were located and without language teachers.

One young live-in governess, Johanna, came with the family when they returned from a year in Germany, where Stewart had been studying neuropathology and psychiatry[3]. Johanna was an especially popular live-in nanny throughout much of Townley's early childhood, but because of her hesitancy in English and poor pronunciation the parents shared evening readings of childhood classics ranging from tales by Rudyard Kipling, poems by Robert Louis Stevenson, and — it must be included — popular stories in simulated "darkie" vernacular about Uncle Remus and B'rer Rabbit.[4] Today, of course, it would be insulting to African Americans and anything but funny to hear it read aloud in this way. Such a book required considerable reading skill, which Margaret in particular learned but Stewart avoided.

Once reading time was finished, each child recited the standard evening prayer before the final "good night." That was the extent of their religious obligation until their primary school in Baltimore included morning prayers and Bible studies as part of the curriculum. Neither Margaret nor Stewart took on Christian teaching at home, making themselves seem agnostic by default and quite different from some of their family's close-friend physicians. The children did attend a Presbyterian church on most Sundays, as well as on Christmas and Easter. Although the best of Christians, they were only churchgoers for celebratory occasions such as holidays, births, marriages and deaths—social conformities which each respected.

In that period, religion was being subjected to daring questions and qualified answers. Agnostics chose to remain unidentified, attending church for appearances' sake and, to some extent at least, for the outside possibility of good luck after death if one were to appear visibly within the fold. However, several of the era's most respected and most capable physicians were devout believers — doctors by the names of Halsted, Osler and Agnew, for example — while many of their peers remained silent with respect to their faith. It was not an era for religious confessionals.

The children understood that good behavior brought warmth and misbehavior was utterly unacceptable and intolerable. Behavior unsatisfactory to the parents was treated as a violation of trust and love. For a sensitive boy like Townley, who was to learn more from experience than from rote, that subtle steering was strongly educational. The fact that there was also a governess in the household did not mitigate against the powers of the parents. Margaret fortified the commonsense requirements of her medical scientist husband, who was not given to the banal details of daily bothering.

In the fall of 1913, a family favorite happen-stance occurred related to a medical meeting at Chicago's Palmer House hotel that included a black-tie dinner. For this trip, Stewart was unaccompanied. He brought a large suitcase to accommodate his change of clothing and the inevitable books and notepapers that might be needed–"You never know!" However, when it was time to open the suitcase in his hotel room, he could not find the key. He searched for it repeatedly—eventually frantically—but he had obviously just plain forgotten to bring the key with him. He immediately cabled Margaret:

SP : "Forgot suitcase key. Send by next train with Pullman redcap. Need arrival time and redcap name." [5]

FMP: "Left top vest pocket."

SP: "Of course. Windy here."

That was how it was with the Stewart Patons. By then he was 48 years old, with a perfectly functioning mind that--simply to be said--did not prioritize domesticity, even his own. His family liked to refer to his quirks of absentmindedness as being "at sea." So be it. Margaret was first mate and navigator to his role as captain. She steered from the stern instead of the bridge. Some might say women in that era were less expressive, more furled, better hushed. In those ways, Margaret was progressively exceptional.

As previously noted, she was a formidable woman. It was she who set the strict standards of family discipline and with that same authority she ruled the roost. An old chestnut that was passed down over several generations was that in their family it was the Paton men who required suffrage. The fact is they got along just fine with Margaret navigating expertly between diverse roles. Actually, this first mate was more the flag bearer than the mender—her domesticity was not based upon do-it-yourself achievements but on vested authority more stolen than presented.

She was never seen in trousers or shorts; she wore dresses well below the knee even for hiking, as family photos repeatedly prove. There are no photographs of her in swimming attire—and few in any form of repose. She had long dark brown hair that was kept in a neat bun secured by several large tortoiseshell hairpins. As her hair became prematurely grey, then white, she took to the common practice of adding a bluish rinse but never a dye job, for that would have been far below her standard of propriety.

Margaret was not the person to have a lukewarm position about alcohol (anti-Prohibitionist, as was Stewart), birth control (Margaret Sanger knew best), and cigars (tried indoors at the Paton home by the heavy-smoking Dr. William Welch, but on one occasion only). As to women's rights, voting on issues began with her announcing her vote as she dramatically and characteristically raised her hand to a full upward stretch, indicating to the family that this would be the only acceptable position to take. As she aged, Margaret became statuesque, with erect bearing and blue-green eyed elegance. In public she wore a large snug four-strand pearl choker that became part of her formal identity, a decorative means of disguising a long and eventually wrinkled neck. In their community of medical friends, she was considered a charming conversationalist, thriving on current events and travelogues, not unwilling to clarify her opinion on the wisdom of small families and how that could be happily achieved.

Margaret and Evelyn Paton, ca. 1915

As home superintendent, Margaret kept a close eye on the quality of staff services, planned the meals and scheduled whatever needed doing in morning staff meetings held in her bedroom. She also the family's authority on a traditional code of manners, being a stickler for etiquette and discipline. Margaret had a low tolerance for "funny business," which was her un-funny generalization for misbehavior. The children were never spanked but were punished by spending designated time alone in the bedroom, or assigned penalties such as being suspended from Sunday car trips to the Bay. They preferred spanking.

The Paton children loved their parents unequivocally. Their father's remoteness in his rapport with them was perhaps all the more provocative because of the distance he maintained. They happily gathered around him as if making him laugh was their obligation. The children equally loved their mother, despite the fact that for all routine disobediences she was the one who meted out the penalties. The parents' devotion to the children was genuine but never maudlin. The children called their father "Father" and their mother "Mother." They left the dinner table after asking to be excused and only in an emergency before the slowest eater was finished.

While Margaret's interaction with friends and acquaintances had a formal graciousness, Stewart was more standoffish, self-contained, reserved–that is, unless someone got him talking about his number one conviction: the corrections mankind would need to make if humanity were to remain alive and well on the planet in coming centuries. His chat was often a bit too psychological and Protestant. He was well ahead of his time in predicting that the damaging ferocity of football was a potential cause of eventual mental disturbances.[6] Townley, being the youngest, may not have understood much of what his father was saying but he listened with the rapt attention of a faithful believer.

Whereas both boys were born in Baltimore, Townley's sister, Frances Evelyn Paton, seven years older than Townley had been born in 1894 in Leipzig, Germany, when Stewart was pursuing post-graduate studies presumably with one of his most influential mentors from that city, Emil Kraepelin.[7] Evelyn may have had the keenest intellect of the three children and certainly was the only one who was mathematically gifted. An effusive individual with a sharp tongue and penetrating mind, she practiced chronic outspokenness with ironclad conviction throughout her adult life and sometimes at near operatic volume while hiding a heart of gold. She did not deploy against her family the sharp and lacerating judgmental tongue that she inherited from her mother; it was only used against those whom she found to be greedy, offensive or as outspoken as she was herself.

When in her 30's, Evelyn married a stout, Virginia-born naval officer, Paulus Pease Powell.[8] Neither blessed nor burdened with children, they travelled the world in his various governmental capacities, serving repeatedly as a Republican appointee naval attaché to American embassies in Manila, Shanghai, and Rio de Janeiro.

Her marriage to a commanding husband could have become seriously adversarial had she not always deferred to him as he reddened in argument. Rarely would she defer to anyone else, even though she was often wrong, or wrong to a degree. Some of Evelyn's valuable and versatile gene pool might have been better distributed to one of her male siblings, if only because in that era men were granted more leeway in their personal assertions.

Shortly before retirement, P's (as he was called, pronounced as it reads) was promoted to admiral. As such he may have acquired a boost in his air of authority that in some circles might have been taken for the sort of hubristic puffiness that comes with high military office, rows of tiny medals on dress uniforms or rows of military badges for daily wear. Matters of importance to him included Navy winning the annual game against Army and the defeat of Franklin Delano Roosevelt in his first, second and third runs for President. However, P's had considerable southern charm, was courtly if not a bit overly intrigued by the ladies, and readily able to demonstrate his authority by taking the hide off his caddie were he to permit the faintest rattle of irons when the admiral was "in backswing."

Evelyn, better than her parents or siblings, spoke Italian, German, French and some Spanish learned largely as a child in Europe and she added Portuguese and Cantonese while living in Rio and later Shanghai. With her linguistic skills and her Anglicized English (her a's just slightly broadened by sophistication and internationalism) upon her husband's retirement she became a personal shopper at the fashionable Lord & Taylor department store on Fifth Avenue in New York City.

The two Paton brothers, Bill ("William" at home) and Townley, were less proficient in their schoolwork than their sister. Bill's poor health persisted after the age of two following the undiagnosed coma. Whether or not directly related, that cerebral shutdown was followed by hesitant speech and rather poor coordination. It was suspected at the time that the illness was the result of polio, complicated by his childhood asthma. At some point during his younger years Stewart was advised to "send William out west" by Teddy Roosevelt, who himself had been a delicate child.[9]

However, there was more to Bill's problems than asthma. He was described years later by his son-in-law as "bright as a button," but school was difficult for him, and in his good-natured way he fought its trials and humiliations. After some home schooling and then attending Colorado A&M, Bill took an extended European tour financed by his father, and in 1927 he met and married an artistic and adventurous young woman, Rowena Stewart, who proved the ideal match for him. Bill was a man of moderate height, thin and wiry who looked like "the Marlboro" man in skinny jeans, wide brimmed cowboy hat and a roll-your-own dangling from a smiling mouth. He was the family's perfect cowboy, and all were pleased with his adaptation to western culture.

Bill and Rowena raised four attractive daughters who excelled in athletics, and before and after graduations from college returned to the ranch to dutifully and happily take their turns in the care and promotion of their parents' moderate-sized dude ranch adjacent to

INSIGHT

the fast and thunderous Shell Creek located in mid-Wyoming. Rowena's own daily chores included cooking three meals a day for everyone, seeing that each cabin was cleaned, and caring for the outhouses by spraying for varmints and bugs, supplying old, non-shiny magazines or outdated issues of the *Farmer's Almanac* to be hung on a long cord near the single "sitting hole", and dropping hay and lime into the pit below. The terrain was beautiful, made more exotic by the howls of coyotes. Along the trails were rattlesnakes, fossils and alleged gizzard stones, mistakenly attributed at that time to edentulous vegetarian dinosaurs whose skeletal remains constituted an exciting drawing card for ranch visitors.

Bill rode a snorting and, at his option, smartly bucking black stallion-the bucking most often prompted by the horse being tightly reined while lightly spurred, the result being a display of horsemanship the dudes were likely to admire and unlikely to fathom. He had a corral full of horses that were turned out every evening and rounded up early each morning for the dudes' plodding trail rides across hills and desert. Each horse had the family brand burned into its left flank. The riders paused when Bill found a discarded antler for a guest's trophy or a snake to behead and de-rattle as a thrill for the tenderfoots, who took such rattles home to Greenwich or Boston as relics of the Wild West. No guns were used in dude season.

Whoever came to know Bill and Rowena admired and loved them both and were impressed by their diligent and well-mannered daughters. Their ranch was as picturesque as a movie set, with its unpretentious log cabins and its corral and hitching posts, a scene enhanced by the fragrance of morning coffee. All hands (that means hosts as well as guests) had their evening meal together in the dining room of the main cabin where there was running water and an actual flush toilet that was all too popular. The William Patons' lives were healthy and long. Bill was a survivor, an uncomplaining but never fully healthy man with pride in his ranch, his children, and his way of life. He was kindly, often amusing, sometimes irascible, but always a caring individual. He was the more raucous, brash and uninhibited person when compared to his younger brother.

Both of Townley's siblings were to select ways of life unlike his or others going back several generations in the bloodline. They were what their father referred to with one of his favorite words describing men of action: "do'ers." In their case, they originated their pathways, proceeding as independently as they might wish, never really at rest. Perhaps from prolonged illnesses, Bill was the least scholarly. He had the quiet demeanor of their father, caring about a quality life but not willing, or perhaps unable, to shoulder more than the most essential responsibility. On the opposite end of the spectrum, Evelyn, like their mother, was acutely aware and absolutely authoritative on all subjects. Townley was comfortably in the middle. Richard Townley was an athletic, impressionable, mentor receptive kind of fellow whose modesty was probably linked to childhood shyness and, later, to a dearth of confidence that his academic achievements would enable him to become the doctor he wished to be. Townley's teachers were no help in that regard. They invariably said nice things about his manners and attitude but less about his comparative class standings. He wanted to be a doctor more than he wished to let on—for he came to realize that wanting to become a doctor was only the first

INSIGHT

requirement and school performance was paramount. As his mother eventually and famously warned, "You should always have alternatives in mind, Son." (Perhaps that may have been intended to make him work harder.)

Nevertheless, Margaret noted that he was playing doctor from the age of five, putting "sticking plaster" on imagined injuries of family members and even willing visitors. At ten, he began learning how to dodge mathematics. According to his father's daily diary, on January 11, 1911, when Townley was in the fourth grade, he came home from school with news for his parents, "We learned fractions today." Right away, Evelyn asked, "If I take an apple and cut it into four pieces, what is the fraction for each piece?" Townley replied, "We haven't come to apples yet."

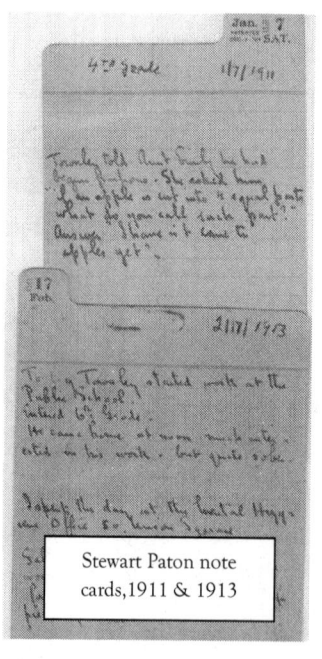

By the time he was twelve, the family had moved to Princeton, New Jersey, for Stewart's new investigative work with college students. Townley entered the sixth grade of a Princeton public school, and the same year he "operated" on two frogs pinioned on a corkboard for leg dissection. He had heard that some doctors operate and others do not. He wanted to cut and sew. He knew nothing of the specifics of gross anatomy, but after skinning the bodies he did a tidy job of muscle separations, appreciating that it was the large ones that made their jumps. There was no real purpose to his project, no scientific breakthrough, just enhanced surgical dreaming.

Stewart Paton note cards, 1911 & 1913

Then, when Townley was sixteen and visiting Baltimore with his father, he was invited by Dr. Frank R. Smith to join him on his Sunday morning patient rounds in the male ward at the hospital. A British-born faculty internist who was especially close to Stewart's brother-in-law, Dr. Lewellys Barker, Smith was the first to invite Townley to join him on patient rounds. The boy knew it was a rare privilege for someone as young as he to tag along as the doctor greeted his bedded patients, examined them briefly and spoke to each as if the patient were an important person rather than merely a poor fellow required to lie quietly while the doctor checked him over as a car mechanic might check the functions of an engine under the hood. That was not Dr. Smith, for he humanized these sick persons and each appreciated the doctor's special caring.

Townley always remembered years later being told by his father that Dr. Smith never turned down any patient because he could not pay the bill. He went on to recall the thrill of sensing that day what being a doctor entailed. He had stood beside the kindly white-coated physician holding his flashlight and stethoscope at the ready — a thoughtful gesture to the boy — as the doctor efficiently inquired of the patients' comfort, appetite, sleeping problems, pain in the surgical areas and, in a lowered voice, about recent bowel movements. That was real inside information, and Townley was a part of it-from somewhat of a distance, but included all the same. In the telling at home, he made sure to explain that he had kept his expression immobile, no matter what the answers.

Today, for non-physicians regardless of age, that kind of medical tourism with Dr. Smith would not be permitted in any hospital, but in that day it was the doctor's choice to bring along such an observer, a nice way to introduce his patients to a good lad who was polite, subdued and interested in every moment of the tour. That hospital visit became a familiar family anecdote that had culminated the same evening in Townley telling both his parents that he was definitely going to be a doctor, "no matter what." Of course, many children capriciously jump to such conclusions, then change their minds in ensuing years as a range of other career options become appealing. But Townley's hopefulness proved genuine, and for the time being that auspicious hospital visit with the kindly and indulgent Dr. Smith left Townley with a sense of belonging.

So it was that Dr. Smith delivered a key nugget of nurture for the boy's future hopes that had first begun when patted on the head as he played doctor in the nursery. That quite obvious parent-planted reward-based inclination had grown and now allowed the boy to envision himself a part — a remote part, but a part all the same — of his father's medical world and the cauldron of excited medical firebrands who were igniting their ancient profession. There was no need for Townley to know the details of the Johns Hopkins medical uprising. By now he knew it was a great affair. If his father was for it, the cause was valid. Sixteen years after his Baltimore birth, Townley felt the warmth and the call of Medicine as he revisited Johns Hopkins with his father, learning more about that sequestered medical haven but almost completely unaware that a national unrest was pervading America. It was the external manifestations of a widespread population illness whose cause and whose cure had a great deal to do with what the Johns Hopkins medical uprising was all about.

TOWNLEY AND HIS PEOPLE

NOTES TO CHAPTER 3:

1. At some time in the mid-to-late 1930s, Stewart made some unfortunate investments that led to a serious reduction in available finance and the need to sell his family house in Princeton, New Jersey. Thereafter, he and Margaret lived a bit more frugally.
2. Stewart had a "weak heart" and often had to explain that he could not accept more responsibility due to his limited capacity for anything strenuous; thus he walked for exercise, sometimes for several miles.
3. Professor Emil Kraepelin in Leipzig.
4. Spoken sources informed the classic book of these stories written by Joel Chandler Harris in 1881.
5. This must have been a name talked about at home, for it was the first year that "redcap" was used for baggage porters and presumably for Pullman porters as well.
6. New York Times article about Stewart: Nov. 26, 1923.
7. Stewart's own thinking fit well with the views of Kraepelin, a psychiatrist who believed psychiatric disease to be a biological and genetic malfunction and not the psychodynamic process of early sexuality, as was the theory of Sigmund Freud.
8. The Internet has a story relating to Powell's attempt to inform FDR and Secretary of War Knox with a message regarding the approaching Japanese fleet in December 1941 that was to be kept a secret by putting Powell overnight in the brig.
9. The comment is taken from a letter of May 10, 1976 from Rowena S. Paton to her sister-in-law, Evelyn Paton Powell. It conveys the information that T. Roosevelt had also been a sickly child and had been sent West for his health, as he now advised for Bill.

CHAPTER 4: MALIGNANT MALAISE

In science the credit goes to the man who convinces the world, not the man to whom the idea first occurs. "Eugenics Review," Sir Francis Darwin, April 1914

Well before the turn of the 19th century and lingering for half a century thereafter, average Americans beyond the protectiveness of an academic colony like the medical community at Johns Hopkins were at odds with the constrictions of their free and opportune country. The *joie de vivre* was kaput. Trust-busting, political reform, the rise of labor unions, and even Prohibition were postulated at one time or another to have a major role in the nation's discontent. Despite being what is now called the Progressive Era (1890-1920), its early years were not progressive for human happiness or for any signs to suggest that things would soon get better. People coped poorly, dragged down by an unexplainable wretchedness that was not attributable to the usual suspects such as politics, education or the social mandates of an under-budgeted everyday life. The country had lately gone through a national depression, but its inching recovery was not improving the persistent malaise.

Social struggles were commonplace. Suffragettes were demanding their right to vote. Poverty popularized prostitution. Small businesses were failing although some big businesses were booming. The Mafia was emulating its overseas mentors. Gambling was rife with swindling and fraud. Child labor was being exploited. Loud-mouthed men—the "hear all about it" barkers—stole jobs from skinny newsboys. Striking workers in mass media, while overworked, demanded higher pay as their overworked presses caused mechanical failures that imperiled their salaries. Newspapers resented radio's "unfair competition" in disseminating the daily news. Inefficiency slowly was succumbing to a new form of intellectual desperation and no one seemed to understand its basis. Economic collapse seemed to be at every corner. The country lay sick without a diagnosis.

The nation's health care was likewise in disarray—probably at its lowest ebb since George Washington awoke with a sore throat and, some say, died from his doctor's overzealous bloodletting.[1] Word was out that "the ranks of the medical profession were being recruited from working men and the lower middle class, to the dismay of the medical leaders who thought such riffraff jeopardized efforts to raise the doctor's status in society."[2] That was an opinion reflecting the elitism and the ineffectiveness of a profession losing its grip and thus in decline. Medical education was at abysmal levels, with an abundance of so-called medical schools, most of which were no more than educational factories turning out "doctors" with little more than a few hours of lectures behind their diplomas, accounting for the incompetence of their graduates. Of the fifty medical schools that were certified, only two or three attained acceptable standards. Competition was arising from other schools of quasi-justifiable health care, such as those of homeopathy, osteopathy and chiropractic.[3]

It was not a good time to be sick, for the medical profession itself was suffering from a lack of self-respect as its standards eroded from the competition of non-medical pseudo-healers. These unprincipled individuals produced an inundation of chicanery that

capitalized on the pathetic vulnerability of the "halt and the lame."[4] Patent medicines for almost every kind of illness were being hawked in the streets. Few, if any, were actually patented and others were nothing more than nasty tasting placebos. The care of chronic diseases—especially tuberculosis—was being neglected and often community contagions lacked quarantines and available immunizations. For the alcohol consuming, cigar chewing male population, bar side cuspidors (spittoons, to be more graphic) served as salivary chamber pots until finally Prohibition (1920-1933) closed the saloons, at which time it is axiomatic that more "spit" simply hit the streets. Even as late as 1930 and during Prohibition, the average man drank 1.7 bottles of hard liquor every week.[5]

As for the medical profession's disregard of principles and conduct, there is a previously published example of unprofessional self-promotion that represents flagrant self-centeredness in an uncontrolled profession. Julius Homberger MD[6] was a young immigrant ophthalmologist, well trained in Germany. He came to America in 1862, when the American Medical Association's Code of Ethics was well known. His initial intent was to further his career in the New World by starting a practice in Manhattan. He was not your typical miscreant, for at only 22 years of age he founded the first ophthalmology journal in the United States, American Journal of Ophthalmology. Yet, for his surgical work he advertised widely, such as in an 1866 Philadelphia daily newspaper: "Surgical Operations on the Eye: Dr. Julius Homberger, oculist (and) editor of the American Ophthalmic Journal (sic), informs the public that he is prepared to perform all surgical operations necessary to restore sight or correct deformity. In no case will he make a charge unless perfectly successful." And so forth.

The following quotation puts the profession's dilemma into sharp focus, for Homberger wrote: "It is an hallucination with which physicians have flattered themselves, namely that the nature of the services of a medical man differs essentially from all other services rendered by members of the community to each other."[7] He may have been an extreme self-promoter, brimming with self-confidence, but he had a point in what he wrote about the clay feet of fellow doctors. Homberger was outraged by the harsh criticism he received for his self-promotion in public advertising, and with no apology forthcoming, the American Medical Association threw him out simultaneously with his resignation. He left New York, reopened his practice in New Orleans, but soon died of heart trouble at 33.

In truth, Medicine did not wish to acknowledge its own traditional elitist attitude, a crust that protected the festering within. The history of self-aggrandizement with pomp and pose goes back far. The medical profession and other well-educated and prominent persons picked up elitism as an appendage to their commendable high manners. In England, in the early 1800s, letters that Lord Chesterfield sent to his son epitomized that sense of elitism that possessed the mannered gentry, which later was mirrored in America. Always addressing his son as "Dear Boy," Chesterfield instructed the lad in ways of gaining social favor, advising that "the scholar, without good breeding, is a pedant" and "every man (thus deprived) disagreeable." Chesterfield's imperative admonitions regarding a gentleman's means for seeking success were the progenitors of an intellectual mindset taken straight from the British that was to grip medical mores in America.[8]

Elitism was not merely the handmaiden of affluence. It was an imbued attitude born of financial and educational advantage but lingering indefinitely even if the money became scant. For physicians it was part of the Hippocratic endowment transmitted by its famous oath. That ancillary whiff of noblesse was particularly present in the bearing and expectations of socially traditional medical doctors whose 19th century societal awareness was out of phase with their proper entitlements. Yet they had too few other strengths in compensation. The merits, rights and privileges of the physician were in need of soul-searching but change of any social kind had become increasingly irksome within the disillusioned profession.

Another example of notorious patient care is based upon a fraudulent operation, a preposterous transplantation. This surgeon is singled out as a "dark" prompter of anti-eye bank associations as supporters of a procedure against the inclinations of human nature that would arise some forty years later. John Romulus Brinkley "MD" (1885-1942) was surgically very active. His single operative procedure over a period of two decades was the transplantation of the testicles of goats into the scrotums of men, allegedly to relieve their middle-aged depression—or for almost any other ailment the patient might wish to be rid of. Many patients felt cured or improved, thanks to the placebo effect that was encouraged by the doctor's assurances. Although many patients had surgical complications and some reportedly died, nothing dampened his fraudulent surgical zest-a charlatan and a quack. It is hard to believe but he performed that operation on some 1,600 men and even planted a few testicles in several women.

The surgeon's charge for this transfer of donor nuggets was a whopping $5,000 a pair.[9] Brinkley had no difficulty finding willing recipients for the useless therapy, indicating their gullibility if not their desperation. For a while, he also obtained human testicles from death row inmates and would implant those into his waiting patients, who paid as much as $7,500[10] for these high-quality human sex glands. In legitimate ophthalmological research, transplantation of animal corneas was being tried abroad and eventually in America, but such incompatible tissues would never be successfully used. Brinkley represented the fraud that was smoldering among countless creative quack physicians profiting from false promises. For a while Brinkley became a millionaire but eventually he went bankrupt from lawsuits against him, and after his varied and eventually unsuccessful career he died a pauper.

The country's failure to thrive had the excuse of wars that were waged at great cost and concern to the citizenry. Over three decades there were seven U.S. presidents distracted by having to preside over the Spanish-American War in 1898 and later World War I and these engagements had to be given priority over domestic issues.

Moreover, there had been a costly national depression that started acutely in 1837 and endured for at least five years thereafter. How much can a population take after becoming accustomed to being optimistic? The "have-nots" blamed the "haves" for their suffering. Muckraking journalists were feasting attention on exploitive profiteers. Only the bank accounts of so-called robber barons such as John D. Rockefeller, Andrew Carnegie, and J.P. Morgan were on the rise, with monopolized wealth that itself was part of the problem-but in this upside down national dilemma, it was also to be part of the solution.

These grievances needed solutions, but first there had to be a diagnosis for the country's miseries and for the medical profession's shoddy condition. Some universal cause was affecting almost

INSIGHT

everything, some sort of insidious dissidence. But why was it so difficult to visualize and pin down? The answer to that was because it was neither something that seemed bad nor appeared to be a reason for anyone's complaints. But coming in a groundswell of realization from numerous sources, first as hunches and later as a certainty, the mystery was eventually and definitively solved.

The disruptive force to account for the basis of the miseries described above was science! The march of science had long outpaced its existing tolerances. But having the correct diagnosis did not make things better automatically, for the subversive effects of science's many misfits with longstanding practices were undermining an already weakened and fed-up society still sluggishly recovering from its earlier national depression. Until the paradox of science deterring social progress could be fully comprehended, the many manifestations of social distress would keep on coming. It still was not a clear-cut explanation. The "aha" moment finally came with the clarification that it was not science as such but new science, with its costs, adaptations and re-education mandate. The last thing needed by the people was a higher bill for its healthcare and for physicians that were too remote and unprincipled to solve the public's collective, as well as individualized, needs. For examples there was a high incidence of tuberculosis, wound infections were as common as the common cold, childbed fever was too often fatal, and syphilis went unchecked from one stage to the next, too often winding up in the brain. There was a dire need for educating the public and for an improved approach to these and other serious diseases.

The medical profession's issues stemmed from quite the same cause as the country's predicament. Starting superficially, something had to be done to establish regulations for clinical practice and research procedures, and to rid the physicians of a prevalent sense of immutable correctness.[11] There had to be a science-based authority that would be precise, appropriate, and sufficiently malleable to evolve with science's continuum of new achievements. This sounds more obvious today than it was at the time, for the medical mindset had its roots in the once brilliant decision of the ancient healer, Dr. Hippocrates—still commonly referred to as the Father of Western Medicine. To better understand the dilemma the medical profession was facing and to explain the harsh reaction that was needed to re-fortify its standing, a quick look further back should be helpful.

The relevance of ancient history to the founding of an eye bank and to the professional restrictions on its medical advocates were conventions from outdated influences of ancient principles. It was Hippocrates who wished to improve the services of doctors by transferring to each community physician an individualized power for decisions and actions. This was necessitated because in Hippocrates' day[12] throughout most of the known Greco-centric world, healings of every sort (including wound care) were exclusively the job of families of the healing deities-especially that of the man-god, Asclepius.[13] Through his example, all healing arts were the province of physicians such as Hippocrates himself, one of whose parents was a healing deity. Here is the point: As history has it, the First Doctor and his sons convinced the gods of human care that educated and honorable men "lacking the blood of gods" should be able to stand confidently by themselves as practitioners of medicine once each had taken an oath to always do one's best and never to do his patients harm-swearing such intent to Apollo, Asclepius and presumably the various gods and goddesses who bore him witness. That big step down from deity level health care to that of the common man physician called for a highly ethical physician willing and able to let responsibility fall upon his own shoulders. It made good sense and certainly increased the availability of care through all doctors thereafter not having to be deities but sworn to their standards by a single oath.

Over ensuing centuries, that transformative arrangement for the oath-devoted physicians turned out to have its own Achilles heel, for the physicians so entitled as free-functioning medical agents took upon themselves an oath-granted exclusivity that brought public regard, to which was added that jot of noblesse. The physicians' proud elitism gave them added self-respect but also a self-aggrandizing attitude that made them feel more competent than they deserved to feel. This formative history facilitates an understanding of the average 19th century doctor: If he were to be controlled by some higher court of medical judges, he would be losing not only his freewheeling professional independence but also the advantages offered by an elitism that had been a part of medical heritage for many centuries.[14] There were no continuing education courses for physicians. But what the freestanding physician might be losing was the trust that, in turn, had endowed his profession in the past with high principles, regardless of how long ago it had been since the physician swore by that oath. It was a grant of permanency, like the word "forever" on today's postage stamps. Those aside, oaths have to be renewed from time to time if doctors' contemporary mores are to depend upon such a "sea anchor" for medical righteousness.

Against this existing status were two absolutes in the thinking of the academics arriving to begin the new medical school in Baltimore and expecting to set the medical profession on a proper course. The first was that medical advertising had to stop. No form of it would be allowed, thus preventing the physicians from the obvious temptations of lucrative but too often false public witness. Even the slightest bit of self-promotion was now being perceived as deleterious to the public's respect and confidence in medical doctors, for advertising invariably leads to overstatement. Second, there would have to be an objective authoritarian source for providing quality control of medical standards and practices. Those two mandates would have to be dealt with as promptly as possible to facilitate the intra- and extra-mural campaign to clean up and modernize the profession.

In 1847, the newly formed American Medical Association became the only centralized potential source of authoritarian judgment of ethical medical principles. A Code of Ethics was promulgated in that year. It was a code with numerous components that related to issues not relevant to this discussion, but it laid down requirements that its member physicians must have nothing to do with anything that could be interpreted as personal promotion. However, the Code initially did not yet remove from the individual physician (nor from medical research) the prerogative to go by independent judgment instead of meeting established and monitored standards.

This lack of requirement for medical surveillance pleased the Old Guard of physicians and outraged the science-aware progressives of the "uprising" faction. The code acclaimers and code abhorrers exchanged irate penmanship in the mid-1880s. Stewart Paton' grand uncle was a fireball ophthalmologist named Dr. Cornelius Rea Agnew, one of most influential and most impassioned of these angered AMA members, representing those who believed that physicians must never depend upon the trickery of assuming a public profile developed by means of promotion—even carefully restricted personal statements—that could be construed as self-advertisement. In this view, Agnew joined squarely on the side of those who demanded the AMA modify its liberal laissez-faire permissiveness by modifying the 1847 Code of Ethics that virtually dictated professional standards to all member physicians.

In a letter to Dr. J. Hayes, an AMA leader, now on file in the Johns Hopkins Medical Archives, Agnew gets right to the point:

August 25, 1885

> My Dear Doctor:
>
> It is obvious I feel sure to any competent observer, that the American Medical Association has got into hands utterly incompetent to manage its affairs in the interests of Medical Progress and the good fame of our vocation. It is obvious that men like Dr. Davis of Chicago are entirely disqualified by nature and education for leading safely . . . What must be done? One of two things, either to get possession of the organization as it now stands and organize it, or to start a new organization...

Four pages later and in highly congested handwriting, Agnew has exhaustively pursued his point that the AMA had better stand up to the surveillance and behavioral conduct of its members. In retrospect, the progressive view was correct the findings of science would be the determinants of the correct course of the medical profession's acts and assessments in the years ahead. Based on the need for restoring much needed confidence in the profession, he and his colleagues took the harsh viewpoint that very little leeway should be allowed the practicing physician in his personal public choices in public. His work and its results should be the demonstration of his abilities, not what he might profess without scientific proof. Therefore, there should be strong restrictions on anything else that could be construed as self-promotion and/or assertions of beneficial patient managements that were not proven to the satisfaction of authoritative leadership.

Without any such objective authoritarian establishment for monitoring medical ethics, the fear was that the risk of granting prerogatives to the physicians and to researchers would surely include some naïve if not blatantly self-promotional decision-making. Agnew was an early advocate of "trust but verify" only if what was to be trusted was clearly defined.[15]

This is the piece with mortifying consequence for his great-grandnephew Townley Paton whose need for promotion of his eye bank would raise stark challenges to AMA conservatism. Agnew and his colleagues had been completely convinced that the AMA must bar all physician from generating the slightest personal publicity in order to preserve a profession's self-respect and patient trust. To put it into a nutshell: No physician should be entitled to make public appearances on behalf of his own interests or any interests that provide him with professional visibility or (as time went by) to use the radio for promoting any cause, no matter how much it needed public education. A physician was not considered responsible to the public and therefore he must not lower either himself or his profession by entering public discourse. That amounted to physicians being seen but not heard publicly.

Dr. Agnew, was what today might be called a religion-driven medical dynamo driven with a fervor to serve mankind as a moral and indefatigable agent of his God. The five-foot five-inch man with wiry sideburns and an incontestable heart of gold was born in 1830, and by 1884 this historically dynamic ophthalmologist had become a noted figure in the evolution of Medicine toward higher standards of professional behavior. Townley was far too young to have met his remote "Uncle Neely," but perhaps that distance made his great grand uncle all the more inspiring as an important ancestor who had a form of creativity, energy and determination for inventing institutions while remaining a fully booked private practitioner of ophthalmology. Townley would be a down-the-line gene-carrying successor to that rare individual—how proud one can be with an ancestor of Dr. Agnew's stalwart correctness and God-driven instinct for benefits to humanity at all levels of existence!

As to be mentioned below, Agnew was, after all, responsible for a great deal of creativity within a nascent medical specialty, and he was one of the leaders who brought about the upgrading of American Medicine at a time when that was critically needed. But many years later when Townley wished to help educate the public to embrace the concept of eye banking, this great-granduncle Neely and the other leading colleagues who had pressured the AMA to strengthen its Code of Ethics in 1885 were the root cause of the frustrating strictness that prevented any physician from any form of public advocacy.

In limiting his clinical practice to eye care, Agnew may have been the first full-time ophthalmologist in the eastern states, but eye surgery had already gained a strong identity with New York, surely making it the most eye-centered location in the country.[16] Agnew's enterprises included variously titled medical activities, such as Surgeon General of the State of New York, the principle founder of the noted U.S. Sanitary Commission (upon whose board Dr. Stewart Paton was later to serve), one of the founders of the New York Eye & Ear Infirmary, and a founder of the American Ophthalmological Society (American's first and still most distinguished eye society). He was also co-founder of the Manhattan Eye and Ear Hospital on whose board Stewart's older brother, William Agnew Paton,[17] also served. Many decades later, that hospital would be the selected site for the first eye bank and, at his retirement from New York, would designate Townley as its first honorary board member-ever.

By late in the 1880s, the matter of objectivity for the conduct, education and involvements of physicians was of such importance to the envisioned goals of the forthcoming Johns Hopkins medical revolution that several of its most distinguished physicians—Dr. William Welch and Dr. William Osler, along with the educator Abraham Flexner—joined Dr. Agnew and his allies at the AMA headquarters in Philadelphia to support the battle for what was being called "scientific democracy."[18] They were all on the winning side.

In summary, on one hand, the physician's separation from public discourse by the well-intended AMA Code of Ethics constituted a stop to self-promotional advertising as a boost to physician self-respect and to the bolstering of its significance with the public. On the other hand, the medical profession's refurbished elitism allowed for snobbish professionals who had no obligation to

INSIGHT

indulge in the serious needs of the public's health; which, at last and at least they were finally not allowed to advocate.

NOTES TO CHAPTER 4:

1. Knox, J.H.M.: "The Medical History of Washington, His Physicians, Friends and Advisers," *Bulletin of the Institute of the History of Medicine*, 174-91, 1933.
2. Starr, P.: *The Social Transformation of American Medicine*. Basic Books, New York, 1982.
3. Today, these health-care variants have assimilated strong medical principles and practices while retaining some of their own characteristics. They are certified, and no criticism is intended.
4. Haggard, H.H.: *The Lame, The Halt, and The Blind. The Vital Role of Medicine in the History of Civilization*. Harper Brothers, New York, 1932.
5. Von Drehle, D.: "The Demon Drink," *Time*, p. 56, May 24, 2010.
6. Snyder, C.: *Our Ophthalmic Heritage*, Little, Brown and Company, Boston, 1961.
7. Ibid.
8. Social clues can indicate biases that persist: It may be coincidental, but the American Chesterfield cigarette with its English name, introduced in 1873, was on course to high popularity in the century ahead.
9. Alton, L.: *The Bizarre Careers of John R. Brinkley*. Lexington, University Press of Kentucky, 2002.
10. In 2015 dollars, these charges come to almost $79,000 and almost $120,000, respectively
11. The AMA was well formed and active but it lacked the mandate of respect that had to come from an understanding of the issues.
12. The following paragraph has been inspired by Stephanie Fleetwood, an authority on the life of Hippocrates. Hippocrates was born an Asclepiad, meaning a genetic relationship to Asclepius with the ancestral right to practice Medicine if he so chose. His parents were respected citizens on the relatively sophisticated Aegean island of Kos; his father was a well-known Asclepiad physician, and his mother's family.descended from an ancient local family. He was educated at aristocratic schools and then crisscrossed the Aegean and Mediterranean seas to study mathematics and philosophy and observe medical practices. He returned to Kos

and studied the religious and practical traditions known only to the Asclepiads from his father and grandfather. But his own emerging concepts of doctoring and healing diverged from the traditional belief that diseases were the punishment of deities and became based on personal observations and research on countless patients - all of which he wrote down. He saw Medicine as a science, not an aspect of religion, but it was his belief in the importance of detailed, written medical histories that distinguished him at the time and secured his position in history. When he established his school on Kos, his sons were practicing Asclepiads. His daughter was married to his most brilliant student, who was not an Asclepiad and technically couldn't practice medicine. However, Hippocrates and his sons convinced the powers-that-be that educated and honorable men should be able to practice Medicine if they took an oath to do one's best and do no harm, swearing by Apollo and Asclepius and all the gods and goddesses. These physicians could never be Asclepiads or participate in their religious privileges, but they could legally practice. It was his democratization of practicing Medicine as much as his introduction of scientific and clinical methods that changed their concept of care.

13. Over time, the physician's prerogatives and the oath itself underwent changes, but as a simplified explanation of the goal that new science had to achieve, the above should be sufficient.

14. Before 1916, when ophthalmology established the first specialty board, there were no forms of medical specialization with specified standards. A few specialty societies were forming, but these lacked authority over their voluntary memberships.

15. The Code changes and its issues are well summarized in these references: Warner, J.H.:"The 1880s Rebellion Against the AMA Code of Ethics"; and Baker, R.B., Caplan. A.I., Emanuel, L.L. and Latham, S.R.:, "'Scientific Democracy' and the Dissolution of Orthodoxy. In *The American Medical Ethics Revolution*, Johns Hopkins University Press, Baltimore, 1999.

16. Rosen, G.: "The History of American Ophthalmology," *N.Y State J. Med.*, 754-758, 1943.

17. William A. Paton, a businessman, world traveler and author of several books about his travels; grandson of John P. Agnew, publisher of The New York World, first business manager of *Scribner's Magazine*; member of the Century Association and the Tile Club whose membershop included most of the leading artists in what is now known as "The Hamptons," located on Eastern Long Island where Townley and Helen would live upon retirement from his Manhattan practive.

18. See Reference #15.

CHAPTER 5: ROSTER OF REVOLUTION

> We are brothers all, in honour, as in one community, scholars and gentlemen.
> "The Prelude," William Wordsworth, 1770-1850

It is a favorite memory of American history that in 1814 after Francis Scott Key witnessed the Battle of Baltimore in the harbor near Fort McHenry, he was inspired to write the "Star Spangled Banner." That the fort had survived the British attack foretold American victory. The flag thus represented the heart of an embattled country.

There is another important American dawn that took place in Baltimore later in the same century. At its heart was not a flag but an ancient Roman watchword, *aequanimitas*, introduced to medical renewal in 1889 by Dr. William Osler[1] upon being recruited to Johns Hopkins University to lead an initial handful of men (sic) committed to an incomparable medical revolution to reconstruct a blighted profession. That single Latin watchword, in revolutionary context, continues to stand for calmness under fire, level-headed grit, and confidence in know-how for achievement.

The challenging mental chaos created in the forthcoming professional struggle in behalf of the medical profession was to reverberate for decades in numerous Paton lives, for it was inseparable from the privileges and uniqueness of their presence at Johns Hopkins. For Townley, reared in its midst, the generated significance of a tumultuous collective undertaking was the equal of a Sousa band playing rousing marches that even a child would want to join.

ROSTER OF REVOLUTION

There were good medical schools and fine physicians elsewhere, in Philadelphia, Boston and New York. But none had the enthusiastic fascination of the new school in Baltimore. To better understand Townley's ambition and to explain the determination that drove it beyond conventional limit, the impact of this extraordinary uprising staged by level-headed professors can only be appreciated by the presentation of a few of its main instigators. Up close, as individual physicians, they were anything but revolutionists; from a distance, their commitment was to resonate throughout the medical profession at home and abroad.

To begin with historical perspective, just before the turn of the 19th century, the leaders of Johns Hopkins University realized the inadequacy of Medicine's public role and became committed to overcome its failings. Their fundamental purpose was to engage the products of new science and to optimize medical education with an excellence that could be championed from within, rather than promulgations to the profession at large. Such optimistic plans for a teaching and research empire of its own making called for building the undertaking from the ground up. The funding of such an ambitious venture was an enormous prerequisite. Wealthy individuals and powerful foundations would have to be convinced of the validity of the university's mission.

William H. Welch.

As with all creative ventures, the ultimate determinants of success at every step would be the mentality of its leaders. For a modernized, science-driven medical school, the primary need was for an assemblage of a diversified but like-minded faculty widely chosen for their unique abilities. The core of this necessarily tightly knit group would be only a handful of physicians, each with his own medical sub-specialty and each with the overriding aim to change Medicine into a continuously evolving first-class profession. The two prime leaders were Dr. William H. Welch and Dr. William Osler, each were young men with inherent and experienced leadership abilities, to form a medical school and hospital that would epitomize the ideals of medical training that included a continuum of research.

Dr. Welch, a pathologist, was recruited in 1884, and Dr. Osler, an internist by today's designation, followed in 1889. Recruitment for the other stars of the revolution had to proceed slowly, for the first need was the structural completion of the new hospital and medical school. In 1892, Stewart Paton arrived from his studies in Europe-uninvited and job hunting. Having heard from American colleagues of the goings-on at Johns Hopkins, Stewart figured that undertaking was too special for him not to become involved in its launching. He was younger than the recruited faculty, yet beyond his preoccupation with the genesis of psychiatry he could afford to be a physician with research and clinical curiosity that would never be frozen, always fluid. It was an atypical status that fit with the spirit of the Johns Hopkins drive.

Stewart had returned to New York by steamship, and in a long-awaited stopover he and Frances Margaret Halsey were married in a Manhattan Presbyterian church before an abundance of relatives and friends. A few days later, they took the train to Baltimore. They did not travel light. The two of them shared two SP-initialed Vuitton trunks. That kind of luggage had to be sent by freight. The bride and groom settled in a row house on Washington Street, a half-mile walk to the Johns Hopkins medical campus under construction. Ahead for them was a half-century of marriage—he, the do-it-yourself psycho-scientist; and she, his do-it-right social adjuster.

Stewart had gambled on the scarcity and need for an "alienist" at Johns Hopkins. That was the name, derived from the French word for "insanity," that identified his chosen specialty-in-development as it reached further than psychology and deeper into fundamental investigation. He was prepared to welcome even the lowest paying appointment if he could simultaneously continue his improvised academic pursuit. A symbol of the new academia was the construction of a building uniquely for the teaching and researches of pathology. Amazing! It was nearing completion and soon to be occupied by clinical modernists in admittedly low paying but gratifying academic employment. Stewart was prepared to teach medical students in neuroanatomy, microbiology and psychology, if those were to fit in the school's curriculum.

The upshot of interviews with Drs. Welch and Osler was an offer he readily accepted: lecturing to enrolled students awaiting the medical school's opening the following year at an acceptable stipend of $80 monthly.[2] A bonus soon followed with his appointment as Director of Research at the Sheppard and Enoch Pratt Hospital (originally Sheppard Asylum) for the insane.

In 1886 and at 27, Stewart had graduated from Princeton University. Four years later, he graduated from Columbia Medical School, and then went on to post-graduate studies in Germany. His goal was to become an alienist. Stewart was serious in his intent to gain clinical understanding of the brain's functions and malfunctions as might be explored in the neurobiology and micro neuroanatomy of animal and human brains and in their comparative physiologies. Those interests applied to the understanding of psychiatric illnesses provided the qualifications of a broad-based teacher, and an evolving psychiatrist.[3]

For the first time in his own country, Stewart could fully appreciate the scientific approaches that Johns Hopkins featured, emanating from plans designed by Dr. Welch that were based upon the systems used in Germany where Welch had also studied. To that foreign influence was added a zeitgeist never before united with medical training. Dr. Osler's *aequanimitas*[4] became the watchword for an educational twist to the anticipated Hopkins medical renaissance.

Over time, his influence and in-put in behalf of the medical enlightenment was undisputable, as indicated much later in a letter to Stewart from Dr. Welsh dated April 19, 1927. He writes, "Rejoice with us in completing our two million dollar endowment for that child of yours, The Phipps [Psychiatric] Clinic." The letter goes on, "We should never have had it but for the interest in the subject with which you inspired me and others, which enabled us to present the case appealingly to Mr. Phipps."[5]

In 1884, William Henry Welch MD,[6] as the first appointee to the medical faculty, became, at 34, Professor of Pathology and Dean of the Medical School—and the fulcrum for the heroic undertakings that followed. As one historian expressed it, Welch "more than any other single person presided over the transformation of American medical education."[7] He created the model academic medical structures for the country, and thus for the world.

One of Welch's most cogent observations was that the advancement of Medicine had become tied to the availability of high finance, and it was the philanthropy of the country's millionaires in making that possible. Paradoxically, the notorious robber barons who had sucked up much of the nation's wealth would now prove to be the nation's most vital salvation by enabling the existing systems to accommodate the advances of science. Reforming was an expensive undertaking, and it was there that Stewart and family members proved very helpful in attracting financial donors whom they helped to sell on the purposes of the Johns Hopkins medical bandwagon. Every personal contact was to be approached with considerable thought and planning. It was an innovative attitude about the need to cultivate the sources of indispensable philanthropy.

Welch was a physician's son but he had never been eager to follow his father into practice. He came to Johns Hopkins from a staff appointment at New York's Bellevue Hospital, having done extensive post-graduate work in several European countries. Welch was short-statured and decidedly rotund but a hale and hearty man with an exuberance and humor that made him an unqualified favorite of many–except for Margaret Paton, who initially took exception to his incessant cigars, noting with disapproval the white ashes collecting on his prominent midriff, always with a cigar "perpetually in his mouth, protruding straight forward, rising and falling during conversations," and in his laboratory pushed to one side as he looked through his microscope.[8] Welch was a lifelong bachelor. He had a strong personal friendship with David Paton, another bachelor and almost career-long Princeton University scholar in residence. Both Welch and Paton

INSIGHT

received honorary degrees from Princeton, one to the Egyptologist for his extensive translation of hieroglyphics and the other to the Dean at Johns Hopkins for his contributions to medical education. That was only one of fifteen such degrees that Welch was awarded in honor of his successful commitment.

To his friends and students, Dr. Welch was known or referred to as "Popsy Welch." In addition to abundant good humor, he was a skilled orator, possessed outstanding leadership qualities, and had a kindness that when mixed with his persuasiveness became an irresistible force in fundraising, maintaining medical standards and avoiding triviality and irresponsible inertia.

Of all faculty members—and cigars aside—Popsy was the most senior and closest friend of the Paton family.[9] Many stories were told in their home about that friendship, including the acceptance of a small clay statue of the oversized Welch mounted on a small pony for a seven-hour trek to visit distant Ming artifacts during a visit to China in his role as director of the China Medical Board of the Rockefeller Institute. The bronze statue[10] that followed the clay model is on perpetual view in the Welch Library of the Johns Hopkins School of Medicine. Stewart eventually gave the model to Townley, who guarded it carefully in his office for a decade or two before it was smashed to smithereens in a cleaning mishap.

Dr. Welch published, lectured, and participated in innumerable projects and programs as a medical leader. The take-home was the good will of a magnetic, enthusiastic man with indomitable academic purpose. His undeniable admiration of Stewart, 18 years his junior, was expressed in an excerpt from the following handwritten letter sent less than a month after Woodrow Wilson's resignation from the presidency of Princeton to accept the Democratic nomination for Governor of New Jersey. Stewart was then 45 years old, in the prime of life, and serving on the Princeton faculty:

"Dear Paton,

I thought that I would not embarrass you, but I am quite sincere in saying that I am of the opinion that you would make an excellent president of Princeton, and if I were writing to anybody else I should say more on the subject.

Very sincerely yours, (signed) William H. Welch." November 14, 1910.[11]

That, indeed, is a memorable letter for its thoughtfulness regarding the highest academic position at Princeton. It was, of course, not an offer but a compliment. Stewart certainly had made some big contributions to Johns Hopkins' medical structure that were not particularly recognized; thus he must have been very touched by that expression of caring from the Hopkins former Dean. What Stewart said in reply is unknown.

To continue introducing members of the senior faculty, the incomparable Dr. William Osler was appointed the sole Professor of Medicine and would become commonly known as the Father of Modern Medicine. Canadian by birth and initial medical training, he was the second appointee to the medical faculty. He had originally wanted to become an ophthalmologist, but that desire was displaced with the realization that a more encompassing medical purpose was to be his destination. Although he stayed only 13 years at Johns Hopkins, his national and international identification became that of the supreme academic clinician who taught and inspired an attitude of rigorously demanding, altruistic and sustained dedication for medical trainees. He introduced bedside instruction and hands-on patient care by his trainees, and they learned to exemplify the iron man endurance that was expected of them. Osler was gifted with a sophisticated vocabulary that reflected his tireless readings of classical literature as well as his intrinsic respect for medical history. Both he and Popsy Welch were in great demand as speakers and advocates of a renovating medical profession.

Dr. William Osler

Fourteen years older than Stewart Paton, Osler was a fatherly friend. He and Stewart both signed permissions for their brains to be studied at autopsy, a fairly innovative voluntary offering of that period.[12] He memorably and jokingly suggested that by age 67 everyone should be retired for a few contemplative years before being dispatched by chloroform. He believed that one's productive years were confined to those before age 40, at a time (circa 1900) when life expectancy was only 59 years.

ROSTER OF REVOLUTION

Osler married Grace Revere, whose paternal great grandfather was Paul Revere, and the Oslers named their son Edward Revere to honor forebears on both sides of the boy's genetic background.

Known by his middle name, Revere became a World War I fatality in France, the Oslers thereby losing their only living child. His biographer postulates that Sir William never fully recovered from that tragedy.[13] He had no inhibitions in speaking about Revere and honoring his military service. That stands in contrast to the entirely different way Townley was later to manage a similar bereavement of his own.

Osler's successor, Stewart's brother-in-law, Dr. Lewellys F. Barker, said of Osler, that "he passed about, gallant and debonair, with a whimsical wit that left the air sweet and gay, with an epigram here and a paradox there, tickling the ribs of his colleagues, none felt him frivolous."[14] Osler left Johns Hopkins in 1905 to accept a professorship at Oxford University as a loyal member of the United Kingdom. There he was soon knighted. Sir William was recognized worldwide as the physician most responsible for inspiring the dedication and commitment of physicians to their profession and for his fundamental role in the movement to alter Medicine's pathway by focusing the mindset of the selected leaders on the task of fashioning new medical mores and enlightened medical education.

INSIGHT

Other leaders of the revolution followed the Welch-Osler precedent with contributions of their own. William Stewart Halsted MD, who was recruited at age 37, as a full professor became known as the Father of Modern Surgery. He and Stewart's wife, Margaret, shared the same paternal grandfather, making them cousins. Like Welch, Halsted was also short, at about five-feet, five-inches, and of stocky build. He was a former Yale athlete and a man of rare endurance, with the steely purpose necessary to succeed as one of the primary Johns Hopkins revolutionaries. By the time Professor Halsted began his surgical career, chloroform anesthesia, as initiated by William Paton's Scottish friend, James Simpson, was soon to be popularized. Halsted selected himself to test the efficacy of cocaine for its anesthetic value. As a result, he would be plagued for the remainder of his life by cocaine addiction.[15]

Welch was Halsted's closest medical ally and was of key assistance in caring for Halsted during his addictive illness that was further compounded by an addiction to morphine used to break the cocaine habit.[16] But more noteworthy, and typical of this remarkable surgeon, Dr. Halsted saved the lives of both his mother and his sister by performing emergency surgeries under anything but customary circumstances. In 1881, when his sister "collapsed from a postpartum hemorrhage" and was in extreme jeopardy, he aspirated a unit of his own blood and injected it into his sister's vein, which she fortunately tolerated without adverse reaction. This was "the first successful direct blood transfusion in America."[17] Clearly, the lack of cross-matching even between siblings is of great importance. For the emergency surgery for his mother and for his sister, Halsted's knowledge and skills had to have luck on his side. One of the Mayo brothers spoke with admiration of this "shy unapproachable perfectionist" and another physician[17] commented that Halsted was "the greatest surgical thinker America has produced."

Halsted's operating room endurance and his attention to the smallest details of each operation were in line with his insistence upon thoroughness and precision. His chief scrub nurse, Caroline Hampton, whom he was to marry, developed an intolerable skin sensitivity to the chemicals of surgical cleanup, and that led to Halsted's historical introduction of rubber gloves for her and eventually for all surgical teams. As a result, wound infections were greatly reduced.

Partly damaged by his addictions, he was less open than his colleagues, but he was ever loyal to the cause for which he was appointed. Although friendly with each other, Halsted and Margaret Paton were not frequent-visiting cousins. Despite the personal troubles that served to isolate him when at work, he was known to be an entirely different, open and fun-loving individual when unencumbered by his work and able to relax.

Professor Howard Atwood Kelly MD was a wealthy merchant's son who completed a strong, award-winning education before joining the Hopkins faculty at the age of 31. He became the first Johns Hopkins Professor of Obstetrics and Gynecology and is commonly known by many as the Father of Gynecology. He was the fourth of the "big four" faculty appointees, honored together by a now famous John Singer Sargent portrait that hangs in the Johns Hopkins William H. Welch Medical Library.[18]

Kelly was original in the use of radium therapy and became widely known for his leadership in its clinical applications. He was an evangelical Christian, father of nine children and an authority on snakes, birds and anthropology in general. He was seven years older than Stewart Paton yet was a favorite Paton family companion, for they shared the love of the outdoors and wild animals. He received five honorary degrees and was honorary member of 15 or more foreign medical societies, as well as being the recipient of countless other high honors and recognitions. Kelly not only collected books but he wrote voluminously, authoring numerous original concepts and authoring several popular medical texts.

Lewellys Franklin Barker MD PhD, like Osler a Canadian by birth, was two years younger than Stewart and was his brother-in-law by marriage to Lilian Halsey, the spunky and avant-garde sister of Stewart's wife, Margaret. Lilian added lively modern pizzazz and spice to Barker's home life — a chain-smoking baseball addict and vocally liberal suffragette, she was an engrossingly cryptic commentator on the affairs of the medical world.

Barker once wrote, "Genetically speaking, humans are polyhybrid heterozygous bastards," [19] a memorable description that emphasizes in his graphic manner a sincere and strong belief in genetic knowledge for human benefit, a belief that led to his interest in the relationships of each disease to laboratory findings. For that and his sustained interest in genetic inheritance, he has been referred to as the classical Progressive Era eugenicist.[20]

When Osler departed from Johns Hopkins to accept the professorship at Oxford, Barker was offered and eventually accepted Osler's professorship as Chief of Medicine on a full-time, expenses-only basis. With that arrangement he was able to continue a busy private practice. Barker was in demand as an internist with a diagnostically acute mind, and he was a popular teacher, with considerable research in anatomy and physiology in his background. His son, William Halsey Barker MD, and three grandsons were to become internists and serve on the Johns Hopkins faculty at one time or another during their careers–each a notable example of familial medical excellence, possibly more common in their days than thereafter.

Called the Father of Neurosurgery, Professor Harvey Williams Cushing MD, was to become known internationally for his many contributions to surgery of the brain, plus other medical interests in his capacity as a classical academician. He came from a prominent Midwestern family, and having graduated from Harvard Medical School in 1895, he came to Hopkins for residency training under Dr. Halsted, then entering private practice in Baltimore in 1901, the year that Townley was born. At age 32, he became Associate Professor of Surgery, responsible for the neurosurgery service. He was clean-

INSIGHT

shaven, somewhat atypical at the time for high-ranking male professionals. He tended to be impatient and brusque but was closely tied to the goals of his companion revolutionaries. In a Pulitzer Prize-winning, two-volume biography of Osler, Cushing wrote of his senior companion, "Whatever may be said of Sir William Osler in days to come, of his high position in medicine, of his gifts and versatility, to his contemporaries, love of his fellow man, utter unselfishness, and an extraordinary capacity for friendship will always remain the characteristics which overshadow all else."[21]

In later years, Cushing taught at Harvard and Yale, both institutions that honored his abilities and skills to the same extent as Johns Hopkins. He was an eclectic physician, a talented self-taught artist, and he made numerous major medical contributions beyond neurosurgery alone. Cushing never lost his love and admiration for the Hopkins faculty and later wrote in his book, "My brief work of 16 years in Baltimore has in a general way pointed directions to my entire subsequent life. I realized that I was in the presence of great masters, and I became not only an ardent student but reverent admirer."[22] That was high praise from one of the nation's most valuable physicians and eclectic minds.

Abraham Flexner (who initially had an even more famous surgeon brother, Simon Flexner, MD) was among those most responsible for the success of the Johns Hopkins medical uprising. An honors Johns Hopkins undergraduate and a well-trained and skillful teacher, Abraham, when with the Carnegie

Institution, masterminded a survey of 155 medical schools in the U.S. and Canada that resulted in the famous Flexner Report of 1910,[23] which "scathingly and devastatingly assailed the faulty conditions that existed" in medical schools. This document was of critical importance in the effort to close proprietary medical schools and inspire academic excellence in the legitimate ones. The survey determined that the Johns Hopkins University School of Medicine was the first medical school in this country of genuine university type. By publishing medical education's deficiencies, that report alone proved the greatest stimulus for medical transformation. Flexner served on the noted Rockefeller Foundation's General Education Board, as had his surgeon-brother Simon He was an effective fundraiser and along with Popsy Welch may have influenced a certain Mrs. Breckinridge's technique of gaining substantial financial support by collecting information about each intended donor and forming personal contacts with them. Eventually he became a patient and friend of Townley Paton, to whom he wrote a dedication in his autobiography.[24]

    The commitment of these academic physicians was not based upon the social prominence of the physician—as typified in earlier eras—but upon the power and justification of ideas replacing old customs, ushering in those of science and sociology. And such new knowledge would not be locked into place, for its delivery system had to be modified by alterations befitting evolving science. The constancy of replenishing authority with new leaders and their modernized ideas would help eliminate the hubris that came with medicine's former intransience.

    As it turned out, the revolutionaries who remodeled the medical profession and were close to the Patons included a number

INSIGHT

of family members whose participation made the Johns Hopkins heroic revolution for them all the more upfront and personal. Those ties brought Stewart and Margaret into the personal zones of the primary instigators. The familiarity and participations that the Patons had with those select and dynamic physicians, including the members of their families, bears inferential testimony to the nurturing environment in which Townley would be raised. The dynamism, creativity, medical achievements and individual leadership of these closely associated men provided a community aura whose radiation not only inspired their own generation of Johns Hopkins physicians but permeated the childhoods of their offspring with irresistible contagion.

It would be quite extraordinary if anyone anywhere would say with a straight face that he or she had an even more powerful medical nurture than that from Stewart Paton and the Johns Hopkins faculty as it encompassed and indoctrinated one very receptive lad named Townley Paton.

ROSTER OF REVOLUTION

NOTES TO CHAPTER 5:

1. Osler first used this word at the University of Pennsylvania Medical School in a farewell address to the medical students. Literally, its meaning is calmness and commitment but its interpretation in the context of its use at the medical school includes dynamism and leadership.
2. In Medical School minutes of March 31, 1898: "Dr. Paton was designated Assistant Visiting Physician to the City Asylum at Bay View. He has for some time been serving in this capacity." In the minutes of May 23, 1901 for the Budget ~ 1901-1902~ the line item entry for Psychiatry is, "Stewart Paton, M.D. Associate in Psychiatry (promoted from Assistant in Neurology; increase of $100) $200."
3. Dr. Henry Mills Hurd MD, LLD (1843-1927), appointed Superintendent of the Johns Hopkins Hospital from the time its doors opened and for 22 years thereafter until his retirement, was a noted psychiatrist who lectured at the Medical School but had become a full-time superintendent of key importance to the hospital and the university.
4. Aequanimitas was referred to as "the Big A" in a letter of Hopkins-referenced commendation from a friend to Townley on his 75th birthday.
5. This letter is on file in the Johns Hopkins Chesney Medical Archives.
6. Possibly the best short summery of the life of William Welch is in Ira Rutkow's book, previously referenced. Others are also referenced hereafter.
7. Fleming, D.: *William H. Welch and the Rise of Modern Medicine.* Johns Hopkins University Press, Baltimore, 1954.
8. Flexner, S. and Flexner, J.T.: *William Henry Welch and the Heroic Age of American Medicine*, page 252. Johns Hopkins University Press, Baltimore and London, 1941.
9. Letters of Dr. Stewart Paton to and from Dr. Welch are on file in the Johns Hopkins Medical Archives.
10. The statue was created by Harriet Mayer and Anna Hyatt Mayer.
11. The letter was saved without the envelope in which it was mailed. Therefore, it is an assumption that the designation of "Paton" referred to Stewart and not to his brother David. The Alan Chesney Hopkins Medical Archives where it is filed has given the opinion that it was sent to Stewart, all factors considered.
12. This did not take place for Stewart, possibly by oversight or inconvenience. No record is found of the Osler brain examination, if it took place in England. He was buried in Brooklyn, NY, as will be noted further at a later place.

13. Cushing H.: *The Life of Sir William Osler*, Vol I, 685 pages; Vol II, 728 pages. Oxford Clarendon Press, 1925.

14. Tucker, A., *It Happened at Hopkins*, published by Johns Hopkins Hospital, Women's Board, Baltimore, MD, 1960.

15. Another physician of that era who developed an addiction to cocaine was Sigmund Freud whose story is told by a prominent medical author. Markel, H.: "An Anatomy of Addiction. Sigmund Freud, William Halsted, and the Medical Drug Cocaine." pg. 33, Pantheon Books, New York 2011

16. Dr. Alexis Carrel. A French physician and 1912 Nobel Prize recipient who was also a leader in eugenics, he died before it was determined whether he was a Nazi sympathizer.

17. Sargent was the son of Dr. Fitzwilliam Sargent, a surgeon who took training at Wills Eye Hospital in Philadelphia and specialized in eye surgery

18. Barker, L.: *Maryland Historical Magazine*, Vol. 38, 1943.

19. Comfort, Nathaniel, *The Science of Human Perfection*, p. 181. Yale University Press, New Haven, 2014.

20. Barker had at first suggested full-time salaried professors in a speech, "Medicine and the Universities," but due to financial commitments he was unable to accept the Professorship without a private practice, as was eventually granted to him upon succeeding Dr. Osler.

21. Cushing, H.: *The Life of Sir William Osler*. Oxford University Press, New York, 1940

22. Ibid.

23. Cushing, H.: *Consecratio Medici and Other Papers*. Little, Brown, and Company, Boston, 1928.

24. Flexner, A.: *Bulletin Number Four*, Carnegie Foundation for the Advancement of Teaching, 1910.

25. Flexner, A.: *I Remember: The Autobiography of Abraham Flexner*. Simon and Schuster, New York, 1940.

CHAPTER 6: COPACETIC MINDS

When I am not thank'd at all, I'm thank'd enough. I've done my duty, and I've done no more. "Tom Thumb the Great," Henry Fielding, 1707-1754

To know Townley's character meant knowing the makeup of his father. Stewart, was an expressive writer and professional social commentator, and was to a large extent his son's intellectual compass, but his son was less verbally expressive. Their values and commitments had the same importance to their lives. Their abilities showed but they were not showmen. When new ideas "turned them on," they were likely to have high amperage but low voltage. That is a formula for big contributions that may or may not be rewarded by obligated appreciation. Neither of them was driven by the need for thanks.

Townley's personal reticence becomes less opaque after examining clues from his father's career. Although they had no professional collaborations, their motivations and choices for their work were obviously akin. Their goals were iconic solutions to perceived needs: an institute for the mentally ill, a school for public health, and an eye bank to facilitate sight-restoring surgery. Those were the kinds of purposes that ignited their energies and challenged their abilities. However, Stewart wrote a great deal and Townley wrote relatively little beyond describing new improvements in surgical technique, outcomes of keratoplasty, and the affairs of eye banking.

The father and son were united genetically and environmentally, but they did not look alike. If they were forced to stand side by side, looking straight ahead in the glare of a police lineup, not even the detectives behind the window glass would suppose they were father and son. But despite the generation gap and

INSIGHT

their physical dissimilarity, Stewart and Townley had inner match-ups as recognizable as a pattern of family fingerprints. They were both kind, gentle and eager to please. They were alert, conscientious, optimistic and both were approachable and attentive, but the tie was more than that.

In the formative early years for Townley, Stewart was an almost constant source of nurture for a son intrigued by doctoring and wanting to be like his sensible and inquisitive father. Nurture was in the air—manifested in Townley's contentedness and intellectual curiosity. Although Stewart was neither a captivating speaker, nor an author memorable for the quality of his syntax, he dispensed good sense about topics that were at the cutting edge of common knowledge, aiming at what was yet to be discovered. He spoke and wrote his views in books and letters to the editor of New York newspapers.

In fact, Stewart wrote in his diary with daily faithfulness, and he compiled six books of several hundred pages each without images or indices, little tomes of psychiatric fact and behavioral admonitions.

Those books were popularly discussed in home and office exchanges—but who knew what the public or the profession found in them? Stewart rarely had a co-author. Unlike his father, Townley was to choose several co-authors to facilitate what needed to be said in print.

Some shared characteristics were as obvious as were their differences. Like his father, Townley was to marry an attractive and socially effective wife. A longstanding Paton family contention by its women (sometimes belittled but not effectively denied) is that Paton wives have always been the family decision-makers, the husbands being too absorbed in their work to assume domestic dominance. To whatever extent such command needs acknowledgment, the maxim is not disputed, merely disregarded as an irrelevance. Neither given to emotional outbursts nor running arguments, Stewart and Townley were highly contented family men, both with comfortable rapport inside their homes and with neighbors, colleagues and essentially all others on the outside. Their characters were as true as their personalities suggested. They were world-news oriented yet fans of jokes if clean and not too subtle—for instance the attribution to Bob Hope that when asked on his death bed where he wanted to be buried his answer was, "Surprise me." They also cherished their Scottish heritance but neither had the ability to tell a joke in brogue.

That brings up another male similarity that set the Paton men apart from the man in the street. By adolescence, Townley had developed his father's preference for personal privacy and as he aged to adulthood and had children, he also displayed Stewart's restraint in avoiding swear words and carnal conversations beyond the birds and the bees. In both households, separated by decades and distance, there was no tolerance for discussion of sexuality in any of its forms unless for gender identification.

In Stewart's day that may have been a not uncommon position to take except when there was a patient in an easy chair (there was no couch in Stewart's office) with a lot to unload. It is probable, however, that Stewart, as for some other alienists of his day, never took the Freudian option of psychoanalysis. And although Townley arrived a full generation later and attended both a boarding school and a college for males only—hotbeds of off-color jokes—he too was a prince of prude. Close family members have enjoyed recalling that Townley's disapproval of public nudity was such that "he did not like to be seen with his shoes off," a phrase repeated hundreds of times as an indication of his amusing bashfulness even at home which became an almost beloved peculiarity.

The two men's Puritanism could have been rooted in some genetic trait causing an antipathy to physical demonstrativeness. As medical doctors, they knew plenty about the biology, physiology and psychology of human sexuality. While the two generations of Paton antediluvian conservatism about common decency may seem reactionary to some, others might feel it preferable to the alternative. In all six of his psycho-observational books, Stewart presented himself as a psychiatric "scold," bemoaning the infinite ways in which mankind failed to perceive its errors, asserting that only with mental adjustments would it survive.[1] Similarly, his occasional dinner speech consisted of a series of facts crowned by thanks and polite inferences to troubled times ahead. He could neither electrify an audience nor restrain interruptions, neither of which had anything to do with the quality of the man who simply lacked the means for a lively delivery.

Townley was similarly limited. There was a time when he and his son exchanged self-assessments about the fun and the troubles of school years. Townley did not have much to say of a personal nature but in searching for a topic of weakness to match the confessions of his son, he chose the most memorable complaint about himself: Failing to have "fast snaps" (meaning quick witted) bothered him. He acknowledged that he was no raconteur, and that seemed to bother him. In contrast, Stewart was a fount of information but he lacked speaker's timing that energizes an audience by tweaking the listeners' minds in such a way as to enlist their concentration. Townley was to become an active show-and-tell teacher of medical colleagues, which he did well, but with personality instead of flourish.

Stewart and Townley deserve considerable credit for what they contributed as teachers, especially because they often did not have the easiest milieu in which to deliver. When called upon to sell their thoughts to laymen, the Paton men were too technical and cryptic to hold an audience. Add to that deficiency, Stewart had to endure conjured terms like "madness," "insanity," "strait-jacket" and "asylum," and to bear the intrinsically "alienating" title of "alienist," which was only slightly less of an affront than "shrink." Townley, in turn, had the disagreeable obligation to advocate the inhuman desecration of removing eyes from the dead. That is no longer what is required of eye bank donors, but in Townley's time it was necessary. Despite the off-putting aspects of their medical sub-specialties, what mattered to father and son was the goal each pursued and the approval of favored peers. While what follows applies directly to Stewart in confirming his professional priorities, it reveals an

INSIGHT

interesting characteristic that at a later time will emerge in his son, more easily identified if recognized in the father.

To begin, a classic Johns Hopkins story involving the reversal of insanity is abbreviated here more for the points to be made than for the history that transpired. In 1912, when working with Yale students, as he had done at Princeton, Stewart met a Yale graduate who was working on another edition of his book, *A Mind That Found Itself*,[2] an extraordinary account of the man's own delusional and maniacal extremes of insanity in the early 1900s. Over more than five years of intense periodic mental illness and asylum imprisonment, Clifford Beers and patients like him were treated as if they were enemy prisoners in the hands of harsh guards without restriction on their cruelty to the patients.

Remarkably, by 1906 Beers had recovered his sanity and in his autobiography he described being retained "insane asylums" where torture by the guards included intentionally over-tightened strait-jackets as the least of his suffering, for he was often brutally beaten resulting in fractures of his nose, many of his bones and on several occasions he was almost choked to death. The book made him widely known within the medical world for the articulately expressed revelations and for the definitive solutions he proposed. Beers became the impetus for long overdue change in the treatment of patients confined to mental institutions.

It was Stewart Paton who became Beers' go-between[3] in introducing him to professors and philanthropists in a drive to establish a "mental hygiene"[4] clinic at Johns Hopkins. As Beers stated in the 1917 edition of his autobiography, it was "through the courtesy of Dr. Paton, who advised me that Dr. Adolf Meyer, then Director of the Psychiatric Institute of the New York State Hospitals at Ward's Island, New York City was the one man of all others in his special field whose support should be secured." That same gratitude to Stewart was reiterated by Mrs. Beers many years later, when sending a letter of sympathy to Townley after the death of Stewart.

Again, in an obituary appearing in the Princeton Alumni Bulletin in 1942, there is this similar statement: "Stewart Paton was the prime influence in interesting Dr. William H. Welch in psychiatry, thus leading to the large gifts by Henry Phipps for the establishment of the Henry Phipps Clinic of Johns Hopkins. Its directorship had been offered to Paton who respectfully declined in favor of Dr. Adolf Meyer." This is more than enough on that topic, but it surfaced again in a letter his wife, Margaret, wrote to her son:[5]

"*Baltimore, May 24, 1943.*

Dear Townley—The article[6] from Hurd [Dr. Henry M. Hurd] enclosed does not state that when Father wrote declining the Professorship of Psychiatry in the J.H. Med School—he did so on the ground that there could be no Psychiatry taught properly without beds—and hence as no beds went with the professorship, modern Psychiatry could not be taught.... Father prepared a paper formulating a plan for a Psychiatric clinic and gave it to Dr. Welch – This paper was quoted (consciously or unconsciously) by Dr. Welch in his letter to Mr. Phipps which the newspaper published at the time of the gift. Dr. Welch made no mention of Father, but appointed Adolf Meyer professor in the new Phipps Clinic.

"*This suggestion was made to Dr. Welch by (your) Father when he*

INSIGHT

formulated the original plan for a clinic. We were in Naples at the time but feelings ran very high in Baltimore... as the profession wished Father appointed. I believe up to that time no one had ever refused a J. H. Med appointment and the President and Dean were sore over Father's action. Somewhere among Father's papers is a copy of the letter Father wrote declining the professorship when it was offered him. Father destroyed his copy of the plan for the Psychiatric clinic, so as not to hamper Dr. Meyer when he found Dr. Welch was giving him no credit for the plan... You need never use this information, but you have a right to know what a knight and gentleman your Father has always been.

F.M.P." [Frances Margaret Paton]

Stewart was a catalyst, to put it modestly. Dr. Welch deserved the great credit he received in realizing the need for a separate institute for public health on the medical campus. Stewart, too, spoke of the importance of public health as a bridge between the health care of medicine and the prevention of human illnesses by the know-how of medically directed preventive social science. Thus, again he became an enthusiastic and active supporter of another Johns Hopkins institution to be proposed, assuming a major role in seeking its financing, finally achieved through a definitive grant from the Rockefeller Foundation with whose board he was closely associated. The Johns Hopkins University School of Hygiene and Public Health opened its doors in 1916, the first school of its kind in America.[7]

There was to be still another passion in Stewart's professional life. He became entranced by the theory that mankind could improve its behavior and intelligence through a process of science named "eugenics." Many of the nation's leading citizens: among them Presidents Woodrow Wilson and Theodore Roosevelt, two Supreme Court judges and literally countless health-care authorities–approved its goals. It won Margaret Sanger's support as a helpful aid to birth control.[8] At Johns Hopkins, Drs. Welch, Meyer and Barker were among its most prominent early supporters. As one author put it, "Virtually every psychiatrist at one time or another believed in the usefulness and expectations of eugenics."[9] It became a collaborative "scientific" endeavor, the product of geneticists, psychologists, clinicians, public-health workers, zoologists and statisticians seeking to use heredity to improve human life. Stewart strongly favored the participation of each of these disciplines, and somehow their mutually created product seemed right up his alley.

When eugenics spread from America to Germany, it was due in part to a large grant from the Rockefeller Foundation. Nazi Germany and its horrific Holocaust were to be the ultimate proponent of the dark side of a venture originally intended to improve the public's health and ultimately to develop its intelligence. Today, it is beyond retrospective explanation how those benign goals turned into restrictive and inhuman measures such as compulsory sterilization of the mentally ill, intermarriage denials, and selective immigrant rejections.

However, Stewart was a holdout against the dissolution of eugenics. In 1919, he accepted the presidency of the Eugenics Research Association. The following is an excerpt from a published commentary about Stewart's inaugural address: "In what is clearly an idealistic concept about improving human understanding by potential modification of behavior, Paton focuses immediately upon the importance of eugenics research being free of propaganda and emotional influences, pointing out that an educated and broadly scientific objectivity is required to make such studies productive. One is left with the impression that his primary interest is in character investigation based upon biological science and the understanding of mental hygiene."[10]

In 1921, Stewart wrote, "There is...some reason to believe that changes in nurture may serve as stimuli affecting the growth of the embryo through the parental germ cells." Written before genes were no more than particles of unidentified substance, this is profoundly speculative but speaks well for the thrust of his thinking. In 1931, he wrote: "It would be helpful to most of us if we could understand better the nature of our inherited capacities or incapacities in order to make the most of our abilities to handle the natural endowments we possess."

Today, eugenics thrives as "genetic medicine" and under that identity, Johns Hopkins' historian Nathaniel Comfort points out[11] that components of predictive inheritance have emerged, gene therapy has been discovered, and studies have been undertaken for the management of certain serious diseases. For better or for worse, old timers such as Stewart Paton were on the track to improvement of inheritance with gene control but too far ahead of what scientific techniques were yet to provide.

To that extent, Stewart was prescient, and his undaunted spirit of investigation gained some justification as the role of genes became honored by investigations and Nobel awards. Stewart's dogged determination to pursue hunches beyond current knowledge kept him a principled eugenicist to the end of his life.[12] Like most other pre-war proponents who did not give up, he had previously allowed its natural science to distract him from the fallout of its social science. Everyone has one or two holes in the fabric of his life, and eugenics became Stewart's most evident misstep at that stage of its development, but its future as a laboratory science would become truly revolutionary.

Unequivocally, eugenics is a complex subject that has a bad side but also a positive side that needs further development over the decades ahead, and whatever services are derived should become available equally to the underprivileged and the wealthy.[13] As one authority in the history of eugenics states on the final page of a recent book, the "impulse to improve human health and happiness with genetics underlies the promise of genetic medicine." However, when considered from different perspectives, the author reminds us that the power of human diversity and the beauty of chance are still more worthwhile than "the illusion of perfectibility."[14]

Stewart's known exploration of eugenics helps to clarify the behavioral traits of father and son, given that Stewart was Townley's primary mentor. Stewart was not driven by the for-and-against strongly held opinions that, for eugenics, changed direction like a wind sock responding to the prevailing breeze. He was a true researcher, which does not mean that his working hypotheses were always correct, but does indicate his consistent dedication to scientific investigation even if threatened by societal misapplications . He was a fighter against mental illness, but never a Holocaust apologist.

In her letter to Townley, Margaret's loyalty to her diligent Stewart related in part to his ready acceptance of being "passed over." Stewart would not be happy that the letter has now surfaced, but at this late date it is only a detail of ancient history and probably contains some statements that are not entirely accurate. Margaret was not usually an angry or a rudely outspoken person, but neither did she bite her tongue—the lioness has her pride and that included her husband, the beloved lion with a short mane. Examples of overlook are sometimes subtle and difficult to discover. For example, in 1941, the year before Stewart died, one of the heroes of the Johns Hopkins medical faculty and another good friend of the Paton family, Dr. Simon Flexner, and his son, wrote a book about Dr. Welch. The text is a thorough history of Dr. Welch's outstanding career and its points of contact with the hoards of persons who helped make the Heroic Age of Medicine heroic.

Despite his interests being so similar to those of Dean Welch, Stewart's name was not mentioned on any page of the book until, in a final appendix with the authors' acknowledgments, Stewart's name was listed on page 460 among many others. Stewart had been by then the originator of the idea for the Phipps Psychiatric Clinic and a strong proponent of the School of Hygiene and Public Health. For both of these entities he was a major supporter and participant in their successful funding. Indirectly, he had helped to attract Dr. Adolf Meyer to Hopkins, the first Director of the Phipps Clinic and Chief of Psychiatry—but only after that appointment was turned down by Stewart. Omitting mention of Stewart would seem a purposeful slight, but instead it represents an unimportant but telling example of Stewart's backseat position for which he expressed no objection whatsoever.

What was it that explained Stewart's several major but largely unsung roles in ideas and fundraising for the needs of the great medical revolution? The best answer may lie in the reality of a metonym. It may sound trite but it gets close to Stewart's painless plight. Furthermore, these observations that applied largely to Stewart form the basis for subsequent comparisons with Townley who also lacked a greed for credit. The interpretation of that characteristic becomes for this writer a challenging explanation. It has no real importance to either of those men, but finding how best to explain them becomes a welcome challenge.

Like his father, Townley would prove to be a hardheaded philosophical idealist, an implementer, and an enthusiast—a "do'er," in Stewart's vernacular. They were both willing to go against the grain of common thought when anticipating what others might not envision. But even if successful in their original thoughts or endeavors, the innate reserve and subdued egos of both father and son made it necessary for their concepts to be unusually explicit in order to free them from the assimilations of other progressive thinkers who by nature tended to identify with the whole of a developing scientific realization as their own. After all, by the very nature of Stewart's and Townley's innovative people-related ideas, neither of them had the urge or finesse to package their notions like personal patents rather than throwaway remarks. Artful embellishment of creative concepts was neither their interest nor their skill.

The contrived observations now to follow as applied to father and son are characterizations exploiting the handy metaphor of masculinity. Stewart is the classic exemplar and Townley here is the presumed genetic confirmation.

Viewing Stewart from a distance instead of close up-as one examines a painting for its best effect-a sign of his times becomes its own social barometer and a convenient way of partly explaining the rather tepid acceptance of these Hopkins devotees. Stewart was a clean-shaven man with a small moustache. That in itself says something about his modesty and modernity. The majority of the older Johns Hopkins medical faculty were quite elegantly bearded. It seems appropriate to postulate that beards and moustaches of those days were iconic tea leaves identifying in unspoken subtlety the presence of society's intellectual Brahmins, the leaders. In an article written in a later year, Dr. Carl Binger,[15] a prominent Manhattan internist, was to write, "It is only a few years since doctors have come out from behind the ambush of their beards."

Binger's comment has a provocative ring to it. Many of the leading physicians at the turn of the 19th century had robust beards. One did not comment on a beard, a form of unspoken bravado. Stewart was beardless in a forest of beards.[16] His small, tightly cropped moustache had no tips to wax. "Facial shrubbery"[17] had a social power for the brazenness of those who acknowledged their own prominence within the profession's well-earned elitism. Why not a beard for Stewart? Call it more of that modesty or shyness, or perhaps just realization of the facts as they existed in the context of his chosen milieu.

Stewart did not seek recognition but, rather, he sought to fulfill goals on his own terms as a do'er of useful work. He wanted to be where the action was to satisfy his incessant curiosity and to settle into a defined new sub-specialty. He was not fulltime or even senior on any professorial staff. And he was only on the payroll as a staff assistant. He was peripatetic and suffered from an alleged weak heart that made him cautious about accepting an appointment whose obligations he felt he might not be able to fulfill. For all these reasons, he was easy enough to bypass politely when credit was meted to the principals. But that is an excuse on behalf of Stewart and it misses the most important point of what is to be explained further, again in metaphor.

At Johns Hopkins, Stewart was the savvy hoot owl among soaring eagles, the latter being what the medical profession most needed in launching its revolution. In academia, the significance of a teacher, researcher or clinician who is not tied down financially to his institution or is without a highly specialized "portfolio" is easily overlooked. A biographical note regarding Stewart in the Johns Hopkins Medical Archives explains that whereas there are many materials in the archives' collection that pertain to Stewart Paton, his propensity to work in the background is one of the major factors to explain why his contributions were easily undervalued.

There are three basic human qualities that serve to enhance an individual's social recognition: "agency," "moment," and "presence." They are also the criteria that either fortify or diminish the reputation of a potential leader. On these, Stewart gets mixed marks. He certainly had a strong sense of "agency," comfortable as he was as a free agent with dedicated purpose. He had a sense of "moment" in living in the here and now and with the realization that there was an overriding opportunity for him to assist the revolution on behalf of his profession. But what he lacked was the gift of "presence." That is the inimitable "it" of optimal leadership, the self-awareness of appropriate compatibility, the ability to be opportune. Such presence comes from personal magnetism contained in the expressiveness of "pizzazz" and "moxie," plus the raw confidence of being "in."

None of those words fit the Paton men. Both men were amiable, kindly and warm; but they were disinterested in showmanship and they avoided personal flamboyance. They did not soar with the eagles but their earthiness brought solid credibility and respect. Stewart was the appropriate parent for a son with calm demeanor and a non-aggressive personality who might nonetheless manage to create an eye bank under challenging circumstances that were both social and paramedical. As Townley matured, his characteristics foretold a compatible, person-oriented nature.

To that base was added just the right conglomeration of nurture from a wise and soft-spoken father, a strong-minded and fiercely loyal mother, and a brave and ingenious brother with crippling academic disabilities, the likes of which were new to the family. His sister, Evelyn, was the wild card in the pack, the loving outlier who was a reminder that there were other life forms beyond the Johns Hopkins walls that were worth knowing better. Stewart held the strongest position of influence. He was a medical scientist whose ambition was rewarded by his work, and whatever gratification it brought was the accomplishment and not related honors. One admiring colleague was to describe him in an obituary as the "leaven" for the Hopkins revolutionaries.[18] If he was the leaven for the major performers, he was also the incubator for Townley.

NOTES TO CHAPTER 6:

1. His writing includes the following books. *Psychiatry: A Textbook for Students and Physicians* (1905), *Education in War and Peace* (1920), *Human Behavior* (1921), *Signs of Sanity and the Principles of Mental Hygiene* (1922), *Prohibiting Minds* (1931), and *Human Beings in the Making* (1942, unpublished). He used various known publishers. He also published chapters, papers, and numerous letters to editors.
2. Beers, C.W.: *A Mind That Found Itself*. Longmans, Green and Co, Fourth Edition, London, 1917.
3. Lamb, S.D.: *Pathologist of the Mind: Adolf Meyer and the Origins of American Psychiatry*. Johns Hopkins University Press, Baltimore, 2014.
4. Mental Hygiene is the name for psychiatric care, coined by Adolf Meyer MD, then the future Professor of Psychiatry at Johns Hopkins Phipps Clinic.
5. This personal letter to Townley from his mother came almost two years after Stewart's death.
6. Article not identified.
7. Today that institution is called the Johns Hopkins University Bloomberg School of Public Health.
8. Baker, J.H.: *Margaret Sanger. A Life of Passion*. Hill and Wang, Division of Farrar, Straus and Giroux, New York, 2011.
9. Stern, A.M.: *Eugenic Nation*. University of California Press, Berkley, 2005.
10. Comfort, N.: *The Science of Human Perfection*. Yale University Press, New Haven, 2012.
11. Ibid.
12. Dowbiggin, I.R.: *Keeping Americans Sane*, p. 128. Cornell University Press, Ithaca, 1997.
13. Stern, A.M.: Ibid.
14. Comfort, N.: Ibid
15. Binger, C.: *The Doctor's Job*. W.W. Norton & Co, Inc., New York, 1945.
16. That Drs. Barker, Cushing and A. Flexner had lived in the Midwest for at least some of their previous years may have influenced their use of the razor.
17. Binger: Ibid.
18. Obituary by C.B. F., "I Remember Stewart Paton," *Amer. J. of Psychiatry*, 117:2, August 1960.

CHAPTER 7: CAREER CRUX

"Over every mountain there is a path, although it may not be seen from the valley."
Theodore Roethke, 1908-1963

So much for the similarities and differences between these two Paton men of different eras. Returning now to sequential history, in Baltimore at age four, Townley was an unremarkable but pleasing child by family recollection. By then, Stewart had spent thirteen years of lecturing and learning as an Associate in Medicine (later Associate in Psychiatry) at the Johns Hopkins Medical School and as a perpetual student taking advantage of all educational opportunities offered in fields related to psychiatry. That was the year, 1905, when Stewart decided it was time to return to Europe for more of the specialized brain education that was not available in America. This time it was a whole-family trip to Italy, to be followed by more such visits in later years to Germany and England.

The Patons departed from Baltimore just as Stewart's major work, *Psychiatry: A Text-Book For Students and Physicians*,[1] was published. In that 600-page textbook he detailed logical approaches to diagnosis and treatment of the mentally ill. The book became a standard teaching text over a good number of years thereafter. It included the panoply of mental disorders and diseases as were then understood, or misunderstood. It was published five years before the word "genetics" was coined and more years than that before genes were identified with chromosomes. The book was immediately perceived within the profession as the most complete, informative and well organized work dealing with Stewart's still-developing medical sub-specialty. As he departed for Italy, Stewart sent a courtesy copy to Dr. Osler and in short order he received the following letter, here abbreviated to eliminate its unrelated chat:

Dear Paton: *July 5, 1905*

A thousand thanks for your book, which came the other day, and with which I am greatly delighted. I think the arrangement is admirable, and you have managed to compress within a comparatively small space a most astonishing amount of good material.... I am sure the book will be a great success. And now take a message, please, to Mrs. Paton, who is, I know, the important member of the firm and able to boss and control you in every way. Ask her, please, not to allow you to get the European habit, but to take you back to establish a first class psychiatric clinic at the Johns Hopkins Hospital. With kind regards, (signed) W Osler.

That was a much-appreciated letter, for it confirmed that Stewart was a fine asset to Johns Hopkins Medical School, and it was reassuring that Osler liked the book that had required three years to write. But Stewart did not stay around to enjoy the book's warm front office reception. With their three children, he and Margaret took off for most of the next five years abroad, interrupted only by his several visits to Baltimore in that interval. Stewart started out in Naples at the Zoological Station on the bay. His primary source of neurobiology was a heavily bearded Darwinian biologist, Professor Felix Anton Dohrn. The animal nervous systems they studied were those from the neighboring sea.

With good luck the Patons were able to rent a small villa on an island just offshore that was reached by rowboat except in bad weather, when they used an overhead cable car. It was a delightful place to live until one day in 1906 when nearby Mt. Vesuvius erupted, throwing airborne noxious gas and hot ash dangerously close to the region where the Paton family was living. They were evacuated from the vicinity of Naples for several months.

Stewart's diary reports that later in the year, among the public swimmers just off-shore of the Patons' island home were two acquaintances he immediately recognized-to his astonishment. Each clinging to a wooden ironing board for flotation were the noted and now wet-bearded American medical academician, Dr. William James; with him was a yet-to-be-knighted, similarly drenched, heavily-mustachioed Scot, Dr. Arthur Conan Doyle. In fact, Doyle was a former Harley Street ophthalmologist in London, a specialty he gave up once involved in the creation of Sherlock Holmes. These three physicians chatted amiably shore-to-ironing board, ironing board-to-shore, making it a merry meeting.

This scene for Stewart was memorable for a togetherness of three eminent former medical school graduates (assuming Stewart was deserving of that ilk), none of whom had chosen a customary way to use their medical backgrounds, each having found an eclectic career stemming from its medical core. Stewart was the alienist-cum-neurobiologist. Dr. James was the trailblazing psychiatrist-cum-psychologist. Dr. Doyle was the ophthalmologist-cum-psychologically astute storyteller (later to become a devout spiritualist). Now all three physicians were figuratively rafting through life in their current of choice. Stewart was greatly amused by their uninhibited public appearance while chatting and chuckling on a calm sea amid others who had no idea who these men might be, but he certainly did not jump in to join them. Anyone who might have imagined such a move simply did not understand Stewart Paton's reserve.

CAREER CRUX

Margaret enjoyed travel, hiking, learning how to converse in other languages, and helping her three children to appreciate the many opportunities that life abroad offered them. Still today, there are within their grandchildren's homes numerous albums of small photographs held in place by black corner stickers showing the family near the shore, resting during mountain walks, picnicking in fields and rarely looking at the camera. Margaret, who is pictured least often, took the photographs. The pictures are reminders that in the early 1900s exercise clothes were yet to arrive. Posed beside high rocks and stony beaches, the Patons appear as if dressed for church in the more modern world, except that Stewart wore below-the-knee knickers and high argyle stockings.

Wherever they went as a family, the two older children attended local schools or had local tutors, depending upon the circumstances for educational programming. There was invariably a nursemaid in tow, speaking to the children in her native tongue, and the children soon understood what they were being told in several languages. By the time they moved back to America, when Townley was eight years old, he spoke Italian about as well as he spoke English.

The family returned to Baltimore toward the end of 1909 and within a year moved again, this time with all of their belongings, to Princeton, New Jersey. For several years they lived in a rented house in mid-town while the only real home of their own they would ever have was being built. It was named Greenlands, an estate of some ten acres on the southwest shore of Princeton's Lake Carnegie. A neighbor who was a distinguished writer wrote at that time the following assessment of Stewart: He "had independent means and was a sort of early freelance psychologist. He was a gallant, thoroughbred gentleman, through and through, and in many ways an inspiring person, but he drove his subject and his pet ideas home to everybody, in and out of season. But I admired him greatly and was privileged to walk with him quite often."[2]

Stewart had returned to his alma mater, Princeton University, to accept a made-to-order staff appointment as "psychiatric consultant," studying the college students for mental health disorders and determining the best choices in their management. It was the start of five years of that consultancy, later to be extended two years at Yale, followed by similar work at Dartmouth and Columbia. He lectured on his sense of continuity between neurology, psychology, and psychiatry and he enthusiastically provided counseling to those students who sought him out—which was actually what he most welcomed as a way of gaining an understanding of the adjustments and difficulties of students' adaptation to college life. He was the first psychiatrist available to college students in that capacity anywhere, and his psychiatric guidance became a model for other colleges to emulate. His extended study was frequently interrupted by back-and-forth's to Baltimore to refuel with his faculty friends.

By age 11, Townley found ice-skating on the lake to be his favorite outdoor winter activity. When it was cold enough for thick ice, he could skate the entire three-mile length of the lake. He was not a truant but schoolwork and ice-skating were a world apart. He had attended public schools upon return from Italy; by age 15 his family thought he would do better at a private boarding school. He was sent to the Loomis Institute,[3] an all-boy boarding school in Windsor, Connecticut, where he entered the ninth grade. At Loomis he

CAREER CRUX

adjusted to school life without difficulty. His marks were quite undistinguished, but at times outright worrisome to his family. That difficulty with grades was probably considered the result of a prior hodgepodge of educational methods and content variations in his European schooling followed by several years in the questionable Princeton public schools. As time passed, it was evident to his parents that he was not a proficient scholar–a poor reader, poor speller and, at best, only "passing" in math.

Loomis Tennis Team, 1919

His athletic skills–skating and tennis in particular–were to become the flags of his school days, yet it is likely that his finest attributes were a compatibility and an energy that led to high popularity among students and faculty. Looking ahead for substantiation of those comments, he was to play each year on the school tennis team and was varsity captain as a senior. Notably, he was elected vice-president of the student council and was president of the senior class when he graduated. In his senior yearbook, Townley himself submitted his then-common Italian nickname that has since become unprintable. It was not meant as a racist slur but as a boy-to-boy tease because he liked using a few Italian words and possibly added typical gesticulations to go along with them.

Loomis Hockey Team, 1919

But in the course of his years at Loomis, troubles arose that had more significance than either his teachers or his family realized, however much they were aware of Townley's academic shortcomings. At one point in his second year at Loomis, Stewart brought up the topic of his son's poor marks. The irrelevant response came back that "the boy had seemed so indisposed" that he was taken into the home of the school's headmaster, Mr. Nathaniel H. Batchelder. That indicates a caring man, but it may also smack a bit of an overindulgence. A few days later, Stewart received the following letter regarding his son (and a reference to the Ulmer case, which evidently was the topic of another correspondence between the two of them):

February 4, 1916

Dear Dr. Paton:

I have your letter of the second about Townley's report. While it is true that his grades are apparently about the same as a year ago, it should be remembered that last year he was doing special work [tutoring] in English and arithmetic, comparable to the last year of grammar school, and special Latin in a group of three boys that was making only about half the speed of the regular class. He is now doing the regular work of the first year; the change in the nature of the work marks a considerable improvement. It is also true that his present report in several subjects is not quite as good as usual. This is very likely to have been because of an off day on a particular monthly test, or some other circumstance of the sort. The average of a number of months is a truer index than any single report. I really do feel that the boy is making about as much progress as we can expect of him.[4] For two days he had a slight sore throat and general indisposition. We took him to the house for rest, and he is now quite all right, and going about his work.

Thank you very much for the assistance you gave in the Ulmer case. I hope that something may come of it.

Very cordially yours,

(Signed) N. H. Batchelder Headmaster

The headmaster probably assumed that Stewart's boy was a limited young man, of much appeal from the viewpoint of manners and appearance but not in possession of a high intelligence. Such an opinion from the headmaster of what was then a partially vocational school for some boys who did not apply to college could mean that Townley's learning ability was not different from some of the other students. College was not for everyone. But if that was indeed Mr. Batchelder's thought, he certainly did not spell it out to the boy's father.

Despite his moderate marks, upon applying to Princeton from a reputable boarding school, Townley's popularity and athleticism surely deserved some consideration. Further, his tuition would be paid in full. Another possible advantage but an unspoken probability may have played a role in deciding upon his application, for Townley was the classical university "legacy." In the first third of the 20th century, a history of relatives at a university definitely tended to bring favor to the selection of their offspring.[5] The admissions office at Princeton University could not help but be aware that this applicant was the son and nephew of Princeton graduates. His distinguished uncle was an unsalaried member of the faculty at the time and his father had been an adjunct faculty appointee for five years when assessing students for mental disorders. In all, his family had ten full-tuition Princeton graduates, plus one current student.

Enough speculation. Townley was accepted to Princeton in the fall of 1920 and his parents, at least, were of the opinion that the university was very fortunate to have him. In college, Townley again became a student with favorable social skills but lacking laudatory academic ability. His sports performances and his consistent "good nature" accounted for notable popularity. He played tennis almost like a professional and loved every game of it. As at Loomis, he was on the university's varsity team each of his four years and was its captain in his senior year. Beyond that, and after three years of membership Townley became president of the Medical Club, indicative of his intense focus upon a future that he dreamed might come his way—and indicative of the opinion of his peers, who obviously found him an outstanding candidate.

MEDICAL CLUB OFFICERS for Next Year — Left to Right: L. Rumford 1926, Secretary; R. T. Paton 1925, President; W. T. Buddington 1925, Vice-President.

Over his college years he worked hard at his studies and as a result limited his extracurricular activities. Little specific information is available about his performance. A few records have been retrieved from Princeton. If he were not interested in medical school admittance, the marks would be acceptable enough to seem compatible with graduation. Townley took little for granted and allowed himself to imagine the awfulness of being rejected by the standards of a medical school he would do almost anything to be allowed to attend.

At some point, his father told him that a physician he had met during the war when stationed at Hazelhurst Field in Mineola[6], New York, was a Dr. William Wilmer, a prominent ophthalmologist from Washington, D.C. who later had become interested in creating his own clinic in Washington if it could get the funding.[7] Townley—for reasons he himself could not fathom—hung on to that stimulating information, imagining that ophthalmology might be a good field for his own medical future, if he were to have one. But previously he had told his parents he wanted to be an obstetrician, like their admirable friend Dr. Howard Kelly. So ophthalmology was not a yearning to be taken seriously.

During summer vacations, Townley occasionally joined Stewart on his periodic visits to Johns Hopkins. It was during his junior year at college — in 1923 — when he and his father visited Johns Hopkins specifically to meet members of its faculty and get an impression as to whether he might be suited for the Johns Hopkins Medical School. By coincidence they happened to run into Dr. Wilmer, with a plan to run a new eye institute at Johns Hopkins and visiting the medical school shortly before he moved there from Washington. Dr. Wilmer was attentive to Stewart's son, wishing him well and saying he hoped to see him again someday at the Medical School. That offhand comment gave Townley a shot of adrenalin, but in his other meetings with members of the medical faculty they were polite about his interest in following in his father's footsteps, but they were not indicating that he seemed a likely candidate for admission. Townley returned to Princeton sensing that his future application to the medical school might not be of any interest to his school of choice in Baltimore.

There he was, an appealing, witty, thrifty, sober and doggedly determined young man. He had become a member of the Quadrangle, one of the oldest University "eating clubs" and one of the best, though not the most social. He was a mirror of some of his father's personality traits-soft-spoken, congenial, intent, thoughtful and intellectually far-sighted--with the addition of a degree of mischievousness, and ingenuity.

Due to living abroad and attending an all-boys school and now all-male college, this naïve young man had had few acquaintances with girls other than his sister. His older and more experienced brother, Bill, was the only family source of tales that whet his appetite for what he had been missing. But girlfriends needed to be chaperoned in that era, which made it difficult to meet and get to know these wonderful creatures. Despite the chaperone situation, early in his college days he did get acquainted with a young lady who seemed at first meeting to find him as appealing as he found her. Beautiful and charming Roberta Roelker turned many a head. But not long after he met her, Townley proudly introduced his girl to a friend who not only had a promising future that was predictable from his academic excellence, but a passion for horses to ride, hunt, and own. It seemed that Roberta was suddenly horse-crazy and sooner than Townley liked to remember, she was riding his friend's mares and taming his stallions, then changing horses in midstream as she

INSIGHT

became his friend's girlfriend and not long thereafter, his wife. The marriage lasted for the remainder of their active lives.

That was actually a good outcome, for in 1923, at a college social event, Townley met a bewitching young New York woman named Helen Meserve, who was someone else's date. She was not only beautiful but playful, full of joy, caring, teasing and flirtatious in a quiet way. She drove him to near distraction. Now, for the first time, he knew that he was seriously in love. She seemed to feel something very similar, but women were less expressive then. For several years while at Princeton and then for two more years thereafter, he remained steadfastly convinced that she was to be his life's greatest love. He had been somewhat of a favorite with other female contemporaries he had encountered. Helen observed that, and she even knew Roberta and would not let him forget that he had been one of her ardent admirers. Call it luck or a fair win, they each had a hunch that they had met the love of their lives. This happy relationship endured the scrupulous scrutiny of numerous volunteer family chaperones. Both accepted this, given that women who were not chaperoned were branded as hussies, persons to be avoided—naughty by implication.

On October 10, 1924, Stewart received a letter from a longstanding friend, Dr. Harvey Cushing, the great neurosurgeon and multifarious upgrade of a Renaissance man who had formerly been at Johns Hopkins and was now a professor at Harvard Medical School. His purpose in writing was to suggest that Townley consider applying to that school. It was a thoughtful suggestion and a tempting idea, but it only crystallized in Townley's mind that what he wanted most was to qualify for the Johns Hopkins Medical School, at a location he thought of as home. And Harvard's admission requirements would be just as stringent as those at Johns Hopkins. That was confirmed by an unofficial assessment of admission standards at the better American medical schools. Johns Hopkins' was especially demanding, for Hopkins had the added requirement that applicants had to have a reading knowledge of two current languages beyond English. Townley knew he could meet the language requirement from his years abroad (Italian and German), but not the academic stipulations, due in part to his inability to finish exams in time periods that were entirely sufficient for most of his colleagues and, to tell the truth, mathematics — even algebra — was simply too abstruse for him to master. He still had enough confidence to decide he was at least an average applicant if not a shoo-in. But Johns Hopkins was not looking for average.

Sometime later, his Uncle Lewellys Barker sent him a copy of the two-volume work *The Life of Sir William Osler* by Harvey Cushing, in which he wrote: "For Townley Paton from his uncle, Lewellys F. Barker. Hoping that the life of a great 'internist' and a 'saint' may be a real inspiration." Townley was being over-nurtured. What he needed was to know why he had such difficulty scholastically–but that he would never know.

Today, it would not take a physician to realize that the cause was familial "dyslexia," [8] an unfamiliar term in Townley's college days and an impairment completely overlooked as the underlying cause for many students' failure to thrive academically. That unfortunately confining name suggests that it only affects reading and spelling, but that is far from the truth. Today, many parents have come to realize that it is a brain dysfunction that at times runs in families and hides what might be high intelligence and outstanding learning capacities once the basis of slowed reading and bad spelling are by-passed, if never cured. Because of its individual-specific range of manifestations and relative severities, the term "dyslexia spectrum" becomes a convenient designation. Unaware of any diagnosis for his learning impairment, Townley's ambition was strong enough to establish satisfactory performance records in boarding school and college, yet hardly enough to enable him to meet the standards of medical school requirements for which a higher degree of candidate selectivity existed among the few top medical schools.

Then, propitiously, what he was to describe as "some authorities" at Johns Hopkins suggested that he consider taking the first two years of medical school at Cambridge, England.[9] Who those authorities were remains unknown. He was told that the Cambridge medical faculty would prioritize the recommendations from the leading American universities if the applicant was given strong endorsement in regard to his perceived potential. Such recognition by the referring source would be taken very seriously. Were Townley to be accepted at Cambridge, then after the second year of medical training in England and if there was an opening at Johns Hopkins he might qualify for a third year transfer to Hopkins without the same emphasis on marks as for students fresh out of college. The British professors could conceivably become the key to a backdoor approach to the Johns Hopkins Medical School.

No young enthusiast wants to be told to consider a more circuitous route to an already burdensome path to completion of a medical education, but the two-step advice was too tempting to ignore. The more Townley thought about it, the more interested he became in the roundabout route to ending up with the last two years of remaining medical education in Baltimore. He was well acquainted with living abroad; that added component would not be difficult. As for getting accepted by Cambridge Medical School, he felt confident that he would get strong recommendations from his Princeton professors with regard to his overall fitness for Medicine. It was also fortuitous that he had been elected president of the Princeton students' Medical Committee.

Townley was faced by a decision he alone could make, and it was related to a rather embarrassing academic limitation about which he had no clue. It was the way he was. Period. He had to consider himself less intellectually gifted than the competition seeking Johns Hopkins Medical School admission, but he could not convince himself that he was less qualified to become a doctor than any other applicant. How does one call upon the inner wisdom that holds one's future goal by a single thread? Go straight and probably lose forever; go around and perhaps have a better chance from a foreign launching.

He decided to submit a Cambridge application. Indeed, he was accepted at Cambridge Medical School on the basis of letters from his Princeton professors in combination with his generally satisfactory but not distinguished marks. As he had hoped, the letters offset the marks with very supportive statements from those who knew the depth of his knowledge and its applications, his attitude of

INSIGHT

commitment and his personal relationships with those who had come to know him.

During his two years at Cambridge, there was ample time for travel and exercise. Townley became a co-captain on the Cambridge Medical School tennis team and was playing well until his second year, when he went with friends on a mountain-climbing trip in the French Alps. Joining with the three experienced climbers, each being roped together for safety reasons, he slipped a footing and slammed his right shoulder against rock that apparently cracked the head of the humerus and badly tore its rotator cuff. It was a painful experience, further aggravated by the return trip to Cambridge, where the shoulder was x-rayed, then tightly and professionally bound. Comfortable at last, Townley underwent a slow recovery at a time and location where physiotherapy was not prescribed. He never again had a full overhead serve but long after healing was stable, he was able to develop a completely unique semi-overhead backhand serve that was remarkably successful for the following several decades, until arthritis in the injured joint necessitated an underhand serve. Whatever writing was needed in testing his abilities may have been interrupted by a right arm bound to his waist over a good many months. Verbal testing was usually easy for him. Perhaps there was a blessing in that injury.

A few months before returning to the U.S., Townley and Helen traveled extensively on a three-week trip throughout former family haunts in Europe—under the surveillance of his parents and sister. This was a getting-to-know-you trip for his parents, designed to make everyone absolutely certain they wanted a marriage to follow.

CAREER CRUX

Today, group input is not a usual request to a bride-to-be, but there was no doubt in the minds of the engaged couple. Engaged or not, during that trip Townley's older sister Evelyn was an alternate chaperone, with other volunteers among various acquaintances. There was one often alluded-to evening—in later decades of fond memories—when Evelyn herself reported that she had eased out of chaperonage for an undisclosed period of time. That was a dead-end story that the Paton children heard about years later and had the nerve to ask for details of the granted freedom. Nothing was disclosed and it may have been a totally uninteresting event made more provocative by its mystery, but the chances are otherwise.

After the summer "testing tour," they returned to Baltimore and Townley began his third year of college at Johns Hopkins. But he took two days off in the fall to visit with Helen and her parents in New York and to ask Mr. Meserve for his daughter's hand in marriage. It was that formal. Fred Meserve gave his hearty approval. They were married on Christmas Eve in 1927 in a Manhattan Episcopal church on Madison Avenue at 71st Street. The large family-and-friend affair was followed by a reception at a local club.

INSIGHT

The couple spent the first night of their weeklong honeymoon at a local hotel and arrived on Christmas morning at her family's house in time for Christmas lunch. Helen's brother Leighton, two years her junior, greeted them with a luncheon toast that ended with, "My sister's husband is so bloody cheap that he wouldn't take her out for their first meal together as a married couple!" Leighton was teasing, but being somewhat stingy was often attributed to Townley's Scottish blood from ancestors never needing to be identified. It was true, however, that he was not a free-spender, nor did he have much to spend in the early years of marriage. As a "descended Scot," he also had a favorite fish: he could not get enough breakfast kippers, something few state-side wives, new or old, would want to deal with in their kitchens due to its penetrating dead-fish aroma, so Helen still had that to look forward to—and to deal with in brave tolerance.

On November 3, 1928, their first of three children, Joan, was born and from the viewpoint of kindness and virtue she was the most perfect of their progeny. In 1929, upon successful completion of his fourth year of medical school—his second year at Johns Hopkins—Townley received his medical diploma, written on sheepskin in Latin. With his classmates, he joined in reciting the Hippocratic Oath and the class was charged by the dean of the medical faculty to abide by the principles of *aequanimitas*, which he vowed to do throughout three years of residency training and for his entire career in Medicine.

His circuitous training had been a risky venture. It left him with an enduring humility in knowing what he could not do as well as some others, but also with an abiding self-confidence in the clinical work that he now knew distinctly he could do better than many of the medical scholars. Those two realizations made him an effective physician whose native modesty was never to be corrupted with arrogance. In 1929, he was accepted by the distinguished and devout American leader of ophthalmology, Professor William H. Wilmer, for three-years of residency training at the brand new Institute that bore Wilmer's name.

NOTES TO CHAPTER 7:

1. Published by J. B. Lippincott Company, Philadelphia and London, 1905. Without explanation, Stewart did not undertake a second edition.
2. Atwood, AW: "These Eighty Years," page 135. Copyright 1961. Privately printed.

INSIGHT

3. In 1970 the school name was changed by a two-school merger, now for both boys and girls and called the Loomis Chaffee School.

4. The Loomis Institute at that time offered preparatory studies for agricultural, business, scientific and academic colleges, with "practical work" for those who did not intend to enter college.

5. To summarize Townley's family connections at Princeton in years prior to his graduation, the following are taken from his yearbook of 1925: S. Paton (Father) 1886; David Paton (uncle and later faculty professor) 1874; Morton Paton 1880; William Agnew Paton 1883; Richard Townley Halsey 1886; Cornelius Rea Agnew ("ophthalmologist") 1891; G.B. Agnew 1891; W.P. Putnam 1819; W. Haynes 1813; A. Rausch 1813; E. P. Halsey 1824.

6. The field's name was later changed to Roosevelt Field, the place of origin of Charles Lindbergh's celebrated transatlantic flight to Paris in 1927.

7. Wilmer served as colonel in the U.S. Air Service, a pioneer in establishing visual requirements and eye examinations for aviators. He engaged in ophthalmic research at the Mineola airfield prior to reassignment in France, 1918-1919, where he spent much of the time in service at Issoudun, the airfield in central France. He was later honorably discharged as a brigadier general in the Army Medical Reserve Corps.

8. Dyslexia was first described in the late 1800s but little attention was paid to it until the 1980s when it was no longer thought to be a consequence of education. However, retrospective diagnoses have commonly been made such as for Pierre Curie (1859-1906) whose symptoms were typical. It was not until mid-20th century that efforts were made to devise optimal teaching for affected children. As well known today, the diagnosis of "dyslexia" identifies reading disability in its name, but that is only a part of the spectrum of learning difficulties that include math, spelling, command of language, speaking skills, etc. The affected Paton family members each differed from the others in the range of affect and its severities. His brother Bill was the hardest hit. Townley's older daughter, Joan, and four of her five children, and his son, David, are all dyslexic.

9. This was confirmed in a letter Townley wrote to Dr. Wilmer on April 5, 1933.

CHAPTER 8: DUO OF DO'ERS

Happiness of a person lies in the freedom for using his prevailing abilities.
Aristotle, 384-322 B.C.

Much of what one does in life is learned from masterful people whose positive example is as much absorbed by their observers through the revelations of character and personality as by what they actually do that is influential. When such people are in line with the same intent as the absorber, they become the best of teachers—whether or not their intention is to teach. The two people—very much senior to him—who are the subject of this chapter were not only that kind of invaluable mentor to Townley but, incidentally, taught him how a new medical organization gets established.

Creative do'ers are needed for the advancement of science as much as are the bench-based scientists. To change the status quo calls for the kind of social persuasiveness that can generate a human force strong enough to move the proverbial mountain in teaching a worthy goal. Such force can have various personal formats determined by individual know-how and related skill. For the creation of the nation's first and foremost eye institute at Johns Hopkins, it took two dissimilar people, with complementary abilities yet different emotional wiring, to provide the undertaking's basis—and a host of others to fulfill their shared dream. Aside from their stark differences, each was aware that the key to success for all advancements in medical science was the availability of adequate funding[1]—and each knew how "big money" could be raised. These two unusual and strikingly committed persons were to play important roles in the life and times of Richard Townley Paton. This chapter introduces them with stories from their early lives.

INSIGHT

So, enter two world-class "changers": the highly talented and charmingly kind William Holland Wilmer — known as "Will" within his own family — and the heady, irresistibly persuasive Ada Marta DeAcosta, aka Aida de Acosta[2] who, through future marriages, was to become Mrs. Oren Root and later Mrs. Henry S. Breckinridge. She is best known in history as "Mrs. Breckinridge," but here she will be "Aida" and Wilmer at times will be "Will," when mentioned in a family way. He was 18 years senior to Aida and 38 years senior to Townley. The shared goal of these two persons is unlikely to have been accomplished had either of them undertaken that goal with anyone else.

Wilmer came to Johns Hopkins in 1925 at age 61, igniting the institute not only with his unique abilities but also with a striking presence. By that year Aida had already completed her work on his behalf, the promotion of her idea and an eye center under Wilmer's command, the first step in fundraising for the establishment of the Wilmer Institute. In so doing, Mrs. B. was far more than an angel in the wings, in fact taking up a weighty burden few men would, or could have borne so effectively — if at all.

In 1881, the fortunate Aida was born in the tony community of Elberon, New Jersey, referred to in the 19th century as the "Hollywood of the East" due to its popularity with leading entertainers and its collection of large estate houses that hosted vacationing VIPs. In that century and for a time thereafter, its seashore appeal brought visits from seven U.S. Presidents. One of them, James A. Garfield, was taken there to recover from an assassin's bullet. But 79 miserable days after being shot, he died in the same house where Aida was to be born 52 days thereafter. The consultant called to consider how the retained bullet could be found and removed was D. Hayes Agnew, MD, the older cousin of C. R. Agnew in New York.

From the first days of her life and for years to come, Aida's developing mind was saturated with numerous variants of social newsworthiness at high *niveau*. She was to learn the power of persuasion not as one might associate with a merely charming woman but as a crafty, well-informed money sleuth with a charitable goal to justify her brashness. Her nature and nurture granted her an upgrade of a silver to a platinum spoon in her mouth and a sharp spade in her hand, a wickedly wonderful means of digging up donor money where few others could find it. If that sounds like ridiculous exaggeration, stay tuned.

Aida's father was Cuban, of Spanish heritage, and her mother's family came directly from Spain. Both parents were highly cultured and wealthy enough to send their eight children to private schools. Aida[3] not only adjusted the spelling of her last name to her personal preference but sometime in her youth she also decided upon 1884 as the year of her birth in preference to the actual 1881.[4] Those three fewer years to acknowledge allowed a beguiling young woman to act and feel her preferred age. To an added youth she added sass and class, an independent spirit forging her life with as few of the customary 19th century restrictions on her gender as she could manage.

INSIGHT

Aida did not speak Spanish, preferring French as a second language. She was sent for one year to the Convent of the Sacred Heart in Manhattan. According to her granddaughter,[5] she, like most of her female contemporaries, did not attend college. However, Aida frequently visited Paris with her parents or school friends, enjoying Parisian fashions and the pleasure of buying the most recently created chapeau.

At 22, during one of her Parisian visits, Aida — by then an alluring and adventuresome young woman — became intrigued with a small, single-passenger airship (dirigible) being flown by its inventor. It took off now and then from a base in Neuilly St. James at the northern extremity of the Bois de Boulogne and flew over Paris usually at some 30 feet off the ground. This innovative achievement fascinated the *avant-garde* of the city's population, and it is safe to say that there were many Parisians who would have given almost anything to fly in one of these dirigibles. From newspapers, friends and other sources, Aida found out as much as she could about this suave and obviously creative fellow. Even then, doing the homework needed was to become one of her most important attributes in pursuing a goal.

The inventor was 30 years of age, and—statistics highly relevant to being an "aeronaut" — he was five-feet, five-inches tall, and slim, with only 110 pounds of weight for his small craft to carry. He was Brazilian but chose to be "stationed" in Paris, where he soon became a favorite of the local press. The news was filled with stories of his piloting of a variety of dirigibles, inspired by the imaginative writings of Jules Verne. Further, this fellow was meticulous in dress even when flying his hydrogen-filled aircrafts. His dirigible project to build and test his aircrafts required a crew of fifteen employees using a hangar just outside the Bois.[6]

Alberto wrote his full name was Alberto Santos=Dumont. He preferred that spelling separating his parents' last names with an equal sign instead of a hyphen, his way of attributing a co-equal acknowledgment to both parents, although this idiosyncrasy was ignored in his press reports.[7] An almost manic proponent of powered flight, young Alberto had a contagious enthusiasm in flying and demonstrating his "wonder of Paris." His Santos-Dumont crafts were already an important part of flight history, and Aida wanted to become a participant in what she, too, saw as a starting point for exciting aeronautic discoveries ahead.

Not the type to require a formal introduction, Aida seized an appropriate moment to introduce herself. She quizzed Alberto about his 30-foot balloon filled with purchased hydrogen and powered by a three-horse power petrol engine that had gears to select one of three speeds. This aircraft could only hold one person, so it would not be possible for her to be his passenger. The mechanized balloon was the first heavier-than-air *powered* vehicle used for human passengers–but only one at a time. Amelia Earhart was two decades from her first flight. In the course of teaching—some might say "preaching"—about his dirigibles, Alberto admitted that other models he constructed had proved fatal to their fliers, both from accidents such as crashes and from explosions from hydrogen leakage combined with ignited fuel, as from the ash of a lit cigar.

After several more trips to the Bois de Boulogne to learn more about her new friend and his flying machine, Aida made it increasingly clear to Alberto that she wanted to take his place and fly the dirigible by herself, a permission he had never given to anyone for this particular aircraft. She was indeed a beautiful young woman—but a woman nevertheless! Little did he know that this was her strength, not her weakness. Her innate, female blandishments and *savoir faire* eventually won him over, as they would so many others in the future. Despite the fact that she weighed 130 pounds, which was more than the dirigible had previously carried, he agreed to let her fly the craft on a day without wind, instructing her as best he could.

Aida explained, "He taught me how to steer the big rudder with a wheel...how to shift ballast and drop weights, and how to work the propellers." He also explained that the motor operated the propellers (called "air screws") and that the rudder for steering was controlled by a wheel near the basket of the aeronaut. He taught her a visual code of signals about how the craft was to be flown with a white handkerchief held in his free hand as he would ride on a bicycle below. He became enthusiastic about her wish to fly his dirigible. If there was trouble, the key to survival was the rope that extended to the balloon's valve for releasing hydrogen, used sparingly in routine descent. He allowed her to figure out that this safety feature had to be weighed against the danger of the highly inflammatory gas in the large reservoir that would be just above her head, a source of explosiveness from the most innocent of ignitions that could obviate any thought about a planned return to earth. But as he reassured her, "If you get too high in the air and become frightened, pull the cord. It will let the gas out of the bag and you will descend. If you faint, your weight will bring it down with something of a crash, but it will not kill you."

On June 27, 1903,[8] a day when the flag atop the Eiffel Tower lay limp, Santos-Dumont helped Aida into the pilot's basket that was a very tight fit due to her 20 pounds of greater weight and bulk than the diminutive ship's owner. And although she was probably two inches shorter than he, at five-feet, three-inches, she was not as slight--and she was wearing a "bulky, flounced black and white Victorian dress" with a "tight, ruffled skirt and wide bustle, a petticoat and fichu,"[9] not to mention a heaped coiffeur topped by a wide-brimmed hat with several roses pinned to the crown. She was always well-dressed, as well as being well-mannered. Alberto considered her a real "society lady," someone who could bring enormous fame to his aircraft if she proved able to fly it.

INSIGHT

She managed to squeeze into the correct position in the basket. Alberto tied a cord to her wrist, the rip cord for hydrogen release which she was to pull if the craft were to rise too high. [10] The increased weight was compensated for by removal of a few pounds of ballast and a full 7,700 cubic feet of hydrogen in the balloon.

Launched, the dirigible carried Aida at a speed that fluctuated between 12 and 15 mph, with the ground as much as 100 feet below. As she flew, Alberto followed her as best he could on his girl's bicycle (his cloak caught annoyingly on a boy's bicycle), giving her a series of handkerchief signals regarding altitude, direction and speed. She relaxed into the gentle pitch and toss, with a reassuring motor puttering away and a view below of pastoral fields, abundant gardens, a race track and a few of the Bois' famous old buildings. This panorama gave Aida a thrill far exceeding anything she had anticipated. The Café Madrid, Lac Interieur in the distance; to the east, boaters on the Seine!

As she flew over a row of poplar trees, she saw the Bagatelle polo field, where an international polo match was being played between the American and British teams, and at Alberto's signal, she descended. The large polo crowd had immediately recognized Dumont's dirigible above them, but now they noticed that it was being flown by "a corseted figure in a large, fluttering black hat festooned with pink roses" — a woman! Congratulatory cheers filled the air, almost a pandemonium of excitement. Several of the horses broke away and no one left the scene to catch them. Aida was later to write, "I will never forget how those people gazed at me as I pulled the valve cord to release the hydrogen gas and started to descend." [11]

132

Alberto raced up on his bicycle and cried out, "Mademoiselle, you are the first woman aviator in the world!"[12] It took several crewmen to help get her out of the basket tipped to its side, but after only a short while on the ground, she climbed into it and off she flew again to the point of first departure. The round trip experience took about 90 minutes and covered approximately a mile, much of that time being taken by the stopover on the polo field. Her flight took place six months before the Wright brothers flew at Kitty Hawk. It was also a quarter of a century before the great American aviator, Charles Lindbergh, flew solo across the Atlantic ocean, in 33 $^{1/2}$ hours of unbroken flying time, arriving in Paris after taking off from the military airfield on Long Island to be greeted in Paris by a vast crowd at the Paris airport. [13] Later that same year, 1927, Aida was to marry Lindbergh's "brilliant and attractive New York attorney," Henry Breckinridge, who would not know about her flight of 1903 until they had been married five years.

Aida's parents were horrified when they heard what she had done. They were not as much upset by the risk (which they probably did not understand) as by the potential publicity. Newspapers were for news, not for social voyeurism. Aida and a disappointed Alberto had to promise that her name was never to be used in connection with the flight. Surprisingly, each of the French newspapers respected their request and Santos-Dumont, too, did not use her name in his book, *My Airships,* although he mentioned that "a very beautiful young Cuban lady, well known in New York society" had flown solo without any external control from the airship's guide rope. A framed photograph of Aida would remain on his desk for the remainder of his life.

INSIGHT

Thirty years later, in the early 1940s, Aida was hosting a dinner party in New York and chatting with a young naval officer who happened to comment that he wished to fly a dirigible, which led to Aida declaring that she had once done exactly that. Telling the story of her flight in 1903 for the first time led to her recognition in the record books as the first woman pilot ever to fly a powered aircraft–and she did it solo.

In fairness, her parents had been correct when they objected to any public announcement of their daughter's feat, but social mores were changing. News of such bellwether accomplishments needed to be broadcast even as late as the 1930s, for society was still awakening to suffrage, public relations, and scientific solutions that needed public recognition of the names and faces of their camera and publicity-shy do'ers in order to advance. At last, such an accomplishment by a woman had become viewed as heroic, but by then Aida was ready for another very different kind of challenge. In the early 1940s, after the idea of an eye bank was conceived, Aida would plunge into the thick of making such a pioneering enterprise a reality–this time, paradoxically, heavily dependent upon her receiving maximum publicity.

In a book written in 1974, Aida's son wrote, "My mother was a very unusual woman...she was a different kind of person. She was the fourth of eight children, all brilliant, all handsome or beautiful (and they) cut a swathe which was in striking contrast to the simple teachers, lawyers, and small entrepreneurs from whom my father was descended. Drawn by Helleu, painted by Sargent, Zuloaga, and Boldini, sculpted by Malvina Hoffman, the de Acosta women were among the most celebrated personages of the late nineteenth and early twentieth centuries."[14] The other children chose social lives confined to a world of affluence and shielded from the public eye.

Aida was the exception. She broke the barrier into public recognition whether she liked it or not—and the part she liked was becoming a prime mover in a culture adapting to the extraordinary advances of science that were transforming both the opportunities and the mores of a modernizing world.

Born in 1863, Dr. William Holland Wilmer II was a different sort of human proposition from Aida, a free spirit driven by gumption and self-confidence who came from a family of numerous siblings. By contrast, Wilmer's spirit was formed by his religious beliefs, formalized by tradition and individualized by his commitment to the medical profession. He stood five feet, eight inches, appearing taller due to his erect bearing. He had strikingly handsome features punctuated by piercing blue eyes. Kindly and congenial, but with genteel inhibitions and scrupulous manners, he could have been cast as the beloved bishop in a Broadway play. The fact is, there were real bishops in his heritage. The apple had not fallen far from the tree.

He grew up near Alexandria, Virginia, in a patrician Anglo-Saxon family that extended back to landed gentry in England.[15] His paternal grandfather was the first William Holland Wilmer, a member of the Episcopalian priesthood and briefly president of William and Mary College in Williamsburg, Virginia. His father was a Yale graduate who spent much of his life in Mobile, Alabama, as an outspoken defender of slavery, widely known for his thirty-eight years as an Episcopal bishop loyal to the Confederacy. There were also other priests in that paternal bloodline.

INSIGHT

As eventually observed by a subsequent medical school dean, Dr. Wilmer was "imposing in stature, un-relaxing in presence, and usually surrounded by a retinue of his junior staff" [16] but, according to the same biographer, "temperamentally uneasy with organization, being less than a genius with the delegation of functions." Religion was never far from his thoughts, nor from the force of his commitment. To Osler's *aequanimitas* he added an element of faith and humanism as reflected in ancient literature by the teaching of the half-god Asclepius.

Will was ten years younger than his brother and twelve years younger than his sister, thereby being almost an only child who taught himself to read at an early age. He loved trees, flowers, animals and children, and rode his own horse to primary school. He learned to be a keen marksman with shotgun and pistol, and along the way he also became a deft billiard player. At fifteen, he and a classmate decided to operate on a dog with a large tumor on his back—Will being the surgeon and his friend the anesthetist. The growth was removed and both boys decided that they had saved the dog's life. That first operation was what made Will want to become a real surgeon in later years.[17]

He attended Episcopal High School in Virginia for three years where he was more athlete than the outstanding student, yet his interest in his studies and his overall conduct made him commendable in both scholarship and sportsmanship. He was most useful to the baseball team in throwing a tricky curve ball. As a result of a fall from his horse, he sustained an injury to his left hand that left him with a stiff small finger. That impairment meant he could no longer reach the "G" string on his violin, and after three promising years of practicing on that instrument, he gave it up.

Fortunately, that impairment did not to bother him in later years when he performed surgery at a high state of the art. In fact, he was manually versatile and became surgically ambidextrous so that either his right or left hand was dominant depending on which of the patient's eyes was being operated upon. In self-imposed ophthalmology training, he used the game of jackstraws to test the steadiness of his hands. From his rural background he had become sharp at billiards and keen in marksmanship with shotguns and pistol, thereby helping to develop the exceptional hand-eye coordination needed by the best of surgeons.

Will's medical training took place partially at the University of Virginia and then at Mt. Sinai Hospital in New York City, followed by a preceptorship with one of that city's most competent ophthalmologists, Dr. Earl Gruening. According to one source, Wilmer was also instructed by Dr. C. R. Agnew in those Manhattan years.[18] After settling in Washington, he began a private practice, with teaching responsibilities at Georgetown University, and during this time he gave 16 years to training and service in the Army Medical Reserve Corps. Thus when World War I broke out, Wilmer's move to active duty eventually took him from the rank of colonel to brigadier general.

In 1917, he was initially assigned to the same airfield on Long Island where Stewart Paton served as a major. Both physicians independently pursued research studies related to pilots' physical and mental preparedness for active duty in the European theatre of war. Six hundred aviators per month were sent from that field to the war zone. They stopped first at Issoudun in central France, where the U.S. established its largest training center for aviators and to which Will himself was soon transferred. For his war service he was awarded the Distinguished Service Medal on March 12, 1918, and over his career he would be the recipient of a senior rank in the French Legion of Honor, four honorary degrees and far too many other prestigious honors to detail here. He returned to Washington and to private practice and with a teaching affiliation at Georgetown University, Wilmer blossomed professionally.

Over 35 years of ophthalmic practice, he was highly praised for excellence in his medical services and for his respectful and sympathetic relationship to his patients. He became the eye doctor for hundreds of influential, often wealthy, politically prominent, and sometimes international patients, some of whom were connected with the nearby Executive Branch of the federal government. For example, Will became a good friend of Teddy Roosevelt, a favorite writer, Booth Tarkington, and is said to have served professionally Presidents Harrison, Cleveland, McKinley, Taft, Wilson, Harding and Coolidge. He would not have liked to have the names of his patients identified, but doing so conveys his stature. His office was on "I" Street, but his patients dubbed it "Eye" Street for their beloved eye doctor, and to this day it is still known as Eye Street among Washingtonians.

Meanwhile, Aida Breckinridge had been working for several charity-based agencies before being appointed in 1923 as Director of Public Relations for Herbert Hoover's American Child Health Association (ACHA) in Washington, where she worked for eight years. This proved to be valuable experience in the furthering of her career.[19] However, her life was to be plagued by a sudden affliction. On a summer day in 1922 while at the beach in Southampton, Long Island, she had been struck by severe pain in both eyes, later recounting that "everything suddenly went dim." That was the start of a long, discouraging trek from one doctor to another. Then, when attending a social event, she met a British viscount, Lord Grey, who also had eye troubles; he advised her to consult with the noted Dr. William Holland Wilmer in Washington, D.C.

Bingo! Washington was her own backyard. Even before they met, she was immensely impressed by Dr. Wilmer's reputation among people she knew or had heard about. Making an appointment, she experienced first-hand Dr. Wilmer's heartwarming manner. When the time came for the patients waiting in the anteroom to be seen "they heard the tinkle of a bell and were invited by his old family servant, William, to walk up a short flight of stairs. Always waiting at the top, having stepped out of his office to meet them, was a tall, gray-haired man with keen blue eyes, a cordial handshake and a pleasant word of greeting."

Upon examining her eyes, his diagnosis was "glaucoma" in both eyes, with very high pressure. Prompt surgical intervention was needed to attempt to prevent its progress. One of Dr. Wilmer's specialty operations was a so-called filtering procedure to relieve and control the eye pressure inglaucomatous eyes. The sight in Aida's right eye was almost gone; sight in the left was failing rapidly. Dr. Wilmer operated on her left eye and the vision was unchanged, as expected, but the eye pressure was lessened. A similar operation was later performed on the second eye. These major surgical undertakings took place over an apprehensive stretch of a few months, and with the patient's sense of appreciation at a high level.

Aida and Oren Root Jr., her first husband, were divorced after fourteen years of marriage.[20] Whatever the cause, there was much to be proud of in bearing the name "Mrs. Root," representing, as it did, a close-knit family with a proud lineage that included the highly distinguished statesman, her husband's uncle Elihu Root.[21] Through her work and her many social acquaintances, Aida Root had extraordinary access to some of the most important and often wealthiest American citizens. Thus, as she lay in a hospital bed with both eyes bandaged following each of her operations, she began to think that Dr. Wilmer deserved his own specialty clinic to better serve the multitude of patients seeking his care, and that she might be able to help him with that.

She soon offered those inspired musings to her profoundly impressive ophthalmologist, suggesting that Dr. Wilmer should have a freestanding building established in his name, possibly in the Washington area. Wilmer acknowledged that it would indeed be desirable to have such an ample facility for both patient care and teaching opportunities, but when she asked for the names of his patients to contact for financial contributions, he balked. Neither she nor anyone else was to approach his patients for money. Wilmer was horrified by the thought of asking his patients for contributions, and that was that.

Such a definitive ruling would have stopped most people from proceeding but Aida moved comfortably among society activists, learning from them the importance of prioritizing sensibilities–aided perhaps by some genetic awareness that even bullfights can have rare refusals, overlooking the wave-off of the matador's misjudgment and allowing the banderilleros to prevent the poor fellow from being fatally gored. Aida had her instincts and her nerve. But she knew very little about eye troubles. That was Wilmer's bailiwick. They each had their strengths.

Therefore, 42-year-old Aida levied a decision against this 59 year-old doctor, whom she was never to call by his first name.[22] Aida merely circumvented Dr. Wilmer's roadblock to his extensive patient information by contacting scores of opticians in numerous states who filled eyeglass prescriptions written by Dr. Wilmer. They gladly provided her with his patients' names and contact information. She also asked William, the longtime loyal employee of Dr. Wilmer, for the names of patients coming for their appointments, and thus many more names were obtained. In all, over 700 letters were sent to these individuals, and the responses were very gratifying. Approximately $200,000 was raised. Now the pump was primed, but several million dollars would be required.

Within a few months of beginning her fund-raising, Aida formed the Wilmer Foundation, appointing to its board such "names" as Pulitzer, Vanderbilt, Proctor, and a certain Henry Breckinridge, who before long became her husband.[23] She then approached some large private foundations, some wealthy individuals who were her friends, and some professional contacts from the Hoover Commission for Children and other non-profit sources she had become familiar with. In one case worth mentioning, she called "a certain person" to say she wished to discuss with him the plan for a Wilmer Institute in the Washington area.

The person in question responded that she should come to his office. When she got there a secretary handed her an envelope with a contribution within. In her words, "I refused to accept it because I hadn't been given the opportunity to tell this man the story."[24] Sometime later this man sent for her and she explained at some length the reasons to help with the funding of the Institute. Once well informed, he gave her a second check. The first was for $1,000 and the second was for $40,000. Not many seeking funds would have had the confidence and technique that Aida showed that supporter.

Aida scored similar successes with other deep-pocketed donors. However, it became evident to her that the most affluent private foundations, such as those of Rockefeller, Mellon, Milbank and others, were run by administrators who knew organizations were more likely to raise large contributions if they were part of an established "mother" institution, and that the ultimate benefits to the public good would more likely be greater if an academic institution were the recipient of their charitable grants. This observation led to encouraging Johns Hopkins' interest in a Wilmer Clinic, with Dr. Wilmer himself as the *pièce de résistance.*

The former medical school dean, Dr. William Welch, quickly picked up on that proposal; as soon as he became involved in raising funds, the results very encouragingly improved. He was not only a near-genius fundraiser but he also represented an exciting mother institution to harbor the building for ophthalmology. Importantly and wisely in the interest of Dr. Wilmer, the funding was deposited in the private Wilmer Foundation that maintained its integrity and its protectiveness for the interests of Dr. Wilmer up to the time he returned to Washington almost a decade later. When a grant proposal from the Rockefeller General Education Fund for $1,500,000 was matched with other donations, Johns Hopkins ended up with an assured five-story Wilmer Institute on the Johns Hopkins medical campus in East Baltimore, which was to become an integral part of its hospital and its Medical School.

That is a highly abbreviated account of the process that Aida had initiated and established, with wise decisions along the way. At the formal opening of the Institute in 1929, she was correctly credited with its basic concept and for initiating the funding that grew exponentially once the undertaking was fully secured by a supporting structure, the Wilmer Foundation, which in turn came into league with Johns Hopkins. Dr. Wilmer's appointment as director of the forthcoming institute and Professor of Ophthalmology at the medical school took place in 1925. It would be four more years before the building could be occupied. Meanwhile, ophthalmology was temporarily taught in existing crowded quarters, but because it had a veritable king in charge, it didn't matter. There was also time for Dr. Wilmer to tour academic eye clinics in Europe to be certain that his Institute would have the benefit of ideas and facilities existent in countries more experienced in this new medical specialty. Wilmer was pressed by time, being older than the usual new departmental heads and in view of a Johns Hopkins rule that faculty members, with few exceptions, were required to retire in the year of their 70th birthday. Therein lay the cause for the most distressing issue that Dr. Wilmer would confront during his Baltimore years. Meanwhile, a total of $4,500,000 had been raised for his Institute, comparable to more than $105,600,000 in current dollars.

INSIGHT

NOTES TO CHAPTER 8:

1. Dr. Welch referred to Medicine as "the stepchild of philanthropy," indicating repeatedly that Medicine had reached a point where its further advancement mandated major funding, not the case in previous eras. See *William Henry Welch and the Heroic Age of American Medicine* by Flexner, S. and Flexner, J.T., page 237. Johns Hopkins University Press, Baltimore, 1941.
2. Spelled D'Acosta, deAcosta or de Acosta, the last being the way she preferred her name to be typed under her signature, therefore considered her preference.
3. Aida, pronounced like the title of the famous opera by Giuseppe Verdi--or, you could say, Joe Green for non-buffs.
4. At 74, Aida's son told her she was entitled to retroactive Social Security benefits, but they could not find her birth certificate and her marriage certificate was intentionally incorrect. He confronted his mother with her almost lifelong lie: "Mother, your lifetime of prevarication is now costing you two thousand dollars, tax free." Her reply: "It was worth it."
5. Considerable information about Aida has been provided in these references: Randolph, M.E. and Welch, R.B., *The Wilmer Ophthalmological Institute, 1925-1975*, Waverly Press, Inc., Baltimore, 1976; Root, O., *Persons and Persuasions*, W.W. Norton & Company, New York, 1974; Hoffman, P., *Wings of Madness: Alberto Santos-Dumont and the Invention of Flight*, Hachette Books, 2003; Santos=Dumont, A.: *My Airships: The Story of My Life*, Dover Press, 1973 and Ashcroft, B., "Aida de Acosta--The First Woman to Fly a Powered Airship," *Air & Space Power Journal*, 2004.
6. As early as 1865--to put that date in perspective, the year of President Lincoln's death and of Stewart Paton's birth--the French writer Jules Verne piqued the public's imagination with fictional stories of man's potential for flights into spaces. One of his books, *From the Earth to the Moon*, described a Baltimore gun club's "space gun" designed for shooting three men to the moon.
7. Gray, C. F., "The 1906 Santos-Dumont No. 14," *World War I Aeroplanes, Issue #194*, November 2006, pp. 4-21.
8. Not until December 17, 1903 did Orville Wright pilot the first powered airplane 20 feet above ground for 12 seconds and covering 120 feet. His brother was to do better when his turn came next.
9. A fichu is a large neckerchief worn by women in those times to hide any signs of the female chest not covered by her dress.
10. From an article by Richard Kleiner in The World-Telegram and Sun, Saturday Magazine, July 11, 1943.

11. Hoffman, P.: *Wings of Madness*. Hachette Books, New York, 2003.
12. Ibid.
13. Root, O.: *Persons and Persuasions*. W.W. Norton & Company, New York, 1974.
14. Ibid.
15. A full-length biography was commissioned by Dr. Wilmer's family and completed in 1942 but never published, the author being Donald Bartlett, Professor of Biography at Dartmouth College. This book was loaned for the purpose of this history by his grandson, William H. Wilmer Esq. of Baltimore, Md. According to a phone conversation with Mr. Bartlett's son, the book was not published evidently because Dr. Wilmer's widow changed her mind about its usefulness to his reputation and the institutions he represented.
16. Ibid.
17. From a New York Sunday Times article by Frank Ernest Hill, July 1, 1934.
18. According to Townley's sister, Evelyn Paton Powell, in a letter to this writer dated September 25, 1966, Dr. Wilmer received additional instruction while in Manhattan from Dr. C. R. Agnew.
19. The ACHA was for Aida the equivalent of residency training for a physician. It was a not-for-profit organization formed from several pre-existing entities, requiring collaborative management and prominent names to attract attention through public promotions that were needed for its accomplishment and its funding.
20. There have been five family generations with sons named Oren Root, Aida's first husband being #3, although he was commonly titled Oren Root Jr., which complicates references to a sequence of distinguished Roots. Aida's husband was a railroad executive. His son, #4, was a prominent lawyer and friend of Charles A. Lindbergh, thanks to an introduction from his mother's second husband, Henry S. Breckinridge, who was the Charles Lindberghs' close friend and personal lawyer, although they did not share his German sympathizing (*Lindbergh*, by A.S. Berg, Berkeley Books, New York, 1998).
21. Elihu Root was a versatile statesman and lawyer who became U.S. Secretary of War and Secretary of State under Theodore Roosevelt. He later served his country as a senator from New York and also became the first president of the Carnegie Endowment for International Peace. Root was awarded the Nobel Peace Prize in 1912.
22. This is not intended to discriminate against the male but to point out that important differences affect the minds of men and women. Today there are approximately as many women in training as men, correcting a greatly unbalanced distribution in past decades.
23. Henry Breckinridge, Secretary-Treasurer of the Wilmer Board, was Assistant Secretary of War under President Wilson and was Charles Lindbergh's attorney at the time the Lindbergh child was kidnapped.
24. Randolph, M.E., Welch, R.B.: *The Wilmer Ophthalmological Institute 1925-1975*. Williams & Wilkins Co. Baltimore, 1976.

CHAPTER 9: A WILMER EYE MAN

> *You have to learn the rules of the game. And then you have to play better than anyone else.* Albert Einstein, 1879-1955

In the fall of 1929, when his residency training began, Townley Paton's future moved from pipe dream to safe bet. Having been accepted for a three-year residency by Dr. Wilmer was for him close to a miraculous happening. Two years earlier, he had come to the Johns Hopkins Medical School from Cambridge with very high commendations from the professors who knew his work. They had expressed their confidence in him with sentences instead of numbers. Having been judged an excellent candidate, he transferred to spend his last two years of schooling at Johns Hopkins Medical School and finally graduated with satisfactory marks. Now he was starting an entirely new field, ophthalmology.

Townley had a lot to prove if he wished to be among the leaders of his profession in the years to come. And that was exactly what he had in mind, not for bragging rights but for the pure satisfaction of feeling he could earn a respectable place as had his father. Townley's highly competitive acceptance for training by Dr. Wilmer was another phenomenal piece of good fortune for him. Had it not been a residency program at its earliest stage (he was in the third year of appointees) when the competition for appointment was definitely less than it would be once the Institute officially opened, his good fortune might not have continued. It was up to him to prove that he was far more qualified that the tests showed. For the moment, he wanted nothing more than what he was to become, a "Wilmer eye man."

Dr. Wilmer was becoming well known as perhaps the leading all-around practicing ophthalmologist, nationally and internationally. But could he also become an equally top full-time academic professor at 66 once the new Institute was functional? If that title of supremacy were to be claimed for Dr. Wilmer, it would rest upon a spectrum of diagnostic skills, surgical finesse, quality of teaching and an exceptional doctor-patient rapport.

Ophthalmology was his passion far more than his livelihood. No question that he was a careful and sympathetic listener to his patients' complaints and unhurried in communicating his advice. He equally served the rich and the poor, a basic intent soon emulated by his trainees. According to his biographer, Wilmer added a catalyst to Osler's a*equanimitas,* for he "believed in religious duty backing up the humanitarian aspect of his work." In one sense he was another Agnew with the strong impetus of religion and the drive of a man capable of achieving greatness across the board. As noted earlier, Agnew had been a teacher of Wilmer when he was training at Mt. Sinai in New York City.[1] Wilmer's biographer wrote, Dr. Wilmer's religion "was never far from his thoughts."[2] As was undoubtedly true of the other residents, Townley flourished under the compelling influences of their easily idolized professor.

INSIGHT

Dr. Wilmer was the Institute's only full-time professor, and while other instructors were also inspiring at times, it was certainly Wilmer who made the training special. As a teacher, he displayed certain elements of the great performers, for he stood apart, staying in character rather than stooping to commonality. His authoritative approach was serious and commanding, the martinet of daily routines; he did not seek to be everyman's beguiler but, rather, the oracle of current knowledge constructively expressed. When he taught extemporaneously, such as at bedside rounds, it was in *ex cathedra* didactics rather than in-house small talk. That level of formality may have reflected his older age compared to other senior faculty members, but its precision and depth drew a respect for his knowledge that came from voluminous reading and many years of patient care.

However, these characteristics of "professing" did not obscure his innate gentleness, despite it being conveyed in the demeanor of a man who felt he well deserved his place of honor. For a starry-eyed trainee at the Wilmer Institute, Townley's new arms-length hero became "the greatest eye man ever."

The Townley Patons lived on Wolfe Street in a narrow row house with white painted steps simulating the white marble steps for which Baltimore, in its more affluent areas, was well-known. East Baltimore was a poor residential neighborhood largely populated by African-American residents, most of whom were becoming dependent upon the all-white Johns Hopkins medical staff for their health care. These two populations lived adjacent to each other, the medics along Wolfe and McElderry Streets and the black residents immediately beside and behind the Hopkins folks, representing only the fringe of an extensive residential community that had become the largest city-segment of Baltimore's total population.

They lived entirely separately but in a kind of mutual symbiosis whereby the learning doctors were dependent upon their black neighbors as patients and the patients in turn had gratitude for the care they received at little or no cost from the hands of their white physicians and neighbors. There was nothing newsworthy in terms of tensions or invasions of one group by the other. For the resident trainees, their lives were cash-poor and intellectually rich. Home was little more than a place to hang the hat, mollify the wife whose loneliness was almost unbearable at times, and tend to an expanding family.

There was indeed a high incidence of new births in the hospital crowd, and hardly had Townley begun his training at Wilmer when on August 16, 1930 the Patons had a son whom they named after his paternal great uncle, David (nmn) Paton, the accomplished Princeton Egyptologist. The young fellow's genes were to prove more medically oriented than his older sister's and—unimaginatively but happily—he was to become an ophthalmologist in his father's footsteps.[3] As gene pools go, David's distribution seemed satisfying but not what one might want to write home about—thus he did that for himself in another book.[4] The Patons' third and last child was Pamela; she was to be born eight years later. Because of the impact she had on Townley's life, much more about her will appear in later pages.

INSIGHT

The hospital's senior staff generally lived in rural communities to the north while the trainees were step-counting distances from the hospital's emergency rooms and on call for all urgencies that arose during the nights. The hospital compound, containing several buildings, was circled by fencing composed of iron spikes cast to appear like an endless alignment of vertical spears. There were several gates in this fence but none on the Wolfe Street side; thus, when urgently summoned at night via their home's party-line hospital telephone, Townley, ever the eager athlete, would climb over the fence in a binary process of heisting halfway up, then thrusting himself higher and further to land comfortably on hospital turf, allowing for far fewer steps to the emergency room. Helen enjoyed teasing that, infrequently but memorably, there were times when he caught his jacket or, worse, his trousers, on one of the sharp spikes, causing rips that could not be closed on the spot and had to be ignored if he was to arrive on time. This he did, but not without enduring the occasional mortification of gaping slashes in his hospital uniform.

The professor's routine has been described by two Wilmer-trained authors, Drs. Elliott Randolph and Robert Welch, in their history of the Wilmer Institute.[5] Every weekday morning at exactly 9 a.m., Dr. Wilmer would arrive in his black Packard car; the senior resident would be standing at his version of "parade rest" to open the car door, grab the professor's briefcase and accompany him to his office, where his secretary would brief him on the expected patients of the day, patients such as Charles Lindbergh, the Governor of Maryland, J. P. Morgan or perhaps the Secretary of War. As Dr. Randolph wrote from personal experience, "let there be no mistake" that Dr. Wilmer expected the senior resident, and only he, to be waiting for his arrival.

After the extended office briefing, the two would proceed to Dr. Wilmer's large examining room where the other residents and several eye nurses would be waiting. The professor then would sit at a desk while the senior resident presented the first patient and his or her history of eye troubles. The findings upon examination were stated and clarified. Each patient always received a kind word from Dr. Wilmer to give courage and confidence before he began his own resident-assisted eye examination. He would upon occasion tell the patient he or she was sitting in the "Presidents' chair," explaining that "every President from McKinley on has sat in this chair." If the patient in question were obese and hesitant to sit, he might add, "Just remember, it held President Taft when he weighed 350 pounds." Occasionally, Dr. Wilmer would tell the most apprehensive patients: "Well, you have come to the court of highest appeal," which, coming from him, sounded reassuring rather than boastful.

On Friday afternoons at 4:00, the professor also led walking rounds illuminated by candlelight so as not to expose eyes recently operated on to any more light than necessary for determining the status of recovery.[6] In preparation for that event on the third floor, a passenger elevator was held in reserve and not even the director of the hospital would be permitted to use it until Wilmer had arrived and met with his entourage. Then followed this procession of doctors, resident staff and a few nurses all going to the ward floor by a series of elevator trips and thence to the wards and from bedside to bedside with almost no voices audible other than the professor's comments and the nurses' instructions in facilitating the eye examinations by the positioning of the patients and the candles. One of Dr. Wilmer's patients, the writer Booth Tarkington, described the scene of walking rounds as reminiscent of "an ecclesiastical pageant" winding its way from bed to bed in semi-darkness, lit by little more than the flickering light from the candles.

At each bedside the professor and his chief resident stood on the right side of the bed while the posse of others jockeyed for a good view on the left side. Townley was to recall a day of crowded rounds when he found himself inadvertently trapped on the right side of a bed, which was absolutely the wrong side for him to be standing. He quickly crawled under the bed to the other side, relieved not to have been noticed by the professor. He also told about an unnamed Senator's wife who had been admitted with a badly infected eyelid injury causing swollen lids and a continuing bloody discharge. Dr. Wilmer prescribed the use of a leech on this festering wound–which Townley "applied." But later, before rounds, when he checked for any change, the leech had become firmly attached to the woman's eyeball, much to her horror—and Townley, being an inexperienced first-year resident, could not get it to release its hold. Fortunately, one of the eye nurses knew exactly what to do, applying drops of topical anesthetic, and soon the leech released its attachment to the eye, allowing easy removal.

Dr. Wilmer's occasional use of therapeutic leeches was a holdover that stretched from the doctoring of Hippocrates (and earlier) to the modern era, [7] when even today leeches and maggots still have their advocates for use in certain circumstances of wound contamination and repair. So the professor deserved no criticism for the versatility of his practical patient management.

As a first-year resident, Townley's job included a physical examination of each of Dr. Wilmer's patients prior to scheduled eye surgery the following day. One of the patients he was to recall in telling Helen about his day at the hospital was an indignant and dismissive woman who refused to let him touch her, saying she would allow only Dr. Wilmer to examine her. The senior resident had to be called, and after prolonged flattery and persuasion he was permitted to perform the most minimal acts of medical servicing before she said enough was enough and what remained to be done would be Dr. Wilmer's concern in the morning. That evening Townley told Helen about his failure to accomplish what was expected of him.

"What was the woman's name?"

"I don't recall."

"Certainly you do. This is not a federal inquiry."

"It was a Mrs. Pillsbury."

"The flour queen?"

"I suppose so."

Helen thought for a moment then came up with a grave pronouncement: "From now on, we'll have no Pillsbury flour in this household." She flashed a smile, then waited for what turned out to be several decades for revenge to take its course.

That episode featuring a fiercely loyal wife prompts repetition of a slightly "ribald" saying taken from Dr. Wilmer's unpublished biography that illustrates the extent of malfeasance the professor would tolerate. It is this: "Someone has said that a wife is like a zero

INSIGHT

to her man, who is the digit. It makes all the difference in the world which side she is on." That may not be a side-splitter and it has a trace of misogyny, but spousal support was always something that Townley could count upon and the same was true for Dr. Wilmer.

It was in 1932 that a particularly memorable VIP sought Dr. Wilmer's care.[8] Because Townley was then the chief resident, it was his responsibility to manage patient issues when Dr. Wilmer was out of town. That is how he met with the emissary of King Prajadhipok of Siam (Rana VII) to make arrangements for an eye examination and possible cataract surgery. Over the years since then, considerable misinformation has been put forth by royalty raconteurs, making this a good opportunity to provide the facts not only as recorded by Townley but also by the unpublished Bartlett biography of Dr. Wilmer.

The diminutive 38-year-old king's arrival was preceded by his representative, whose job was to learn the layout of the Institute, such as the location of Dr. Wilmer's office and various other locations, presumably for security concerns and for maximizing conveniences for His Majesty. In touring the Institute, Townley was asked about the floor immediately above the operating rooms: was it for storage or patients or what? The king's aide was told that the floor above constituted the Institute's research department, containing cages of numerous animals of several species, such as rabbits, mice and cats. The emissary asked to have them moved out, for neither animals nor humans were acceptable at a level above the king's head.

Townley made inquiries and had to reply that nothing could be done about the research laboratory and its vivarium of animals. This threw a wrench into otherwise easy planning, and it led to the decision in advance that King Prajadhipok could not be operated upon in that location, although His Majesty definitely wanted to be examined by Dr. Wilmer. An appointment was scheduled and Dr. Wilmer met and examined this relatively young man whose ripe cataract was declared ready for extraction. Arrangements were made for Dr. John M. Wheeler in New York to operate at a leased private mansion on a large Long Island estate where, in fact, the operation was performed in all due comfort with social and surgical compliances. No person or animal was above the king's head. A second procedure was needed to remove some of the retained cataract fragments which was not unusual in those days. The king returned for a final eye exam by Dr. Wilmer.

The Wilmers invited the royal couple to their home in Guilford for a home-cooked dinner. It was an uneventful and evidently satisfying evening both for both the royals and the Wilmers, but a problem arose. Cora, the Wilmers' longstanding black cook who was held in considerable affection by them, observed that her white employers were dining at the same table as the dark-skinned visitors. She was so emotionally overwrought—so shocked and distressed by the inappropriateness of this—that she quit her job, then and there, never to return. [9]

As to the ending of the King Prajadhipok story in Baltimore, when asked by his aide what Dr. Wilmer's bill amounted to, Dr. Wilmer reportedly answered that "the king can do no wrong." But, according to Townley, no payment was made to Wilmer but a very generous one equivalent to $700,000 in today's money was given to Dr. Wheeler. That detail is mentioned to correct a Wilmer tale that he was given a huge gift of money from the king, not so. There was no eye follow-up but in that same year, 1932, a revolution in Siam

INSIGHT

(present-day Thailand) led to King Prajadhipok's abdication and to his spending the remainder of his life in England, where he had much earlier become fluent in English while attending Eton College. He died in England of heart failure at age 48.

    Cataract surgery in the 1930s was far from the only eye procedure soon to gain radical replacements with upgrades of instrumentation. Dr. Wilmer performed glaucoma (trephining) procedures in no more than ten minutes of operating time. He was the first in America to perform a successful retinal detachment operation with the technique of Jules Gonin of Switzerland, soon to be the basis for all modern operative detachment procedures. He insisted that his assistants use rubber gloves but he himself refrained from using them. As reported previously, the surgical use of rubber gloves was devised by Townley's great-uncle Dr. William Halsted. Other surgeons began to use gloves for reducing the prevalence of wound infections, and eventually surgical gloves became routine. However, for the delicate surgery demanded of the ophthalmologist, Dr. Wilmer and some other fastidious operatives believed that the gloves affected the dexterity of masterful hands.[10]

    Decades later when such gloves were made of latex, almost all surgeons in the United States used them, except for a few ophthalmologists. Such a rare finicky surgeon may not have had the worldliness to realize that modern condoms are made of surgical latex and that even hardened murderers have learned to their regret that their fingerprints can leave an impression through such gloves and thereby identify them.

    Today, it is hard even to imagine the limitations and challenges eye surgeons faced in the early 1930s and for their entire careers, for it would be three decades before the use of operating microscopes and related finer instrumentation. Sutures in Dr. Wilmer's time were comparable to a hawser when compared to the almost spider web-like strands of nylon used in the modern era.

Post-operative recovery began with ten days of hospitalization and bilateral eye bandaging, usually followed by months of gradual vision recovery. During this time the cataract extraction patient was fitted with "bottle bottom" lenses as "aphakic spectacles." These were eventually replaced by contact lenses and finally by intraocular lenses placed immediately within the eye after the cataract extraction.

Furthermore, finding retinal holes whose closure is essential to the cure of retinal detachments was extremely difficult when confined to the use of a hand-held ophthalmoscope compared to the state-of-the-art new instrumentation that was produced in the 1960s and thereafter. In short, Dr. Wilmer and his contemporaries examined eyes and operated on them under the severe handicap of very low power magnification if any.

Thus, what Dr. Wilmer and his peers were able to accomplish were near miracles in their time, and he was among the most knowledgeable and successful of eye surgeons of his day. He taught his surgery by demonstration accompanied by running discussion. Some of the residents, such as Townley, took to eye surgery like ducks to water. A paper by a former Wilmer resident includes the following comment: "R. Townley Paton...showed signs of great surgical skill, with a delicate sense of touch, excellent judgment and fine technique."[11]

As in the other ophthalmology training programs, the trainees had not had their manual skills tested in advance of appointment, but with eye surgery still in a "gross" versus its "microscopic" later phase, the need for exquisitely precise hands was not yet a defining qualification. It was in the late 1950s and early '60s when those with outstanding manual ability were identified and encouraged, while all others came to realize that alternative aspects of their specialty were better suited to them.

In his day, Professor Wilmer was enlightened but also academically conservative with respect to his trainees' education. Regardless of his own interest in medical advances related to precedents abroad, he was not willing to grant his trainees free rein in taking their own ideas into clinical practice. Despite reports of increasing success with corneal transplantation in several European countries, Townley was forbidden by the professor to perform that operation at the Wilmer Institute. Thus, determined to do an operation he had read about in foreign publications and had experimented with in the laboratory, Townley obtained permission to do several such cases in early 1933 at the nearby University of Maryland Hospital. Unfortunately, in Townley's three corneal transplants on volunteers only one was reported to be successful, arguably supporting the wisdom of his Johns Hopkins professor. As for the patients, success for one of three was at least an achievement for that one patient's otherwise incurable blindness.

What Dr. Wilmer did champion was an early trend toward patients' roles in the understanding and management of their own illnesses. This was a change from the aloof dictates of 19th-century physicians to the more communicative and collaborative role advocated by medical doctors like the professor who realized that the patient himself had a major responsibility for his illness outcomes, especially when there were difficult management hurdles to cross.

On the one hand, the medical profession was educating the public about the exclusive role of medicine instead of valueless alternatives "on the street," and on the other hand medicine would increasingly need public information and implementation of medical practices. It was probably too soon to promote that distinction but *sub rosa* entries into the yet undefined realm of social science became a gradual evolutionary change in American health care.

Townley's three years of training went smoothly, feeding his appetite for more and more opportunities to cure by cutting, as the surgically-oriented physicians might casually proclaim. He knew how to refract for optimal eyeglass corrections, how to use eye exercises for relief of the common causes of children's eyes that crossed, how to diagnose glaucoma and treat it with medication if that proved sufficient, how to probe lachrymal ducts to reduce tearing, and how to address many other eye issues that did not require surgery. However, as for many ophthalmologists, the surgery was his greatest fascination.

Dr. Wilmer (front-center) and Townley Paton, ca. 1933

INSIGHT

Dr. Wilmer's 70th birthday was to be the date of his retirement from the Institute, in accordance with the university's age limitation on its faculty. However, his departure after less than eight years in Baltimore as full-time Professor of Ophthalmology and only five years after the Institute's construction was completed was too soon for a man in excellent health who wanted as much time as possible to form the eye department in line with his own concept for its future. After all, the Wilmer Foundation, created well before the founding of the Institute, had been the source of its financial achievements, and his Hopkins career had been transferred from an exceedingly successful practice in Washington. Moreover, Dr. Wilmer knew that Dr. Welch was not required to leave the faculty at age 70, so why did the rule not apply to him?[12] According to Maumenee in an oral history, that question was never answered. Wilmer was unsatisfied. Even though he was required to step down as Director- he accepted that ruling — he still hoped that he could continue in a peripheral role in the Institute and thus complete his further plans for research development.

That possibility was torpedoed on April 10, 1934, with an announcement in local newspapers of Dr. Alan Woods' early take over[13] as Acting Professor and Director of the Wilmer Institute. The fact that medical politics and the human need to prevail were to mar the ending of Dr. Wilmer's tenure in Baltimore became a communication lesson learned too late. Hurt by the published and premature announcement of his successor, Dr. Wilmer wrote a letter of resignation to the president of the Board of Trustees of the university dated May 17, 1934. According to his biographer, he left the Institute in "pain and bitterness" having felt "shoved out" and having expected to be the one to select his successor. [14] Informed of the decision, he had met with the administration and others to acknowledge Dr. Woods as his "choice," but he had expected to retain some level of authority in the further advancement of his Institute. The kerfuffle that ensued took off from the unfortunate error in bypassing the viewpoint of the retiring Director. There was an unwritten but well-known mutual frigidity between the Director and his designated successor. They were two men of distinctly different personalities. The younger man was said to be tactless and gruff at times although a popular Johns Hopkins faculty member. Wilmer, by contrast, was reportedly poised, sensitive, shy about self-promotion, and easily victimized by outspoken brashness. His biographer concluded, "Doubtless he was a little naïve among those of his friends who did not like each other, or whose interests clashed." Re Wilmer, his wife, did not want the biography to surface for fear it would reflect badly on a great institution, but her feelings were clear: she detested Dr. Woods." [15]

Thus, Dr. Wilmer returned to Washington feeling dispatched rather than ceremoniously retired. Mrs. Wilmer was devastated by the treatment of her beloved husband in his final months in Baltimore before returning to Washington. It would be less than two years later, on March 12, 1936, when Dr. Wilmer died of a heart attack. He was interred in a chapel crypt of the National Cathedral of Washington on whose board he had served and, incidentally, where in the 20th century alone more than a dozen presidential funerals were held. It was the resting place of numerous other noted U.S. citizens, including another special person — especially for Townley—

INSIGHT

whom he would meet in New York only a few years before her death, the world-famous, totally blind Helen Keller. In those same years before Dr. Wilmer's death, he was to keep his word in referring many patients to Townley, thereby facilitating his entry into private practice by providing him with interesting and unusual patients who invariably were both worldly and challenging. By 1933, the Townley Paton family was ready to split for an entirely new medical world.

The Stewart and the Townley Patons, with Evelyn, 1933

NOTES TO CHAPTER 9:

1. Late 1930s: Letter to Townley from Evelyn re Agnew teaching Wilmer.
2. Bartlett biography
3. Princeton University--Johns Hopkins Medical School--Wilmer Institute.

4. Paton, D.: *Second Sight: Views From An Eye Doctor's Odyssey.* Create Space, 2011.
5. Randolph, M.E., and Welch, R.B.: *The Wilmer Ophthalmological Institute 1925-1975.* Williams & Wilkins Company, Baltimore, 1976.
6. Low light meant less squeezing from the lids, thus less risk to the surgical wound.
7. Leeches were supplied from leech farms, a very distant cousin of eye banks.
8. There are two chief references, the first being readily available: Rones, B., "The Wilmer Institute: The Early Days," *Survey of Ophthalmology,* 19:3, pages 169-178, 1974; the other is the unpublished Bartlett biography of Dr. Wilmer referred to above, as yet not publicly available. In 1971, in answer to a letter from Mr. Edward Bogert of Princeton, New Jersey dated April 13, 1971, Townley wrote that as the chief resident when the king visited the Institute he could recall the facts accurately, as recorded in this chapter. In addition, he emphasizes that all of the eye surgery (two operations) was done by Dr. John Wheeler in New York upon Dr. Wilmer's referral due to the animal lab issue. He goes on to say that a check for $60,000 was sent to Dr. Wheeler (not to Wilmer) for the surgery.
9. From the Bartlett unpublished biography, see above.
10. Dr. Halsted and Margaret Paton shared the same grandfather.
11. Bartlett biography.
12. Rones, B: "The Wilmer Institute: The Early Days" Survey of Ophth. 19:169-178, 1974. Again the Bartlett biography covers this topic quite thoroughly.
13. Ophthalmology Oral History Series: "A Link With the Past. An Interview with A.E. Maumenee conducted in1990 by Sally Smith Hughes, Regional Oral History Office, University of California, Berkley in cooperation with the Foundation of the American Academy of Ophthalmology, 1994.
14. There are two chief references, the first being readily available: Rones, B., as above, and the other is again the Bartlett biography.
15. In the unpublished biography, the writer reports that Dr. Wilmer was "temperamentally uneasy with organization, being less than a genius with the delegation of functions," thus suggesting Wilmer had a share of the blame due to prior indefiniteness. According to a New York Times article about Dr. Wilmer's retirement (July 1, 1934), he was made both Professor and Director Emeritus of Ophthalmology at the time of his departure to Washington. What Dr. Wilmer would not know was that when Dr. Woods retired from the Directorship, his successor, Dr. A. E. Maumenee, gladly permitted him to retain an office in the Institute and active in his patient care. This is discussed in Maumenee's oral history referenced above.

CHAPTER 10: THE TRANSFORMATIVE CITY

Whatever you are, be a good one. Attributed to Abraham Lincoln

By the end of his third year of residency training, Townley was the typical product of an *aequanimitas*-infused, Hopkinsonian boot camp. His deep submersion in ophthalmology had prevented him from developing the urbanity that comes from more direct dealing with the real world. His subsequent transition to self-determination was a more wrenching experience than for residency graduates today, who enjoy more normal living standards than those of the slavish trainees of Townley's era, from whom the Johns Hopkins faculty expected total conformity to emerge as ideal doctors— which they were. At an age when his former school contemporaries in business, law and other professions were living comfortably and maturely, Townley was only just beginning to conduct his life without institutional command. In current vernacular, he was a well-turned-out, naïve "medical nerd."

The Townley Patons were headed to Manhattan, where Helen's parents lived at the time and where Townleys's parents had lived previously. In America's notorious Big Apple, creative opportunity was virtually unlimited, but at the price of a transition in attitude and style from a southern to a northern American culture. If Townley wanted to excel professionally with the personal assets he inherited, he would have a social learning curve that would take him from being a pleasantly nurtured medical trainee in Baltimore to a socially savvy medical authority in New York. That was no curve; it was an almost straight line up. But a primary incentive to "think big" about the New York move was Dr. Wilmer's plan to refer his Northeast VIP patients to Townley as soon as he opened his

Manhattan office. Why he was so sure that Townley would be the best recipient of his referrals is not known, but he must have given it careful thought.

Johns Hopkins Hospital

It was for Townley a thrilling prospect, even though the move north was, for him, like leaving a matinee and emerging from a half-empty movie house into a crowded sunny street: momentary disorientation and dazzle, soon followed by adaptation. However, adaptation from the enveloping enclosure of Dr. Wilmer's residency would be a much more prolonged happening, further complicated by the upward mobility required to establish a medical practice in—arguably—the country's most sophisticated city with respect to its intelligentsia. If Dr. Wilmer's referrals were to be promotional of Townley's career, it would require that he attend to the certain accompanying requirements: a well-located office and an affiliation with a hospital with high standards and strong administration.

INSIGHT

Manhattan for the sheltered young Townley Patons would serve as a do-it-yourself finishing school for cultural experiences, one that brought no guarantees of friendships or success but enormous possibilities. Nothing there would be spoon-fed to them, or charitably excused. There were medical immigrants to the city who saw no reason for social assimilation, and they would remain at the edge of this unique Northeastern society. Others, such as the Patons, would choose to merge with the group they felt most comfortable in joining, were it also to offer opportunity.

In 1933, portents of war were scaring Europeans as Adolf Hitler became Chancellor on his way to leading a fatal aggression against the Jews, and the Nazi party introduced a law to legalize eugenic sterilization. In America, in contrast, Franklin Roosevelt assumed the Presidency, instituted the New Deal and said optimistically, "The only thing we have to fear is fear itself." It was a year when Prohibition was repealed, Albert Einstein immigrated to the United States, and construction in Manhattan was key to hastening the downfall of the Great Depression. The American zeitgeist was epitomized by five-year-old Shirley Temple who that year began rehearsing for the first movie written just for her, *Bright Eyes*.

Manhattan was inundated with European immigrants. The location of the city on the Hudson River and the port of New York with its large bay allowed for thousands upon thousands of fresh arrivals. They were sent to a harbor landfill called Ellis Island and from there—upon passing various inspections — they took available jobs in construction, dock work and similar labor. Whereas the just-arrived Paton "immigrants" sought freedom and independence, the real immigrants from Ellis Island counted on constricted lives that provided guaranteed wages and affordable housing. That dichotomy was and always will be the source of a universal discrepancy within every nation, but the adversity it created for the less advantaged could be lessened by those more advantaged. Townley was soon to begin providing his diagnostic and surgical skills to many patients not to be billed. Such free medical care has largely disappeared in modern day's complex of health insurance and legal constraints.

Little things can mean a lot, like the forceful timbre of the natives' voices, which now seemed foreign even to Helen, despite her upbringing there. The contrast between Baltimoreans' modulated, reserved tone of voice and the feisty, brusque, accented and outspoken utterances of Manhattanites was striking. If indeed the meek were to inherit the Earth, there would be damn few New Yorkers as beneficiaries. Moreover, Manhattan folks seemed disinterested in newcomers, if not actually annoyed by their differences. Crime was far greater than in then quiescent Baltimore. This was made apparent by the newspaper reportage that sensitized the population to the presence of the many bad apples among the citizenry. It was a population whose description seemed at odds with the Statue of Liberty, St. Patrick's Cathedral, the newly opened St. John's Cathedral, the Empire State Building, and the New York Public Library, whose two guarding lions would be named by Mayor-elect Fiorello La Guardia, Patience and Fortitude, qualities essential for living in that city.

The city's clustered residential zones represented numerous identities—Germans, Italians, Jews, Chinese, Irish, and African-Americans.[1] Each modified the English language differently; each used flags, songs, bands and parades to celebrate being outposts of an "old country," or a separate race — all except the native New Yorkers, some of whom, as the Patons had not fully appreciated prior to moving there, lived comfortably on the Upper East Side, with second homes on the Gold Coast of Long Island. Their versions of flags and parades were formal parties with orchestras–hardly bands–and dance steps like the London-originated Lambeth Walk. These were valuable residents–style setters, sports enthusiasts, Wall Street moguls — and, as if the old-time robber barons had switched priorities, the wealthiest among them initiated most of the greatest artistic, architectural, educational and health-oriented philanthropies.

Over time, Manhattan became a city the Patons would grow to love, not just for expanding its array of skyscrapers and progressive modernization but for its people, in spite of themselves. Their gruff-sounding voices belied warm hearts that beat forcefully and actively. The Patons embraced it all: wily bargainers, street musicians, the three baseball teams with their constant infighting and summer streets teeming with children playing in water shooting at them from a hydrant.

Each city group had its own accent; one in particular was to become familiar within the Paton circle of acquaintances. The Gold Coasters, who in Manhattan clustered in the Upper East Side, conversed in what in that era was referred to as "Eastern Long Island Lockjaw." There was no other form of lockjaw, only Eastern. It was spoken with the chin thrust slightly forward and the jaws almost closed. The words were delivered with some help from abdominal contraction that forced a mildly nasal sound, the intermittent breathing for which added a measured modulation embellished by a rich and sophisticated vocabulary[2] and — one might feel compelled to say—quite often inbred thought. These were Manhattan's social elites, and most of them lived in the neighborhood of New York where the Patons first settled.

It was in the early fall of 1933 when Townley, Helen, and their two children made the long drive north across the Mason Dixon Line into America's Mecca for entrepreneurs and financiers. Even before leaving Baltimore, Townley had been accepted to the medical staff and given admission privileges to the Manhattan Eye, Ear & Throat Hospital. In an exchange of letters with Dr. Wilmer that preceded his acceptance, Townley wrote:

April 5, 1933, Dear Dr. Wilmer

I did not want to impose upon you and have you fill out the form that was sent to me from the Manhattan Eye and Ear Hospital. However, I shall attempt to answer your questions. After graduating from Princeton in 1925, I spent two years at Cambridge University in England **on the advice of the authorities here at the Hopkins** *[emphasis added]. Three vacation periods of about six weeks' duration were spent studying at the following clinics: La Colle d'Anatomie in Paris; at Salpetrierre in Vienna under Dr. Chiari in Pathology and under Dr. Wenchiback in Medicine; and then in Edinburgh at the Royal College of Surgeons. My four elective quarters on my return to the Hopkins were spent in medicine. That summer I also substituted in the Wilmer Clinic before beginning my internship. Thank you very, very much for your interest and unending assistance.*

Sincerely yours, [signed "Townley"]

INSIGHT

This letter documents that it was "authorities" at Johns Hopkins who advised Townley to apply to Cambridge Medical School, thereby indicating their wish to assist his medical career-whoever they may have been.

With Helen's tasteful choice of location and facility, they initially rented a house on East End Avenue at 80th Street, and a medical office in mid-Manhattan was also rented and furnished, including some instrumentation Townley had purchased in Baltimore. Within a few months, however, that office proved too small and a new office was selected at 927 Park Avenue at 81st Street that remained his office until his retirement. There was space in the new office for an assistant ophthalmologist, two secretaries and an ophthalmic nurse, whose presence allowed for minor surgical procedures to be done on the spot.

Soon after arriving in Manhattan, Townley began making arrangements in Manhattan for hospital privileges. Their first home location was just two blocks from Doctors Hospital, and he thought — erroneously as it turned out — that it might a convenient location for his surgery and postoperative visits. He was almost automatically accepted to the medical staff and he soon discovered why. The Doctors Hospital became Townley's first brief exposure to a form of medical exceptionalism. That may sound favorable but it was not. The hospital was a private surgical sanctuary for those who considered themselves to be Very Important People—and some definitely wanted to avoid publicity while undergoing elective medical cosmesis: actors, politicians, socialites, famous writers, and eventually at least one infamous murderer. At least one very wealthy woman lived there for several years at enormous daily cost, as if it were an inn, and, strangely, the hospital administration could not muster the authority to discharge her. The medical achievements that characterized this hospital were more palliative exercises in smalltime elective feel-good plastic tucks and only rarely real surgical interventions. There is no point further blemishing its nugatory reputation, for the hospital was torn down a few years thereafter. That was certainly not what Townley sought either for himself or his patients and he decided to turn to the hospital that had been his obvious choice, the Manhattan Eye, Ear & Throat Hospital (MEETH).

Gracie Mansion, the home of New York mayors, was across the street from the Patons' rented home. By 1934 it was occupied by Mayor La Guardia, who famously entertained the city's children by reading the weekly "funny papers" on the radio — two personal touches of caring in a cosmopolitan metropolis. The mayor's mansion was located in Carl Schurz Park. One day, Townley's almost-five-year-old son hit into another child of similar age when riding his tricycle in that park. Although the child was not injured, the kid's irate father followed the Paton boy and his nurse back to their temporary home across the street on East End Avenue. He rang the doorbell so vigorously it signaled that whoever it was had something urgent on his mind.

The door was opened by the alarmed Dr. Paton, whereupon the grocer-father launched into bursts of Italian abuse that sounded like foreign gibberish to all but Townley, who continued to be fluent in the language. Townley responded to the infuriated father in what must have been passable Italian. The rage vanished. The doctor and the grocer were suddenly almost embracing acquaintances. All was forgiven. There it was in a nutshell: something about Townley went beyond broken language, either English or Italian. He had a touch, without touching.

These Patons were not independently wealthy, as Stewart had been before his finances became depleted, and Helen's parents were on the borderline of being adequately fixed for a comfortable retirement. Helen's capable father, Frederick Hill Meserve, began life too poor to afford college until he could earn the money to pay his own tuition at Massachusetts Institute of Technology. He did that by becoming a land surveyor in Colorado and later a draftsman for the Elks Hotel in Colorado Springs, before joining a textile firm in New York. Neither he nor others in the immediate family had money but they were successful in non-financial ways.

The Townley Patons were "middle-class, medical," according to their own assessment. Within that calculation was the assumption that the "medical" designation implied a higher ranking than "legal" or "intellectual" at that moment in history—so great was the appreciation and admiration the medical profession was earning then and over a few more decades to follow. Thus, in Manhattan, Townley and Helen were being received cozily by "people with names," given a step up the social staircase—that is, if one measures "up" by wealth, power, and the reassurance of that clubby indicator, the so-called Eastern lockjaw which is a lifelong attribute that is confined to those who speak it from childhood.

Certain formalities of Manhattan's characteristic Upper East Side began to appear once the Patons' arrival on Park Avenue was known by what Townley privately referred to as the "Hoity-Toity." From mid-morning to mid-afternoon, a time when the husband was least likely to be at home, smartly dressed women wearing white or cream-colored gloves plus an assortment of designer-labeled fall or winter furs rang the doorbell and extended the community's welcome to Helen who dutifully asked them in for a cup of tea and crust-free watercress sandwiches. If no one answered the door when they rang, the lady in question would leave her calling card on a silver plate on a small door-side antique table used for the delivery of mail from downstairs. As part of the ritualistic process, it was up to Helen to return their calls in the near future. She did not particularly enjoy doing this but knew it was her responsibility to play the social game.

As with many physicians whose wives are their most valid brag, Helen was Townley's bowsprit and rudder, a formidable helper and his greatest fan (as she was to him). From a non-flamboyant, industrious family, the former Brearley student had the charm, style and pizzazz that made her among the most clever of her contemporaries. Helen's mother, Edith Turner Meserve, was a loving

Mr. & Mrs. Frederick Hill Meserve

person with common sense and good intentions, but she was not the family's leader-that was Fred's role. Frederick and Edith Meserve lived comfort- ably enough in a house just east of Lexington Avenue on 78th Street. Eventually, he became known for his hobby as one of the greatest collectors of photographs of the Civil War period. Lincoln, who died the year Fred was born, was his special interest. Lincoln biographer Carl Sandburg became his close friend and Fred provided most of the illustrations for his and Sandburg's book, *The Photographs of Abraham Lincoln*, on which he collaborated in 1941, and for Sandburg's six other volumes on the 16th President.

Helen and Townley did well in their adopted city. By 1936, with the office at 927 Park Avenue at 81st Street and a new home address in an apartment building at 823 Park Avenue at 75th Street, the Paton family's fortunes were becoming increasingly favorable. Their apartment was a duplex with three bedrooms upstairs and two small bedrooms off the kitchen for "the help," consisting of only Scandinavians or Eastern European immigrants, among whom there was some turnover in early years. Daughter Joan attended the same highly regarded school her mother had attended, Brearley. David was sent to Buckley, a shirt-tie-jacket, preppy boy-only institution.

While Townley had not been as much of an on-the-page academic as some at Johns Hopkins may have wished, an eye surgeon he demonstrated the best of skills, provided by an excellent pair of hands. He also had a dedication to patient care as ardent and profound as exemplified by a Greek graduation oath intensified by an Oslerian byword. Therefore he possessed two major assets for a successful practice, primed by doctor-admiring individuals whom Dr. Wilmer began to refer as soon as Townley's office door was opened, almost faster than he could accommodate.

THE TRANSFORMATIVE CITY

Some doctors have to wait years to develop a practice of this nature. These were all affluent, educated people from the New York area who knew of Dr. Wilmer's forthcoming retirement and were in need of follow-up by a doctor closer than others in Baltimore or Washington. Generally, they were coming to Townley with the hope of having him as their eye doctor indefinitely. Usually older than most eye patients who need a change of glasses, these referrals were more worldly and more in need of medical or surgical management. They made Townley feel not only needed but welcome in an eclectic group of established New Yorkers.

RTP's 927 Park Ave. Office

No one had health-care insurance; thus the financial aspect of patient care was dealt with in Townley's office. His secretary (a job not yet referred to as "assistant") had her hands full making appointments for people who were not accustomed to being kept waiting. To Townley's prolonged chagrin, over the years there was a much-parodied and possibly exaggerated phone exchange that took place in his office in the fall of 1933. It went something like this: "Godammit, I told you who I am. I want to talk with the doctor! Yes, I heard you, but who the hell are you to tell me that I can't be seen by him today? What's that? He's with a patient? Tell him to get on this line right now so that I won't have to have you fired. I can't be expected to wait any longer! OK, I'll hold while you go get him."

Long pause, then softly, kindly spoken: "Oh, yes, hello, Dr. Paton. I'm Jack Morgan—John Pierpont Morgan, Jr., as she must have told you." Pause. "I've been told you are the best eye doctor in this part of the country. Excuse my voice. I have a little cold. . . You say you read an article about me in The Herald Tribune a few days ago? Very good. Look, I need an eye operation. Cataract trouble. But it has to be removed out on my private and very comfortable yacht. I'm superstitious about hospitals. The captain can help out. Put me to sleep. Have you got a cute first mate who'll hold my hand until I'm asleep?"

"Mr. Morgan, I do thank you for calling and I would be delighted to be your eye doctor and operate on your eye if that is needed. . . Why are you laughing, Sir?"

Another long pause, followed by: "OK, OK, you caught on. Well, almighty God, Paton, it took you a long time to remember your college roommate. You've only been in New York two weeks and already you don't recognize old friends. Too many big shots in your office getting themselves listed for surgery and fussing you up like a fancy Fauntleroy. I think they've turned your head, Old Man." Pause. "Well, I like you, too. Just wondering if you're the same fellow I knew years back and am calling to see if you can stop working long enough for lunch at Schraft's, two blocks from your office on 79th Street."

They ate lunch together, happily.

A week passes, then: "Yes, Dr. Paton. Thank you for speaking with me. This is Pierpont Morgan. Your secretary said I could talk with you directly to arrange a trip out of town to care for my horse's eye. She's in Connecticut. The horse, Sir. The vet says she has a corneal ulcer. I need you to take over before she loses her eye."

Long pause for the doctor's response. "What do you mean, 'If you're Morgan, I'm the tooth fairy?'" Sputtering, then indignant. "I'm sorry, Doctor, but I think I am being made fun of, and that is not what I expected after talking to Dr. Wilmer, whose Institute I've supported, or from your friend, the president of the Century Club. Rest assured, there are other well-qualified eye doctors to call about my horse. Goodbye!" Slam!

A weekend was about to begin and, mortified that he had not recognized the real Morgan, Townley spent much of it taking care of a corneal ulcer on Mr. Morgan's favorite horse. Working long hours and on weekends was the price to be paid for the benefit of the near deluge of VIP patients who made him fair game for a good deal of ribbing by longstanding friends. For the horse there was no bill, but Townley did hear by a later phone call that its owner was grateful for the upgrade of veterinarian services and was "terminally amused" by the phone call.

Not being regular churchgoers, Helen and Townley were Protestants by default—Episcopalian and Presbyterian. Still, within only a few years, thanks especially to Helen's New York history and

INSIGHT

Townley's recognition as a good citizen as well as a good doctor, the Paton name was added to the New York Social Register, which in those restrictive Upper East Side times implied entrance into the chic Old Family-Old Money in-group: society's Eastern Establishment that included a few borderline candidates without intrinsic wealth to identify with the established social set under certain conditions.

Social climbing was not their aspiration, but both Townley and Helen realized that being identified with the elegant-home crowd of privileged people would add patients to his practice and, later, donors to other causes they might soon be pursuing. For this social distinction, the métier and character of the breadwinner had to be well-respected, the family had to have substantial local roots in the region (such as Helen's), and its behavior by reputation and social performance had to reflect cultural "breeding" (not a genetic actuality). After that there was leeway in requirements for inclusion, depending on whether the people in question were wanted or if it was the other way around. Nevertheless, these unwritten prerequisites might have come straight out of an 18th-century comedy of manners.

Though it was, in effect, a caste system—one that was not much written about in America's early 20th century—the unwritten mores existed, paradoxical though they may have been to a democracy's liberalization. These were unique, highly educated, interesting and welcoming people. Townley and Helen became mutually good friends with these kind and sophisticated individuals. But it was always fun to tease them a bit for the slight crustiness that needed good spirit and friendliness to melt completely.

Townley invited one of his patients, Emily Post, for dinner one evening. At the time she was the highest potentate of Victorian manners in the United States and probably only secondary to Queen Victoria herself internationally. Townley thought she would be a fun guest for Helen to meet and especially informative for the kids. However, his last-minute invitation almost caused apoplexy. One didn't "enjoy" such a person, one "prepared" for her.

"Tonight, Townley?"

"Sure, why not!"

"I can tell you why not."

"Too late, she's coming."

Recovering, Helen laid the linen tablecloth and matching napkins, put out the polished silver and only the un-chipped china from the matching set, the small butter plates and butter balls instead of butter squares. Very *comme il faut!* With cut flowers added to a bowl in mid-table, it soon looked like a layout fit for royalty. Mrs. Post arrived a polite ten minutes late, looking like just another sweet older woman. She was relaxed, conversational and once dinner was served by the uniformed maid, she was observed picking up the asparagus and eating it from her hand—a move she explained was the way of the French. Would she have done the same thing at Mrs. Roosevelt's house in Hyde Park? Sure. No one felt uncomfortable and there were evidently no major code infractions; of course, had there been any, Mrs. Post would not have mentioned them. She was so at ease being just plain normal and upbeat that the Patons knew from then on that beyond the basics, manners were more about caring than behaving. For want of a good memory for names, Townley usually referred to affluent dowagers as "Mrs. Umpty-Ump" who was high amid the "Hoity-Toity," but Mrs. Post was actually a breath of fresh air in an environment that could be quite stuffy.

What can be called Greater New York, the city as an entity, had a bustle and bravado that made it intriguing to someone as action-oriented as the now 32-year-old eye surgeon and his wife. While he was preoccupied with patients, medical associations and soon enough the demands of the eye bank birthing, Helen became an enthusiastic, non-credentialed interior decorator by studying magazines and books about design while also befriending one of the city's leading decorators, Walter Johnson. He was a bachelor of unusual charm, who sang annually as a lead in the Gilbert and Sullivan operettas put on by the Blue Hill Troop—an amateur company made up of lawyers, businessmen, artists and others with time in the evening for practice and a love of singing on stage.

Helen decorated the Paton apartment expertly and advised others, using her flare for colors and design. However, without a license to sell her skills she conceived another occupation that proved a good solution for earned income: she decided to become a shop owner. After considerable preparation and with the daily help of her enthusiastic mother, Edith, she soon opened a business called Helen Paton Wool Luxuries on the second floor of a building near the corner of Madison Avenue and 60th Street. Every article in the store was made of the highest-quality

English wool: scarves, throws, baby clothes, small blankets, even booties.

To advertise her business, Helen enlisted her sister, Dorothy Meserve Kunhardt—who, while also becoming a successful Civil War authority and co-author with her father, wrote popular children's books, such as *Junket Is Nice*, *The Green Aardvark* and *Lucky Mrs. Ticklefeather*. For Helen's store promotion, Dorothy created a flyer to be mailed to existing and potential customers of Helen's store. It consisted of a cartoon that she drew showing from behind an elegant woman with a broad-brimmed hat riding a horse in Central Park. The rump of the horse had a tail made of Helen Paton Wool Luxuries' finest imaginable English wool. The tuft was mounted through a hole in the card where it was unobtrusively taped on the backside. The verse on the card pointed out that passersby could not resist stroking the horse's tantalizingly soft and beautiful tail. Such a mailer was very innovative form of advertising in those days, and it drew many customers to the store. It also was the precursor to Dorothy's most important and hugely popular children's "touch and feel" baby book, *Pat the Bunny*, that still sells in various iterations.

Helen's creative way to become well-dressed would not have been applauded by the social register set, although many of those women would probably have done the same thing if they could. Top-quality designer garb was generally beyond the budget of a doctor's wife, and with private schools, an expensive apartment and a doctor who ranked money lower than surgical achievements, another source of revenue had to be found if she wished to be stylishly turned out.

INSIGHT

She was unfazed. When their live-in cook, a refugee recently from Central Europe, asked if her two teenage daughters could live in the apartment in the small room downstairs next to hers, they were readily granted that opportunity. Though they scarcely spoke English, each was clever with needle and thread, and had inherent good manners and a winning, unspoiled personality. With strong guidance from Helen, the two girls rapidly learned to become seamstresses and applied, as Helen advised them to do, to Mainbocher, the 57th Street store of one of the most sought-after women's clothing designers in America.

The girls learned the requirements with the tricks of the Mainbocher fashion house and reproduced them perfectly for the store and just as perfectly at home by copying the suits and jackets to be selected by Helen in "payment" for their occupancy of the tiny bedroom.[3] They delighted in the sense of exchange and were proud of what they had learned. Helen bought the fabrics for her new clothes relatively cheaply at fabric stores. It was not long before she became what in the jargon of the day was a "looker," well-qualified–the family teased–to appear on magazine covers and in advertisements.

Poised, slender, beautifully dressed and joyful, Helen had the warmth and charm that made her the family's drawing card, while Townley was the medical ace. All the two of them really cared about was the other's level of happiness within the structure of the lives they led together.

THE TRANSFORMATIVE CITY

NOTES TO CHAPTER 10:

1. These residents who concentrated abundantly in northern Manhattan section called Harlem expected at that time to be referred to as Negroes, never as "blacks."
2. By the late 20th century, their characteristic tone of voice and pronunciation of words would become almost non-existent. Today, it is only found in occasional words, expressions and sounds that are its residuals in families that have unconsciously perpetrated the memory of its affectations.
3. These young ladies became highly commendable Americans, and they remained in touch with the Paton family for many years – ideal immigrants, inspiring citizens.

CHAPTER 11: PRIVATE LIVES

The unexamined life is not worth living.
Socrates, 470-399 B.C.

With Manhattan surrounding them, the possibilities for mind-bending experiences ranging from the best of museums to the thrill of Broadway plays were constantly available but too rarely attended. Helen had her store and the home to keep her busy. Townley was remaining an all-too-typical Wilmer graduate, a workhorse and a dabbler in ideas in whatever spare time he could carve out: designing modified handheld instruments, writing reports of clinical studies that were published in eye-related publications, teaching surgical techniques to trainees and attending state and national medical meetings for ophthalmological organizations. He was getting close to formulating a plan that would solve the need for donor corneas to be used for corneal transplantation. His optimism was always a major asset to his work and his play, such as playing tennis with every confidence that he would be the winner. He was far more often right than wrong. Most weekends were free of obligations and the children, now five and seven, needed the air and freedom of wider spaces.

So Townley rented a summer house in Armonk, New York, for his city-bound family. It was just an hour's drive from the city, an old but roomy house with a large porch and a surrounding field. No other houses were visible in any direction. For the next five years, Helen, the children and most of their furniture would spend the summer months in Armonk, joined by Townley on weekends. The house belonged to Cornelius Rea Agnew, the ophthalmologist grandfather of the current man of the same name. The present C.R. Agnew was already in his 70s. The Paton children called him "Cousin Neely," as his grandfather had been called, a derivative of Cornelius; his wife was "Cousin Blanche."

The Agnews lived in a large stone house about a mile from the rental cottage. They kept riding horses cared for by a groom who taught Joan and David to ride during the months of several summers. The groom would arrive on horseback with a smaller, saddled horse on a lead line. Each child had a thirty-minute ride twice a week. Everything seemed to go well on these horseback experiences, except many years later Joan admitted that the groom frightened her by making advances and behaving inappropriately toward her. She was totally unprepared for such an unexpected and unnerving experience, no matter how minor or brief it may have been. Her innocence, unpreparedness and resulting repressed silence might have been avoided had Townley or Helen ever discussed such things with her, but those conversations never took place.

During the summer of 1938, when Joan was ten and her brother was eight, their sister Pamela was born. Pamela was a welcome addition to the family and a wonderful surprise to her parents. Wore quickly than seemed possible, she was to grow into a beautiful teenager with a fun-loving disposition and a captivating friendliness that won over all who knew her. Pam was her parents' bond with youth, their amulet of family love-invoking just by her existence the coziness parents thrive upon as older children begin to go their separate ways. Pam had the perfect disposition-thoughtful and well mannered, cheerful and good-natured she was the family's sweetheart, especially adored by her father.

With three children, it was time for a summer house of their own. After an extended search, they found Spring Point in St. James, on the north shore of Long Island, a two-hour drive from Manhattan. The property included sixteen acres of undeveloped largely scrub oak land located near a high bluff above Stony Brook Harbor.[1]

The white clapboard house was set back from the bluff by a small field, with a lawn bordering the house in the back and on the two sides. There were six bedrooms, two of which were for "the help." After several years, Townley finally had his most wanted addition to their summer home life: a tennis court was built where scrub oaks had been. No longer did he need to be a guest on other courts. His became the social and recreational focus of their lives in St. James. Over the years, many neighbors and visiting friends joined the almost continuous daily play on summer weekends.

Townley was indefatigable, playing a remarkable number of sets whenever time permitted and opponents were available. In fact, he was known to have played thirteen of his usually vigorous sets of community level tennis in a single day. The underhand serve he used due to his old right shoulder injury from climbing in the Alps was a nasty one, with variable bounces, and it was accompanied by a mischievous chuckle that added to its threat. His "cannonball" tended to inflame powerful competitors who, often enough, would drive the ball far out of court with their overconfident returns.

Gussie Moran, the popular tennis star in the late 1940s, used the court several times for practice before the U.S. Open at Forest Hills. She was photographed there by the fashion photographer Toni Frissell, who with her husband, McNeil ("Mac") Bacon, was a frequent competitor on the Paton tennis court. Another rising young player with national ranking, Eugene (Butch) Scott began his tennis on Townley's court, later became the country's third best tennis player in 1963 and a member of a Davis Cup team. Still another player was Townley's close friend and frequent opponent, John ("Jack") Sculley, whose young sons also were early learners on Townley's court. John Sculley, Jr. became a world-renowned expert in marketing and as CEO of Apple famously clashed with the visionary Steve Jobs over management styles and priorities. Sculley ultimately moved on to a successful career in other creative businesses.

The RTP Family in 1941

INSIGHT

Spring Point was an ideal place for exercise of every muscle. One of the fall workouts for Townley and some of his men friends was cutting wood for winter fires with axes and saws and stacking the logs. Some eye surgeons would have been aghast that he would take such risks with his fingers but not Townley, who managed the tools as if they were just another set of instruments, each with specific purposes. One of his most admired ophthalmological contemporaries abroad would not even carry a full briefcase when traveling. Townley evidenced no signs of muscle fatigue or loss of fine hand movement surgery as a result of his "heavy lifting." And as a surgeon, he had learned the skill of sewing and knotting, which came in handy as he repaired rips and replaced lost buttons on his clothing. There was a time when he set about beekeeping for home honey, but that led to bee stings from poorly managed smoke puffs and the lack of enough netting for the heads of those seeking to retrieve the honey. Truthfully, these problems stemmed from not knowing enough about the safety measures of beekeeping. In those days, when honeybees were not in shortage, one could simply release a queen bee in some convenient location and the swarm would move out with her.

Townley was a contented homebody who loved his family, and was especially "nuts about" his tiny daughter, Pam, as older fathers tend to be about their youngest offspring. Anyone familiar with that side of his life would agree that he did not thump his chest with joy, exclaim to the world his levels of pleasure, nor speak to anyone in glowing terms about whatever he clearly enjoyed. It was his body language and his expressions that best spoke his feelings. That was so much his nature that no one thought twice about his conservative attitude toward verbal expression. One could know him, however, by observing his actions and appearance.

Townley was always fun, optimistic, jovial, and twinkly. He liked telling and hearing stories that made him laugh, and in general he was a man's man, at play and in work. Townley objected to off-color jokes, for they embarrassed him. By the time his two older children were grown and worldly, they would have liked to share a

RTP-summer of 1956, Martha's Vineyard

few "good ones" with the Old Man, but they knew what was not on the welcome list. Helen often teased him at home, about his degree of personal modesty, which was linked to his family's prudishness. The most risqué of his expressions came when needing to relieve a full bladder, "My back teeth are floating"—anatomically inaccurate but not a salacious confession.

INSIGHT

By that description Townley sounds exasperatingly stodgy. There were ways about him with people, and especially with patients, that were quaint but always charming and gentle. One might argue for the sake of objectivity that his warm rapport was a result of not having exuberant compliments at the tip of his tongue, but that deficit in itself was an attribute of honesty and friendliness avoiding a manufactured kind of self-centered blather. It is difficult to find fault with a man who kept himself rather closely fettered.

Stewart and Margaret had moved from Princeton to live in New York City by the time Spring Point came into the lives of Townley's family. They enjoyed a calm life filled with books, afternoon tea and a quiet house, enjoying visits with old friends and new acquaintances. Margaret remained a lively conversationalist, thriving on current events and travelogues. At 45, Margaret had fallen in a bookstore and broken her right hip, a break that in those days could not be surgically repaired. For the remainder of her life, she was dependent upon a cane and she walked slowly, in great pain and with a bobbing gait, her set expression masking her agony. Stewart and Margaret were welcome family members whenever they wished to visit Townley at Spring Point and sometimes that was for a month or more.

Early in Helen's and Townley's years at Spring Point, Townley purchased a Comet, a sixteen foot sailboat with a centerboard, jib and mainsail. It required a crew of two, such as father and daughter or father and son, but it could hold up to four people if they did not mind being crowded together as three of them sat on the deck with their legs dangling into the cockpit, Townley being toward the stern with his legs similarly placed and holding the main sheet in one hand and the tiller in the other. Townley soon felt that as the ship's captain, he could sail it just about as well as anyone else. He was almost right. He and the children (not Helen) became enthusiasts in competing with local friends who also had Comets, racing them on Wednesdays and Sundays during the summer months. There were a dozen of these sailboats and some of their skippers were experienced boatmen. In time, the Paton boat became a contender and Townley found a new diversion that he and his children enjoyed to the maximum from spring through late autumn.

The Stewart Patons when visiting wanted nothing to do with the Comet. Just talking about it suggested to them that Townley might want them to go sailing, so they avoided the subject. His mother had a good excuse with her bad hip, and his father, as always, had a heart problem that he did not speak about, but "let on" about. He was not aquatic. Helen's parents were less forthcoming with their son-in-law. When they were visiting late one October, Townley indeed asked them to take a sail with him and "the boy" on Stony Brook Harbor in the safe and entrancing Comet. With plenty of weight in the boat, Townley figured the wind would not tip the boat excessively and the blanket-wrapped Meserves would find that they liked sailing, even though he could tell that they had accepted reluctantly.

His prediction was incorrect. When they had sailed to about the center of the harbor, a sudden gust of wind capsized the boat, tossing all four into unseasonably cold water. Their flotation devices were tightened and the Meserves clung to the gunnels as best they could. It was their first dunk in salt water in at least twenty years of staying safely ashore. But rescue came in the form of the harbor policeman in a flat-bottomed skiff powered by a small Evinrude outboard. It took lifting and grunting to get two sodden elderlies into the rescue boat. The day ended with hot showers and hot toddies, and although all was forgiven. "The day Townley tried to drown his in-laws!" became the taunt by which the day always would be remembered.

With that story of Townley's recreational and adventuresome spirit having been told, he deserves another with a better ending. There was a day when he could not resist a sudden urge of impulse buying so he purchased a second-hand, four-cylinder Indian motorcycle previously used by the Manhattan police. It had a sidecar that surely Helen would enjoy riding in. He had not previously driven a motorcycle, but he drove this one from the garage where he bought it in Manhattan to St. James, a precariously wobbly two-hour ride with a nervous 12-year-old son as ballast in the sidecar. Townley sustained a burn on the inside of his left ankle from contact with a red-hot exhaust pipe, but otherwise the trip went better than one might have anticipated. No matter how determined he was to avoid that exhaust pipe, the burn site was revisited numerous times over ensuing years. It became a scar-a personal brand that the children enjoyed examining as if it were a vestige of valiant deeds of war.

Townley was no Evel Knievel, but over the following decade he never had an accident with his three-wheeled Indian. The motorcycle became the family's primary means of transportation in St. James—good gas mileage and just the one headlight that had to be taped to limit its light to a slit so if there were Germans flying overhead they could not spot the vehicle. Helen would be stuffed into the small sidecar, even when they went out to formal dinners in evening clothes, as then was customary, Townley in tuxedo with an ankle clamp to keep his left trouser leg from the exhaust pipe and Helen in a full-length evening gown, arriving at the hosts' home looking windblown and bursting with patriotism. They were soon the talk of the neighborhood, the kind of superficial chatter Townley tolerated happily, even welcomed, for he had no interest in sharing intimacies, his or others.

On December 7, 1941, Stewart Paton heard the bad news on his small radio upstairs and in descending the stairs for dinner he announced in a voice somewhat louder than usual: "We are at war!" Simple and straightforward, it was an unforgettable pronouncement. The family grouped around the walnut-and-ash Philco radio the size of a juke box, with only one small lighted dial and two knobs—one for station selection and the other for volume—and listened to the news of the Japanese attack on Pearl Harbor.

It was not long thereafter that the war in the Pacific reached full pitch and Townley volunteered for military service, signing up with an offered Army commission as major—as had his father in World War I. However, after being assured an appointment with a first posting at a California hospital, he was later rejected as the result of a required physical examination. His lungs had x-ray opacities considered tubercular, and possibly active pulmonary disease, likely the result of extended work in post-mortem dissections while in medical school at Cambridge. He was offered a waiver to sign that would free the government from responsibility for his care if the illness were to become clinical, but decided not to accept the appointment.

By then, in preparation for a move to the West Coast, he and Helen had entered their two older children into boarding schools so that Helen could join her husband in California. With the cancellation of their travel plans, she would remain happily involved in her Wool Luxuries shop in New York and as for the ophthalmologist, maybe the time had come to resurrect an old hunch and make it into a project to keep him extra busy for a year or two. Somehow that was his compensation for remaining a civilian. With Pam still at day school, they moved to a smaller apartment still in eastern Manhattan, just off Lexington Avenue on 79th Street. It would be a quiet and especially loving life with daughter Pam but without her older siblings for most of several years to come. Spring Point would remain their identity as "home."

In November of 1942, when Stewart's last book that had taken almost two years to write was almost ready to be published and two years before his son's eye bank would begin fighting for survival in Manhattan, the 77-year-old Stewart had a fatal heart attack on that same staircase where he had made the war pronouncement. He was buried not far from uncle Cornelius Rea Agnew in a family plot at the Green-Wood Cemetery in Brooklyn. In 1948, at 81, Margaret died in a one-room retirement apartment in Manhattan on the eighth floor at 79th and Park Avenue. By then she had no interest in others who lived in the same retirement facility, having become a partially bedridden recluse by her own choosing. That was certainly not as she had been throughout her active days as the family hawkish historian. With her death, the Paton family lost its primary genetic link with the Johns Hopkins medical revolutionaries.

One day during the war, Townley took his two older children to see the Ringling Brothers Barnum & Bailey Circus at Madison Square Garden, and there they observed firsthand one of the most remarkable systems of human communication ever conceived and achieved. The circus performance began by offering its usual exciting pandemonium of opening sights and sounds. Immediately after a loud announcer's voice had prevailed over thunderous marching music, into the arena came yodeling yells and enthusiastic screams from the clowns; elephants in daisy chain formation, trunk-to-tail; horses in costume with riders that included a monkey and a dwarf; men and women on stilts, whose costumes covered them from head to toe, making them seem fifteen feet tall; gorgeous girls in tights and feathers; athletic men showing off their physiques and waving their arms, as if victors in some competition; and dogs barking as they entered, surrounding a girl they appeared to adore, taking turns jumping into her arms, one giving way to the next. And there were the famous Flying Wallendas, performing their daredevil high-wire skills of balance and coordination with no safety nets below them.

In the pandemonium of sight and sound, Townley noticed that Helen Keller and her companion Polly Thomson were in the audience, enthusiastically enjoying the performance. Helen, totally deaf and totally blind, was being informed of the circus proceedings by tactile information passed to her by Polly. Their fingers were flying,

INSIGHT

using their original "digital" communication long before that word was adapted for other purposes. Helen sat bolt upright, twisting her body as if watching where the events were taking place, smiling and reacting appropriately to the acts and the sounds of the music. All the time, her right hand was in contact with the rapid tattooing of her companion's fingers; it was their two-way conversational synapse.

Her friend Samuel Clemens (Mark Twain) had said, "Helen Keller saw more in her blindness than others could see with their eyes."[2] Some of the most profound lessons in life come from the observation of creativity in solving seemingly incurable human predicaments, and Helen Keller was among the most inspiring of such people of all time.

Townley was ready for testing his own creativity as it related to the cure of blindness. He knew that nothing could be done for Ms. Keller's blindness, but she was the perfect inspiration for using ingenuity to solve a supply problem without much precedence.

NOTES TO CHAPTER 11:

1. It has since been renamed St. James Harbor.
2. Herrmann, D.: *Helen Keller: A Life*. Knopf, 1998.

CHAPTER 12: THE QUARTERMASTER

It is hard to fail, but it is worse never to have tried to succeed.
Theodore Roosevelt, 1858-1919

Townley had mixed feelings about the Army's rejection of him on the basis of presumed tubercular lungs, despite the absence of symptoms. He felt perfectly healthy, he could be a tireless weekend warrior on the tennis court, but he had adjusted his priorities to being involved in the defense of his country—and he was to be a major in the Army, eventually with probable service in the Pacific. When that was no longer lying ahead, he continued his medical practice in New York. Only Pam lived at home with her parents, her siblings at boarding schools. Helen had her projects to keep her busy indefinitely and Townley always had as much as he could comfortably handle, with a daily slew of patients and plentiful surgeries of various ocular varieties.

Still, an initially vague thought was shaping up, soon to become a nagging pipe dream possibly fraught with risks of failure but straight-forward and temptingly applicable to what he anticipated would be surgical amplification. Its dream kept getting more vivid, and he spoke of it to Helen but to no one else. Townley imagined that he and others interested in corneal surgery could create a strong and well financed, legally approved, socially acclaimed, technically feasible public service organization to vastly increase the frequency of keratoplasty, not only through the promotion of eye pledges for post-mortem retrievals but by putting in place a solid system to encompass aspects of the promotion, eye retrieving, processing and distributing donor eyes to awaiting eye surgeons—all components of the donor and recipient process that would use an existing term, "eye banking." That basic need was too obvious to claim originality for its resolution. What was needed was to put together all aspects of a complex requirement and use every means conceivable in gaining approval and for its implementation. A timid approach would be worthless in a socially difficult environment for the so-called harvesting of donor eyes.

He realized that no matter how highly qualified his prior ophthalmic training and clinical work had made him, even just one critical misstep could lead to professional disaster persisting long after the fact. At a time when only Helen knew of his gathering thoughts, Townley was well aware that if he were to undertake an expensive venture as "CEO" of a "free" eye banking establishment, the cost of failure would not only be the loss of tens of thousands of dollars of other people's money but a personal reputation as an impractical dreamer whose judgment would not be trusted should he have other brain bursts in years to come.

Clearly, to establish an entity that would take on all aspects of donor eye collection and distribution would involve extensive social interaction. It would also be thinking big and once started to move into a full-blown system, the whole enchilada. For such an undertaking to survive among predictable critics, it would obviously have to produce some immediately favorable results to prove its validity, then promptly proceed to become an efficient, systematized process accompanied by enough publicity and material evidence to make certain that the curses of disgruntled opponents would fall on at least a substantial minority of favorably turned eyes and ears. The key realization at that time was the difference between a medical breakthrough judged and accepted within the profession as opposed to a novel public-dependent system with medical rationale. It would be like talking lockjaw to the New York Yankees—some of the words would be mutual but not the level of technical understanding or any particular degree of interest.

Townley eventually decided that goal was well worth the risks. With a proper launching and a groundswell of supporters, a sustained achievement would bring cures to an incalculable number of blind people by virtue of increasingly successful surgical transplantations. It would mean that the clear corneas of donor eyes would be delivered from where they were retrieved at any hour of the day or night to the next listed surgeons waiting to perform a transplant operation. The mechanics of the early plan were very simple. Townley rationalized that what he had to do at the start was to have its purpose publicized, hire technical manpower, and ask ophthalmologists to persuade their patients to pledge their eyes for use after death. Then he could quietly enjoy the satisfaction of being a "supply side eye guy," evolving from medical major to a helpful medical quartermaster.[1] That would be rank enough — he would be the undertaking's sequestered junior officer instead of an Army major on parade.

But the trouble with dreams happens when you wake up bereft—in this case bereft of donors from patients of the eye doctors or the availability of other existing sources. Well, Townley must have rationalized, effective promotion of donor pledges could be encouraged in hospitals, church congregations, old folks homes, morgues, prisons and so forth—always with the proper permissions obtained. Once that system were to catch fire, it could become popularized at the instigation of local corneal surgeons, wherever they were located.

Soon, Townley began to realize that someone, a figurehead, would be needed to champion the cause from out front. He himself would be only the unidentified deviser of the not-for-profit, non-affiliated undertaking so there would be no need to defy the AMA's strict position against a doctor being named in the promotion of a public purpose. He would ask Helen to help raise enough money to launch his idea. In this approach, Townley was on his way to becoming what the English have generally called a "backroom boy."[2] Even in the Heroic Age of Medicine, innumerable heroic acts were never publicly known, and Townley's father, Stewart, was a good example of that attitude. In creating an eye bank, Townley was thinking first about the need in his profession, also a benefit that would feed his own obsession for corneal surgery.

Starting such a project in Manhattan as opposed to its long-term viability should be easy enough, at first he figured. Innovation in eye care would not be new to the city. One author was to write, "There is little doubt that the appearance of ophthalmology as a specialty was intimately linked with New York City."[3] It seemed the perfect place to test his hunch that a socially aware segment of the public, once informed of the need, would willingly pledge eyes for the dramatic blindness-to-sight gift of corneal transplants. Manhattan provided a contrast to the more traditional city of Baltimore, so ideally suited to fostering an initially sequestered medical revolution in education and training—an academic enterprise in a cozy caldron. If his hypothetical model were to be easily emulated elsewhere, it should always be functionally complete and financially independent through charitable support. In distinction to an exclusively medical audience it had no alternative but to function publicly. However, he soon came to his senses in discovering earlier eye banking kind of efforts, even a few contemporary ones, that had not been promising because they had lacked the heft to overcome cultural prejudice and common misconceptions. It would take a large manufactured wave of educated conviction ultimately to reshape public assumptions and the invariable preconceptions.

There was no question that Townley's venture into structuring the corneal surgeon's Valhalla was not going to be as easy as he had initially supposed. It would have to break social barriers far more significant than what would someday be faced by donor skin or even donor organs, and these surgeries had no surgeons leading the way despite less onerous requirements. It was up to the eye doctors to make the use of donated human tissue happen effectively and with regularity. If they were successful in persuading donors, other human tissue components might follow very naturally into the new form of so-called banking.

But could the proposition of an eye bank be sold on its high-minded rationale to overcome its eerie fundamentals? Should it be framed as an intended scientific concept that generates backing from the appeal of its philosophical as well as its technical sophistication? After all, the cornea has been referred to as the window to the soul, suggesting that the reality of a person's vision becomes the metaphysical perception called insight. Townley, as a dedicated eye surgeon, probably considered the sanctity of the human eye above any other portion of human flesh, but to provide an articulation of philosophical ocular bravado would be ridiculously out of the question for him. Indeed, he was a common sense unvarnished advocate, and for better or for worse that was his limitations and even his strength.

INSIGHT

Townley asked the administration of the Manhattan Eye, Ear & Throat Hospital if the hospital could provide the space needed for his undertaking's independent headquarters. Once again, he had the advantage of legacy, if that held any sway, for his great-grand-uncle Cornelius Rea Agnew had co-founded MEETH when it was MEEH in 1869. Whether or not that was a factor in the hospital board's agreeing to do so, his request was granted.

Being one of only the two active corneal surgeons in New York at that time, he had few close allies in facilitating the availability of donor corneas, let alone explain their need. The other keratoplasty surgeon, Ramon Castroviejo, was by far the more active and more experienced of the two. He was a dynamic, fervent Spaniard with an incredible talent for ophthalmic surgery, conspicuously little interest in medical societies, a referral base predominantly from Latin countries that would be the envy of any keratoplasty enthusiast, and it was thought by colleagues that he had a notable ability to acquire donor tissue by constantly shaking down personally nurtured and privately held sources. "Cassie," as he was known to most of his colleagues, was an independent operator in every sense of the expression. He had begun performing keratoplasties in animal eyes in the 1930s, and by 1941 he reported that he had performed an estimated 200 human operations—without specified outcomes.[4] It has been postulated that many donor corneas were efficiently imported from Hispanic countries.

Both Castroviejo and Townley were skillful technical surgeons, and both had considerable pioneering spirit. "Cassie" was an early proponent of square instead of round grafts, particularly for a corneal disorder known as keratoconus, a thinning and cone-shaping of the cornea. He believed that chronic sinusitis challenged the immune system and thus required many of his transplant patients to submit to extensive sinus surgery as a preventive measure against transplant rejection. His surgical techniques and the hand instruments he invented to facilitate the surgery brought him deserved global recognition and he became a popular speaker at society meetings. As years passed he would have the self-confidence, the animus and the evidence to become a popular advocate of keratoplasty, but he was also an iconoclast lacking the modesties of the American common touch.

As for his surgical technique, Townley had little to claim at the start, but as time passed he was to speak in favor of overlying sutures until they were replaced when finer sutures for direct suturing, and he later would report successful keratoplasty for relatively common Fuchs' endothelial dystrophy.[5] Largely, his advocacy of keratoplasty from the very start was for many causes of corneal blindness, and as for other surgeons who performed frequent operations the percentage of successful transplants increasing rose to well of 75% clear grafts. Never mind that today the percentage in most series is well over 90%.

While Cassie was an ingenious innovator who fashioned instruments to suit his needs, Townley's contributions became more of a one-to-one educational nature among fellow physicians and would-be corneal surgeons. He was much admired by the residents and medical staff whom he actively trained over many years in his Manhattan practice. The relationship between Townley Paton and Ramon Castroviejo was professional and somewhat reserved. Either for reasons of competition or acclaim, Cassie was not interested in lending a hand with establishing an eye bank unless it were to become demonstrably successful.

INSIGHT

Both surgeons were popular with patients—popularities fundamentally dependent upon surgical outcomes but also on doctor-patient relationships. In those days a successful transplant might mean only slight or moderate visual improvement, and many transplants failed. On one occasion, a corneal surgeon visited Dr. Castroviejo in his private medical sanctuary, actually a row house in a swanky neighborhood just off Fifth Avenue and north of the Metropolitan Museum. The once residential house was converted into an eye care facility with an operating room and recovery rooms where he kept pot-operative patients for as much as a week or more. Cassie was making his rounds on recent surgeries. He had come to the bedside of a one-eyed patient he had operated upon three days earlier, whose entire upper half of her face remained bandaged in the interim. When the attending nurse removed the patching, the woman appeared stunned at first, then looked around, and now able to see well enough to know where Cassie was standing—her first eyesight in many years—she proclaimed, "You are not only a surgeon, Dr. Castroviejo," she paused to control her emotions, then said forcefully and dramatically, "You are a god!" Cassie's response was classical Castroviejo. He bowed as if in modest concurrence, saying with a sweep of his hand only this: "I am at your service, Madame."

The third most active corneal surgeon in the late 1930s was another newcomer to Manhattan, John Milton McLean MD MPH. Another Wilmer Institute residency graduate, he was the newly appointed young chairman of the eye service at Cornell University Medical College at the New York Hospital, a few blocks from MEETH. He was an unusually talented academic ophthalmologist who, upon finishing five years of residency training and then two more years as a fellow under Dr. Wilmer, spent a final year on the

Wilmer full-time faculty. Recruited to New York in 1942, at 32 he became the youngest chief of a clinical service in the school's history. He remained in that medical school for his entire eclectic, highly productive career. His work included excellence in both research and clinical academics. But he had had little exposure to keratoplasty under Dr. Wilmer's tutelage, sharing Townley's experience of Dr. Wilmer objecting to transplant operations, knowing of their limited success at that early time for such an undertaking. Wilmer had a point, but that was to change as European eye surgeons led the way.

At MEETH, Townley was well into his primary venture when John McLean became interested in the concept of having an inter-hospital agreement for obtaining donor eyes. Together they attempted to establish a group of collaborating city hospitals to share donor corneas as the individual needs arose, but that effort never gelled. At one point in 1944, Dr. McLean and his hospital's administration kindly agreed to have the fledgling eye bank occupy a space at his hospital when MEETH was still lacking a proper refrigerator for short-term temporary storage of donor eyes and for around-the-clock telephone answering service that was essential in eye banking routine. After a few months, the Eye-Bank returned to MEETH, by then fully qualified to meet its needs. Beyond that, John chose not to be a participant and rejected Townley's offer of an appointment to the board of what had become the Eye-Bank for Sight Restoration.[6]

What was it about corneal transplantation that was so tempting to these New York eye surgeons? Most of the original conceptualization came from European countries in particular, but in 1838, Dr. Richard Sharp Kissam in Manhattan used a pig's cornea to patch the cornea of a patient's seriously damaged eye. The donor cornea remained clear for about two weeks, with improved vision in that interval.[7] Before Kissam, there had been numerous trials with animal corneas, the use of glass as a corneal substitute, and even a few human donor transplants, but none had been successful. As always with animal tissue, Kissam's graft failed not only because it was done without sutures, but because no animal corneas of any species can be successfully substituted for human tissue.

An Austrian physician, Eduard Zirm, is usually credited with performing the first successful human corneal transplant in 1905.[8] He used a fresh human cornea from a donor eye that had to be removed because it had been irreparably destroyed although its cornea remained undamaged. The surgery was a success, and that became a definitive demonstration that human corneas could be transplanted. Except for blood transfusions, it was America's first successful human tissue transplant on record.

Over the following two decades, however, not many such human keratoplasties were known to have been performed until 1930, when Dr. Anton Elschnig[9] in Prague published the results of 174 grafts he had done with freshly obtained corneal tissue, about half of which were successful in restoring sight. In the early 1930s and increasingly in the 1940s in Odessa by the Black Sea,[10] the noted Russian ophthalmologist Vladimir P. Filatov reported hundreds of successful keratoplasties that demonstrated conclusively that corneas taken from cadaver eyes worked well in transplantation. He and others reported that donor corneas should be removed as soon after death as possible, then used as soon as the operation could be carried out. His source of corneas for transplantation was a morgue where no official permission was required to recover as many eyes as he needed from recently deceased bodies. He did not report any donor family issues arising from that source of human eyes; perhaps the families were not consulted and therefore did not know about the eye removals.

The concept of "eye banking" by any name was not original with Townley. No idea remains pristine if one examines history deeply enough. In the early 1940s, there was a concomitant effort to establish a system to facilitate keratoplasty in Daly City, California, where two pioneer workers on behalf of eye banking activities deserve recognition. George Hanson and his second wife were a carpenter and retired Swiss governess in everyday life but they were also secretary and assistant secretary of the Dawn Society—volunteers who sought people willing to pledge the use of their eyes for keratoplasty by a few Californian eye doctors. The Hansons had a small printing press in their basement that they used to produce promotional material to further the purpose of gaining public support for this exciting but poorly understood mechanism for restoring sight to certain patients.

The Hansons' work included the delivery of donor eyes to ophthalmologists known to be awaiting an opportunity to perform surgery. No information has been uncovered as to the later lives of these two energetic people, nor is there any known reason for the demise of the Society. What is known is that the Hansons received financial assistance from the Grand Lodge of California of the International Order of Good Templars, from a Christmas seal promotion,[11] and from private donors "from people like you," to echo the PBS appeal for donations "from viewers like you."

Old newspaper stories can be excellent sources of historical information. According to an article written in 1964, James E. Smith, president of the Staten Island Central Lions Club's Sight Restoration Society, told his fellow members about a chemist who 15 years earlier (presumably 1949) [12] needed a corneal transplant and was taken to a Manhattan hospital to have the operation, using a donor cornea from a convict at Sing Sing. However, the death sentence was commuted so the deal was off. The cornea was later obtained from a deceased infant. It seems probable that the surgeon for that case was Townley Paton.

Smith went on to recount that the Dawn Society in California had been brought to the attention of his Lions Club, which, as a result, began to seek pledges for the use of eyes after the owners' deaths. He concluded that there was more need for an organization to assist in this work on the East Coast than on the West Coast, so the Sight Restoration Society of Staten Island's Central Lions Club was established in December 1944, thus becoming another preliminary, non-medical, volunteer eye-pledging endeavor.[13] By then, Townley's organization was already named the Eye-Bank for Sight Restoration. Today, it is widely known that Lions Clubs were the original organized supporters of the needs of eye banks, but when that interest was first kindled remains an ill-defined segment of eye bank history. As with the Dawn Society, very little information about the earliest efforts on behalf of pledge cards and related volunteer activity has been uncovered.

In the United States, as well as in most other countries, there were social, legal, religious and logistical impediments that had to be circumnavigated for donor corneas to be used for transplants. Did Townley have the character, personality and know-how to accomplish a project of such multifarious complexity? He was an idea man, with little experience as the organizational type in charge. Meeting with non-medical people as a speaker with lectures and illustrated demonstrations seemed absolutely essential, a conduct not permitted by his profession. Great-Grand-Uncle Agnew and his associates in the 1840s could never have imagined that what they had fought so hard to achieve among dissenting colleagues to enforce the AMA's corrected Code of Ethics had now become almost as much of an impediment to the advancement of clinical science as the Code had once been to the salvation of Medicine as a distinguished profession.

When Townley first began thinking of eye banking, of considerable help for the concept was the banking of blood. The idea of short-term blood storage originated in Leningrad in 1932.[14] The first functional blood bank was instituted in Barcelona in 1936, prompted by a need for blood transfusions using citrated whole blood with a preservative. In the ensuing Spanish Civil War, such donor blood was safely stored for several days under specified conditions. The first blood bank in the United States was organized at Cook County Hospital in Chicago in 1937.[15] Transfusions became prevalent across the country after the American Red Cross Blood Bank was established in 1941. Whereas donor blood has to be matched with the blood of the intended recipient, that is not necessary for corneal transplants because the cornea has no blood supply.

Importantly, the development of blood-banking introduced to the public the concept of giving human "tissue" (blood is properly classified as a tissue) to benefit those in dire need. It demonstrated the infrastructure that is mandatory for safe and efficient functioning of such a bank and it attracted national organizations to assist in the collection and distribution of the donor blood. Therefore, blood-banking became a networked system with the extensive involvement of volunteers and non-profit agencies such as-and in particular-the American Red Cross. Blood banking had the distinct advantage over banks for formed or so-called solid tissues in not requiring either a dead donor or the removal of a vital organ. Blood is renewable, making its donation a gift without usual consequence.

There may have been something about American initiative represented by men like Henry Ford, dedicated to efficiency and effectiveness, that played a role in formalized eye banking's organized and timely processing in the United States. Townley took up the practice of speaking of it among colleagues and other willing listeners not as a small-time model but as a lofty long-term goal in which "millions of people" with white scarred corneas could be restored to sight once keratoplasty became a routine operation. Some thought the young eye doctor was talking through his hat.

In the United States during the 1940s, it would take enormous public persuasion to overcome the envisioning of flesh from the dead being sewn into living eyes. While facial disfigurement of a corpse was a desecration more imagined than real, it was to be easily joined in opposition to the concept of eye banking by religious customs of honoring the deceased and a desire to remember the person as a beautified spiritual body in some sort of awesome transmigration, no matter what his or her religion dictated. Moreover, the removal of eyes was an entrenched punishment in certain cultures, including the Polynesian Hawaiians. It was also feared as a real threat by those sons of Allah who interpreted the Koran's assertion that "It is a sin to break the bones of the dead" [16] as less of a sin than removing the eyes.

Although the Catholic Church was not on record as opposing the principle of eye banking, it would not be until 1956 that Pope Pius XII referenced the plight [17] of the blind man of Jericho whose sight might have been restored by a corneal transplant, thereby giving his tacit blessing to the procurement and use of donor eye tissue. Many altruistic Evangelicals, conservative Jews and seemingly all Muslims at that time, along with—and this was the worst news—many persons without faith who needed no excuse to find eye removals intrinsically abhorrent. Then, too, there is a tempting negativity some muster regardless of rationale, seemingly more for the satisfaction of dissent than from serious conviction, and those recalcitrant people can be as firmly oppositional as those with specifically stated reasons.

To establish a viable not-for-profit organization to solve those challenges, it would have been helpful if Townley had been all three of the following: a social "glad-hander," a medical politician, and a fundraiser able to convince the wealthy to hand over big chunks of their money. But, like his father, he did not have the kind of presence that magnifies the persuasiveness of so many of the major, usually academic, achievers in their search for support of institutional projects. His best professional identity was that of a relative newcomer to Manhattan who was a respected and well-liked eye surgeon who had trained at the Wilmer Institute "Mecca." That last could be a two-sided consideration when it comes to raising money locally, even in a large community.

Townley was going to need much help from non-medical supporters willing to speak out loudly and clearly, since unlike him they would be able to do so without the slightest infraction of any code unless it were a blatant advertisement of the behind-the-screen doctor himself, his personal work, or an advertisement of his clinical interests. The latter exception was equivocal enough to be subject to interpretation, but even if the AMA were to accept Townley's role as a technical advocate for a non-profit enterprise, he would have to expect some remote fellow professionals would to express their objections impersonally but effectively. It was a bizarre position for this would-be trail-blazer to be in, for the infrastructure and public face of an eye bank called for administrative, fundraising, and general public relations—each of huge importance but to be done by a non-medical person.

An angel in the wings in the fullest sense of that term was what he needed the most—but on-stage, not in the background. It will be no surprise to the readers that a very special presence was to come on the scene, a Johns Hopkins heroine. Her seemingly magical abilities had previously guaranteed the success of a finance-predicated scientific "start-up" that she herself had conceived, the Wilmer Institute—Aida Breckinridge.

When Aida swooped in to help materialize the first eye bank, in that same year a famous child's book[18] was published that dealt with the arrival and magical abilities of the incomparable Mary Poppins who descended from the sky on a kite string, took a position with a family named Banks (sic) where she served as the incomparable governess: empirical, stern as necessary, deeply dedicated and supernaturally talented. Aida was to become the eye bank's Mary Poppins.

THE QUARTERMASTER

NOTES TO CHAPTER 12:

1. That is an interpretation from the evidence of his actions.
2. According to the Internet, an expression first used to describe the anonymous technicians and scientists who worked behind the scenes in the UK during World War II. Lord Beaverbrook coined it in a speech in March 1941.
3. Rosen, G.: New York City in "The History of American Ophthalmology," NY State J. of Med., p 754-758, 1942. Also, Rogers, B.O.: "Manhattan Eye, Ear and Throat Hospital: History and Contributions," NY State Journal of Medicine, Sept. 1976, pages 1555-1562.
4. Castroviejo, R.: "Results of Corneal Transplantation," Arch. Ophth., 19: 834-835, 1938 and "Comments on the Technique of Corneal Transplantation," Amer. J. Ophth., 24: 2-20, 1941. This is a classic article in the history of keratoplasty but lacks details on donor eye sources and post-op outcomes.
5. Paton, R.T. and Swartz, G.: "Keratoplasty for Fuchs' Dystrophy," Arch Ophth., 61: 366-369, 1959.
6. John McLean was distinctly interested in keratoplasty (McLean, J.M. Symposium: "Corneal Transplantation II_Technique." AJO, 31: 1310-1374, 1948.) He offered temporary space at his hospital for short-time use to fulfill MEETH needs until they could be accommodated at MEETH, a period of a few months. Some sort of transient misunderstanding must have arisen between McLean and Paton, for no joint venture into eye banking existed; that became clear once the eye bank's services were relocated and the work expanded; special containers were made and printed instructions for removal of eyes were made available, and the publicity campaign was started with the approval of the Census Bureau of the Academy of Medicine (Cordes, F.C.: "Federation of Eye Banks," Amer. J of Ophth: 41, No. 1, January 1956; Also Rhoads, K.B.: "Meeting the Challenge," Newsight. Eye Bank Association of America. November, 1965). Some degree of inter-hospital competitive spirit may have been in play. Nothing more need be mentioned on this matter unless there is further information not available to this writer in which case new information would be thoroughly acknowledged in the second edition (if there is one).
7. Kissam, R.S.: "Keratoplastics in Man," NY J Med., 2:281, 1844.
8. Zirm, E.K. (1906): "Eine Erfolgreiche total Keratoplastick: Albrecht v Graefes," Arch. Ophthal., 64: 580-593.
9. Elschnig, A (1930): "Keratoplasty," Arch. Ophthal., 4:165-173, 1930. Cited by Leigh, A.G.: Corneal Transplantation. Blackwell Scientific Publications, Oxford, 1966.

10. Filatov, V.P.: "Transplantation of the Cornea from Preserved Cadavers' Eyes," *Lancet*, 1, pages 1395-1397

11. Farge, E.J.: A *History of the Eye Bank Association of America. Its Origins and Development, 1930-1991*. Manuscript available from EBAA, 1001 Connecticut Ave., N.W., Suite 601, Washington, D.C. 20036-5504.

12. News clipping on file in Eye-Bank for Sight Restoration: from the Daly Record, date not available.

13. This truncated reference is from a brief mention in an article of the Staten Island, NY Advance, October 29, 1953, which reads: "Growth of Eye Bank Idea Told to Central Lions. How the eye bank idea originated by the club with the formation in 1944 of the Sight Restoration Society in of Staten island is spreading throughout the country, was told last night to member of the Central Lions Club at a meeting in the Rivera Chateau, Oakwood Heights."

14. Oberman, HA.: "The History of Transfusion Medicine" in *Clinical Practice of Transfusion Medicine*, Petz, L.D. and Swisher, S.N., 2nd edition, Churchill Livingstone, NY, 1989; and Diamond, L.K., "History of Blood Banking in the United States, JAMA, 1965; 193:40-44.

15. The first blood bank in the United States was organized at Cook County Hospital in Chicago in 1937. Fantus, B.: Therapy of Cook County Hospital: "Blood Preservation," *JAMA*, 1937; 109: 128-131.

16. From the Hadeeth, as has been ascribed to the Prophet: "When someone breaks the bones of a Muslim man who is dead it is as if he has broken the bones of a Muslim man who is alive."

17. Pius XII, "Allocution to a Group of Eye Specialists" (May 14, 1956) in *The Human Body: Papal Teaching*, ed. Monks of Solesmes (Boston: St. Paul Editions, 1960),382.

18. Travers,PL: *Mary Poppins Opens The Door*, Harcourt, Brace, New York, 1943.

CHAPTER 13: THE HYPHENATED BANK

Education is not the filling of a pail, but the lighting of a fire.
William Butler Yeats, 1865-1939

It was late in 1944 by the time organizing an eye bank structure was well underway in the space designated for Townley's use on the third floor of the nursing residence of the Manhattan Eye, Ear & Throat Hospital. By then, an eye bank board had been constituted: The chairman was Stanley Resor, president of the MEETH board, and Townley was elected vice president. With the exception of a lawyer friend of Townley's, the other members of the board were also directors of MEETH.[1] On February 21, 1945, the bank was chartered under the laws of the state of New York as a voluntary organization devoted to the collection, processing and distribution of eye tissue for transplantation, research and medical education.

The Eye-Bank for Sight Restoration was soon given its unique hyphen that has since continued to characterize this bank as the first to be created anywhere in the world. State regulators in 1944 and sustained in 1945 made the picayune assertion that an eye collecting entity could not be incorporated as a bank if it was not primarily involved in financial transactions, never mind that blood banks were not required to be hyphenated. Paton's bank thereby resolved its first of many skirmishes with authorities upon agreeing to a hyphenated name and getting the point across that it was an humanitarian, not-for-profit entity. It, admittedly, was not a bank in the depository sense in that the corneas of donor eyes had to be used within a day or two, once obtained.[2] Over the years, the Eye-Bank for

INSIGHT

Sight Restoration (EBSR) elected to maintain its hyphen as a proud birthmark symbolic of its historical identity.

From the early months in 1943, the eye banking concept was given secretarial assistance by the efforts of Eleanor M. Lehr, a patient of Townley's and the widow of a physician. She was its first Executive Director. Her job soon became more complex than she had anticipated, more outreach than intra-office, and she had to work in tight quarters. The space for her desk, a secretary (who was not appointed for several months), two telephones, a filing cabinet; and, before long, a small refrigerator were inadequate for the demands of launching an organization. There were soon to be managerial responsibilities in one of the hospital's laboratories for pathological examination of donor eye tissue. Mrs. Lehr was also burdened with the recording, advancement, and responses that a defender of eye banking required.

She did her utmost to orchestrate, sustain and grow the entity into the structure of an actual agency, but it was too much for that well-intentioned woman to accomplish. In retrospect, what Townley concluded was right on target: She lacked sufficient assistance, but she also lacked the experience and ability to deal with the machinations of a non-profit's birthing. She was an accommodating and kindly woman, although not without strong feelings of her worth and responsibilities.

Those were sometimes hectic days for the recovery of donor tissue. Townley himself would be called during the evenings or even late at night to perform enucleations[3] at private homes, hospital beds or hospital morgues, often enough that he kept an enucleation (eye removal) kit in his desk at home. In later years, young doctors seeking additional and paid experience would perform this service, for in New York State technicians were not given the right to enucleate eyes for the eye surgeons until 1969.

Townley was responsible for informing ophthalmologists of the rationale for creating the Eye-Bank by means of publications, mailings and talks, but to adhere to the AMA Code of Ethics in that regard as supported by all medical agencies, his promotions and talks had to be limited to within the medical and nursing professions. How could he promote the Eye-Bank and obtain corneas without personally talking to or otherwise corresponding with the public? How could he raise money in the public without advocating the Eye-Bank?

One solution became very helpful, not only because it was a source of some donor eyes but also it was a newsworthy story that did not require but could not deny the use of his name. Townley took what in retrospect was the incredibly important step that was described in the Prologue, the obtaining of donor eyes from electrocuted prisoners, called "Townley's Sing Sing caper" by family and friends. Although the story as told earlier contains a few improvisations, it is an accurate portrayal of his endeavor to secure donor eyes with as little personal publicity as such offbeat action would allow. From 1940 through 1944, there were 78 electrocutions at that prison, all male with one exception. There is no accurate record of the frequency of Townley's visits to the prison, but family recollection is that the trips were made often in the early 1940s until 1945, a year when there were no electrocutions, and 1946, when there were only a few. [4]

INSIGHT

Scarcely had the bank become hyphenated when an issue arose related to the need to establish legal precedent for obtaining body parts, termed "anatomical gifts." Eye-Bank lawyers saw to it that laws were amended to allow the individual or the responsible family representative to determine the manner in which his or her body should be disposed of after death.

By the time of the second board meeting, on March 8, 1945, the need for major philanthropic assistance had become dire. The bank was entering a period of grace when not much productivity was expected but at the end of that ill-defined period it would have to be moving along well or fold its tent. Townley, to the despair of his wife, was in daily involvement with issues that had to be fitted into a busy office practice, family obligations and a night's rest.

It was all too apparent that the Eye-Bank needed more expertise in its management, more outlets for publicity, and much more financing to meet its growing needs. Once again, the years when Townley was at Johns Hopkins gave him the source for his solution to the challenge of finding just the right person for this critically important assignment. Any medical person who had spent even minimal time at Johns Hopkins Hospital knew the name of Aida Breckinridge, the conceiver and the primary inducer of funding for the revolutionary Wilmer Institute. They would also probably be aware of her eight years as head of the Public Relations Department of the American Child Health Association under the leadership of Herbert Hoover and her volunteer service in public relations capacities with the National War Fund and the National Red Cross.

When Townley contacted Aida to ask if she would like the job of setting up an eye bank, the first of its kind, he explained that an executive director experienced in organizational ability, public relations and fundraising was what they needed. Would she take on such responsibility?

"No thanks, Townley."

But then, about a month later: "Yes, I'd be glad to give it a try." In that interval she had done her homework well, knew all about the office where she would work, understood what would be expected of her and had a good idea of how she might go about the undertaking. She accepted the executive director appointment early in 1945.

"Mrs. B." did not hide an intellectual loftiness born of a demanding forbearance that did not please the long-suffering, well-meaning, overwhelmed Mrs. Lehr, who now could barely wait to quit her job. In a letter to Townley written a decade after ending her work at MEETH, Mrs. Lehr did not mince words: "I do feel that allowing Mrs. Breckinridge to ignore me completely was the height of discourtesy and lack of gratitude, and frankly I have always felt that you should not have allowed it to happen."

By the time Aida Marta de Acosta Root Breckinridge responded positively to Townley's recruitment, she was 63 years of age—although she still lived the life-long fiction of being three years younger. By today's standards, she was a small person, and she had limited eyesight due to the retinal ravages of her glaucoma. But she had black hair, direct gaze, bold moves and a confident manner. She was neither wallflower nor blushing matron, descriptions that had too often characterized female volunteers in that era. She was a well-salaried executive able to take care of herself as well as, if not better than, the majority of men.

INSIGHT

Aida may have been too much the dynamo for each of her two prominent husbands, who would have been justified in not feeling in full control of their lives, as husbands can feel if they themselves are also "do'ers." She was divorced from her first in 1922 and would be divorced from her second in 1947. At almost mid-century, the inimitable Aida Breckinridge was a traditionalist with turn-of-the-century manners and a portent of end-of-century working womanhood, a phenomenon in her era.

Her dynamism and familiarity with the needs of non-profit agencies were just what Townley and his Eye-Bank allies needed. Aida ran the office as she ran herself: diligently and perceptively, with a certain hauteur and elegance befitting a noblewoman willing to do a demanding job on behalf of humanity, which is not the same as doing it with humility. It seems right to say that by nature and nurture she was a uniquely qualified and inspired person with the audacity of Susan B. Anthony.

Aida came in the nick of time, for the wheels of the directorship had been spinning without much traction, and that was not a good situation for potential supporters to discover. Through her contacts, she quickly got an outstanding article written about the bank in the magazine section of The New York Times, thanks to her friendship with its editor, Lester Markel. She also oversaw the creation of a pamphlet about the Eye-Bank that would be reprinted for over a decade, written by an employee of its publisher, J. Walter Thompson. Her contact with medical writers was thorough and lasting.

As must be obvious by now, Aida was no pussycat, and she was a full 20 years Townley's senior. Helen Paton resented her commanding attitude about Townley's need to do this or that, and did not like orders issued to herself with a no-holds-barred inference and a polite "Mrs. Paton." However, those sometimes exasperating attributes accounted in no small part for Aida's extraordinary productivity and success in providing whatever the bank required, and there had been the previous employments at non-profit organizations that also reflected her skills.

It was she as Executive Director who set up an Eye-Bank Advisory Council, a classical "Breckinridge" accomplishment. Although officially it was Townley's job to invite the Council members, she picked, pursued and successfully recruited them, including Herbert Hoover, representing his non-profit prominence prior to his presidency; Ethel Barrymore, representing leadership in the entertainment field; Abraham Flexner, the person most responsible for upgrading medical education; leaders in the field of national art, high officers in the Army and Navy, distinguished businessmen, the head of the national Red Cross, presidents of the important airlines and, not least, senators and congressmen. Many of these names were almost household words at that time although now they would barely be recognized.

Aida was just getting started. Letters were written asking all seven of the living wives of the ex-Presidents of the United States to join the Eye Bank Council, and all but Mrs. Woodrow Wilson (who was in poor health) accepted. They were: Mrs. Benjamin Harrison, Mrs. Thomas J. Preston, who was the widow of Grover Cleveland, Mrs. Calvin Coolidge, Mrs. Franklin D. Roosevelt, Mrs. Theodore Roosevelt, and some years later Mrs. Dwight Eisenhower.

To these Council members, Townley added 15 well-recognized American ophthalmologists, making a total of 99 members of the Council. Aida needed a president for the Council so she visited Albert Milbank, who was a friend of hers and her husband's, with fundraising and the Council on her mind. Mr. Milbank not only agreed to become president of the Advisory Council but he contributed from his Milbank Memorial Fund $25,000 (about $330,000 in 2016 dollars) with a promise for equal donations over the following two years, followed by $15,000 a year thereafter.

Such accomplishments that Aida scored in a very short time after her appointment were soon followed by others, both financial and organizational. Once funding had begun in earnest, the Eye-Bank office was moved to a larger space on the first floor of the hospital. Over the early years and with the organizational approach led by Aida, the Eye-Bank for Sight Restoration developed affiliated hospitals both locally and nationally and Townley helped them train their own residents and fellows in "retrieving"[8] eyes and in performing keratoplasty. Research studies on the enucleated, post-operative, cornea-less eyes were an important component of eye bank-based activities.

The state's autopsy law permitted surgical procedures for the sake of post-mortem examination but did not permit body tissue to be permanently removed from the cadaver. Aida, with the help of a state senator and a lawyer, had that law changed to facilitate the needs of eye banking. Thereafter, 170 affiliated hospitals joined the list of active sites for eye banking. But medical politics and a related paranoia became counterproductive at times. Aida began to realize that even mentioning the name of the Manhattan Eye and Ear Hospital was being perceived by some doctors and hospital administrators as if MEETH was "trying to build itself up" by its cornea programs. She settled on excluding the hospital name from her correspondence and instead just used the name of the Eye-Bank and its address, 210 East 64th Street.

THE HYPHENATED BANK

Pledges of eyes for the Eye-Bank soon after death became plentiful after numerous bank promotions. Pledge cards were distributed in mailings, brochure accompaniments, and during Aida's talks and talks given by others. The public, in doctors' offices and handouts by many volunteers, easily noticed the cards. Thousands of signed cards meant many more thousands of people who were informed. Just how useful they proved within the families of signees cannot be estimated, but the reminders to the public of otherwise uninvolved persons constituted a practice quite uniquely identified with the Eye-Bank in that era. Taking a pen in hand and actually signing a pledge made a signer a member of the movement, a card-carrying participant.

During the ensuing decades, eye pledges were never to become a primary source of donor material, but even if the signers did nothing more than carry the card around with them, it meant that an army of protagonists for the Eye-Bank carried that card in memory, introduced it in conversation, and urged others to assert their humanitarian concerns. In some ways and at that point in history, the originality of carrying a pledge card as a non-binding, wallet-borne codicil was almost as beneficial to the cause as newspaper publicity, for it was personalizing the challenge to each signing individual in deciding that he or she really wanted to have eye removal at the time of death.

The Eye-Bank also benefitted greatly from Aida's help in arranging and promulgating the public availability of lectures and surgical demonstrations so that Townley and a few medical colleagues could teach beyond the surgical details of eye banking and be available to answer questions that related directly to eye bank expertise. A clever dodge of the AMA's mandate of professional muteness was to invite a corneal surgeon from abroad to give a few public talks as well as professional lectures in the U.S. That speaker would not be bound by American rules. Townley or other hosts could be there to answer questions if the visiting colleague turned over the

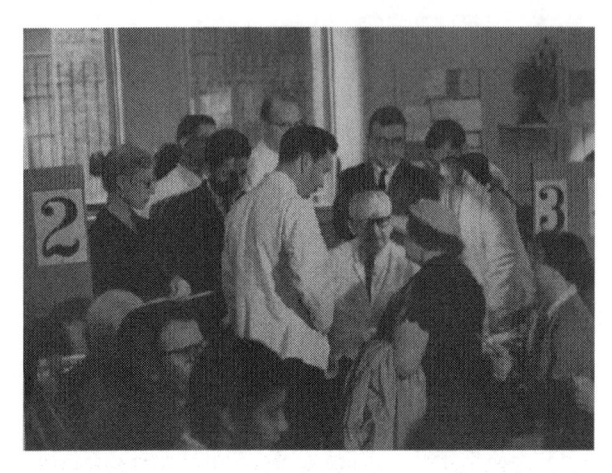

floor. Who could argue with that? With different audiences, such as nurses, administrators, journalists, technicians and potential donors, Aida, too, was frequently a teacher and spokesperson on behalf of the organization, which she knew in great detail and spoke of fluently and effectively. Good as she was as a public speaker, she was unbeatable as a one-on-one fundraiser, with all the couth and charm of an Emily Post and the conviction and forcefulness of an Eleanor Roosevelt.

By 1946 and for the two decades to follow, Townley's free weekly clinics for pre- and post-operative eye care and for doctors interested in the teaching and examination of patients' eyes, meant that his plate was overflowing with the details of eye banking. Aida was similarly swamped by tasks and responses ranging from minor questions to legal threats, which she sorted out as best she could, often becoming the problem solver herself. Those responsibilities were the natural by-product of a very successful undertaking.

However, the situation was not without harsh criticism. The Eye-Bank received irritating accusations related to obtaining the donor eyes or the prioritization of recipients who may have thought they were not people who had to wait. Townley himself was not immune to sharp criticism. Try as he did to avoid it, he was too much in the public eye. To prove his personal commitment to avoid publicity, an article first appearing in The St. Louis Post-Dispatch in 1948 and later condensed for *The Reader's Digest* is a good example, for Aida had cleared the journalist's purpose with Townley, who had given his hearty approval as long as his name was not used. The article was titled "She Deals In Human Eyes," [9] creating the impression that the bank was not under medical control. The journalist, Lois Miller, did an excellent job of describing the Eye-Bank, while also mixing in a very readable biography of Mrs. Breckinridge's earlier life. The article states only that "a group of prominent ophthalmologists came to her [Aida] with an idea" for an eye bank. That was a concocted avoidance of Townley's name. No one is known to have asked just who were those un-named miscreants responsible for pillaging the dead, not identified in print ? It was left to the readers to figure out and there are always the obtuse reader looking for attributions to be corrected,

That article was distributed to every seat flap of every flight of Eastern Airlines for a full year. The airline was to become the carrier without charge for the delivery of eyes from the Eye-Bank for Sight

Restoration to surgeons waiting in other cities across the country. The refrigerated container with the eye or eyes for delivery was taken to and from airports by *gratis* services provided by the American Red Cross.

It may be difficult for current readers to grasp the intensity of criticism that Eye-Bank promotion precipitated in its early years, yet there are only a few entries in the literature where criticisms of Townley's efforts on behalf of related public education are mentioned, and in those places only by his allies rather than his opponents. In an undated and unpublished talk to an ophthalmology group, Townley wrote, "At first I found the greatest opposition from the ophthalmologists. The reason for this mule-like stubbornness exhibited some thirty years ago [about 1945] was no doubt due to the fact that corneal transplants were only being done by one or two eye surgeons and most ophthalmologists had no experience in performing this type of eye surgery. In fact, very few eye surgeons at that time had ever seen a successful corneal transplant."

The instructional sessions by Townley for national and international visiting ophthalmologists were a weekly event, given regularly and funded by the Eye-Bank. These clinics were invariably jammed, as potential patients and referring doctors were crowded into a MEETH teaching hall. Similarly, clinics with post-operative patients were also open to visiting ophthalmologists.

According to Aida's notes,[5] "Doctors came from all parts of the world to attend Townley's corneal surgery clinic every Thursday afternoon and to learn about his eye banking effort, for it was the only one of its kind in the country" and "when the clinic takes place it is hard to get to see Dr. Paton with the crowd of men around him and with the group of patients on whom he had operated successfully." She continued, "In the eight years the clinic had been going, 6,000 cases have been examined in this clinic and many letters written back and forth to the doctors who sent in their patients."

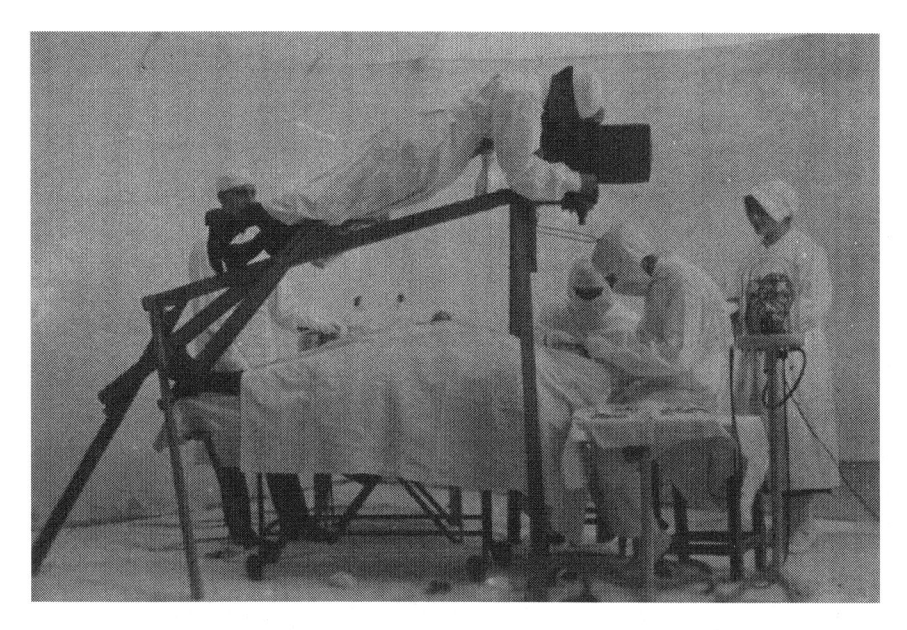

Photography became a vital ingredient in the teaching of eye surgery due to the need for magnification of the surgeon's technique and eventually to include moving pictures that could be copied and projected, thereby providing the highest expertise wherever it was desired. Professor Joaquin Barraquer in Barcelona was for many years one of the greatest pioneers for eye photography, not only because of his advanced skills but also because of the quality of photography that evolved under his direction. The earliest efforts in the difficult challenge of obtaining close-up pictures while not endangering the surgery's need for sterility is illustrated in this 1947 photography sent upon request from the great surgeon himself.

INSIGHT

Teaching eye surgery, specifically corneal transplantation, became one of Townley Paton's primary missions in relation to the developing need for eye banking. The following photograph taken at MEETH in 1948 shows the cumbersome but—for that period—an effective means of teaching corneal transplantation for those who could not be present in the operating room.

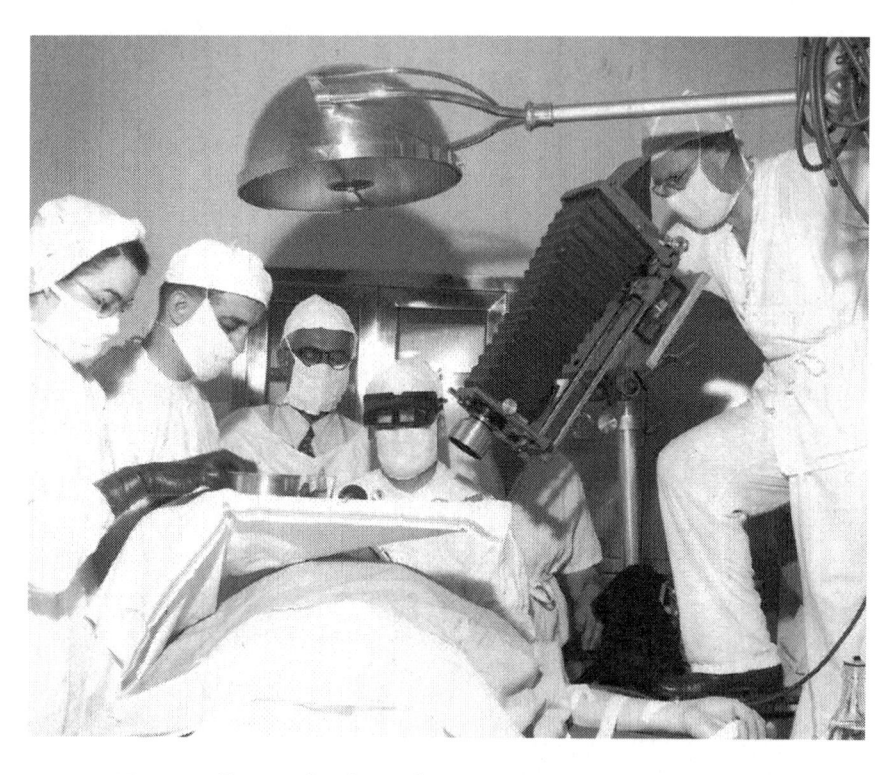

Eventually, with the advancement of photography and the introduction of the operating microscope in the 1950s and 1960s, video eye photography became an enormous contribution to surgical instruction and rapidly advanced the appeal and popularity of ophthalmology as a medical specialty. Even in its most primitive iterations of the 1940's eye photography had a major catalytic effect on the demand for ore keratoplasty and thus ever-more donor corneas.

Townley supported his family on the income of his private practice, while his weekly work with the Eye-Bank was voluntary, regularly scheduled and usually over-booked. As a teacher of keratoplasty in both the operating room and clinic, his concern for thorough instruction meant straightforward explanations in his plain beans-and-bacon style. But in the course of Eye-Bank promotion, Townley's inability to give a rousing talk expressed in smooth sentences with a flood of helpful words to make dramatic points began to frustrate him more than he wished to admit. He made an unusual decision, registering himself and his team for the Dale Carnegie course to learn more about how to influence people through the spoken word. Helen was amused by his independent effort but not surprised later to hear from Townley that the skill of an expert widely commended across the country for his instructions on verbal communication had been of little if any benefit to Townley. He would have to do without the blarney of Carnegie.

Townley's delivery was even less effective than that of his articulate father who droned on in a dull monotone. What Townley projected was a mildly staccato, plainly worded improvisation of running thought, backed up with the kindest and most sincere expressions that saved his efforts from a thunder of rude feet or premature departures in the audience. Not only did those things not happen, but most of the students and colleagues he instructed would remember positively the information given in his presentations, his patient relationships, his animated expression, and the simple frankness of his explicit delivery. Many wrote him letters of grateful appreciation after attending his free clinics at MEETH.

INSIGHT

All his life, in every recital or organized talk or formal speech, he spoke with a slightly faltering delivery punctuated with smiles, a quick nose pull, or a reassuring nod. He was almost as animated as soundless movies but in this case the accompaniment of words was like a dubbed translator who only caught the essentials. That may sound unfair or overly critical but consider the effect of a man much involved in his responsibility, pursuing it in earnest with the resulting effect being an informative, scientifically unique, easily understood presentation that listeners at all levels of medical knowledge could appreciate and fully absorb.

Looking back, one can assert with confidence that his were the expressivity traits of a place on the dyslexia spectrum, a form of familial dyslexia that typically varied from one generation to the next, both in manifestations and intensities. The components of dyslexia that plagued him in the days of his schooling were unaltered but no longer troubling in his office work. The unvarnished information he presented so matter-of-factly spoke louder for him than contrived hyperbole. In fact, as it turned out, a pledge of one's eyes, a decision of deep-rooted conviction, was elicited most effectively from a non-aggressive and indisputably sincere eye surgeon.

More often than not, Townley's operations were voraciously observed by visiting doctors to his right and left as he stood at the head of the operating table. The operating microscope had not yet become a part of eye surgery, and he wore a loupe for 4x magnification. Of course it was also before television was to facilitate the view of onlookers who under the circumstances of unaided vision often had to be cautioned against approaching too closely to the surgical field. On one occasion, a portly Egyptian doctor standing on a stool, leaning forward to get a good view of the operation lost his balance and fell forward across the patient's chest. It was an alarming occurrence but fortunately, after the surgical field was restored to its proper plane and with changed periocular draping, the operation itself was otherwise uneventful.

That was not quite the easy out in another mishap that became a classical story for caution and prevention. With only one donor eye available, its cornea was trephined and the disc of tissue to be used was set aside on a covered Petri plate as the patient's opaque cornea was then trephined to provide the hole to be filled by the donor tissue. Somehow in the surgical process, the top was off the dish and the intended graft got caught on the gown of the scrub nurse. Before it could be retrieved, it dropped to the floor of the operating room—actually next to a foot of the O.R. radiator against an adjacent wall. The panic of losing the graft once the eye had been trephined was only partially relieved when it was found to be lying on the floor backside-up. Townley broke scrub, lifted it into a sterile dish, rescrubbed and repositioned himself as before, then soaked the donor button in sterile saline solution and sewed it into place as had been intended. No infection or other adverse effect on healing and recovery was to follow. [6]

This incident underlined the necessity of top-quality assistants and the intraoperative care of the donor cornea as a sacrosanct responsibility. Aside from those two potentially disastrous occurrences, no other such operative complications are known to have taken place, and Townley's published record of successful surgery was among the best, both nationally and internationally.[7] Typically, he did not try to deny or excuse such incidents, and over his long career he was never sued by any patient. That was a record to be especially proud of in a city all too notorious for having a litigious reputation in the health field.

He summarized with exaggeration: "I had nothing but failures for a number of years. I was always having to wait months at a time until by chance some diseased eye had to be removed, which yet retained a cornea sufficiently healthy for my purpose." Although that was an overstatement on his part, it was not long before even receiving corneas from the pledges of deceased prisoners was conveyed as pressured and inappropriate. [10]

Dr. Derrick Vail, a distinguished and influential colleague from Chicago, wrote: "The plan and organization (of Townley's Eye-Bank) met with many difficulties and much opposition by many ophthalmologists at first. These hardships were chiefly due to the publicity that perforce accompanied the venture, for its spectacular nature in all of its aspects intrigued and fascinated the people. It attracted the newspapers, whose reporters, at first at any rate, exercised little calmness, discretion, or even accuracy in their news stories. A few publicity-seeking ophthalmologists showed little or no ethical restraint in not only permitting their names to be used but, in some cases, volunteered their patients and even themselves as subjects for the news photographers. This was very bad for the cause." [11]

This quotation describes what Townley faced as some medical friends and less-known foes joined with a chorus of opponents in the tumultuous advent of early Eye-Bank promotion. He understood the basic nature of the doctors' motivation to resist change in professional decorum but concluded that he had to press ahead because of the public's need to have a doctor speaking about donating the eyes of the dead. He violated the Code on numerous occasions, what else was he to do? He had to carry the message while avoiding as best he could any circumstance that appeared to entail self promotion, a difficult separation adjudicated by the bias of the individual witness.

Often enough, Townley came home exasperated not so much by patient care as by having to calm the troubled waters at the Eye-Bank among those who fell short of Aida's expectations or failed to understand the urgency of their work. But it is too easy to overlook the constant struggle that she was having with progressive blindness and its related frustrations and limitations. She was, after all, a woman past retirement age and still in a position of unique responsibility. Townley knew all this to be true and had an overriding respect and gratitude for what she provided.

Aida relentlessly admonished Townley to speak up and take whatever flak was necessary. She did not go so far as to say that he should speak up when his own medical future could be at risk, but she implied the need for some intensity for the sake of his project. He, indeed, gave many talks, either formally or informally, to what amounted to hundreds of listeners. Gradually, with prolonged positive advocacy, extended public education, and the appearance of the "eye option" on drivers' licenses in most states, eye banking was finally to become a household word. It was an eventual victory hard won.

The privately opinioned Helen Paton knew that her husband suffered inwardly from professional slights, sarcasm, and indifferent attitudes of certain of his peers and critics. For the occasional self-appointed detractor who tried her husband's patience or criticized his purposes, Helen held the cudgel in a feminine hand. Not a fighter, Townley chose silence over revealing his complaints. But when

INSIGHT

Helen caught wind of any annoyance, she wanted the details and wrung them out of him, scowling and grousing on his behalf. With his pique absolved, Townley slept soundly. Helen was a poor sleeper, but she had her own little ways to resolve criticism of her husband's effort to champion eye banking. Her microcosmic revenge had no substance to it whatsoever, but it was her infallible placebo: she would go out of her way to misspell or mispronounce the critic's name or, if she shook hands with him, she offered only her fingers (as Victorian women used to do instead of giving the full hand). These insignificant acts became her social shibboleth, absolving any lingering irritation.

Townley and Aida were a fortuitous team, totally different in almost every respect but locked together by the broad requirements of eye banking. They were infrequently glimpsed simultaneously, and there are no known extant photographs proving their dedicated togetherness. But despite their rather independent fields of operation, each had his and her own responsibility which usually called for communication several times a day, year after year.

During their partnership, and for the remainder of their lives, Aida, of course, addressed Townley by his first (actually his middle) name and spoke to him with briskness if she felt it was called for. She likewise called Helen by her first name when she was not annoyed by Helen's defense of Townley. But at no time did Townley, her boss, ever come close to calling her "Aida." To Townley, she would remain a leading lady in his life known quite simply as "Mrs. Breckinridge." She, in turn, never overlooked the leadership of her younger associate or the fact that he alone was rightfully the Eye-Bank's founder. Just to be sure that others heard it from her, on July 13, 1945, for the record and for a meeting of the Eye-Bank board, Aida Breckinridge spoke these recorded words: "I do want to say that the founding or idea of an eye bank is due to Dr. Paton's imagination and he should get the credit for it."[1]

NOTES TO CHAPTER 13:

1. The MEETH board members were not there to run the Eye-Bank but to allow their hospital to share a gratuitous identity with the freestanding bank.
2. Some methods of prolonging the interval for holding a donor cornea have since been discovered but essentially eye banking is not an extended process.
3. Surgical eye removals. Alternative words in lay language are retrieving or recovering eyes for the Eye-Bank.
4. Teeters, N. K.: Sing Sing Electrocutions, 1881-1963. Pamphlet. Ossining Historical Society, Ossining, 1989.

5. From an 18-page summary of her Eye-Bank work not long before Aida's retirement, on file in the Eye-Bank.
6. Almost certainly, the donor cornea was from a young donor with a normal layer of endothelial cells, for had that layer been sparse the graft would unlikely have cleared due to damage to endothelial cells from the cleansing irrigation with saline solution after the fall to the floor.
7. RTP's early report of PK results.
8. Several words have been used such as retrieving, reclaiming and rendering.
9. Miller, L.M.: "She Deals in Human Eyes," *Readers Digest*, August 1948, p. 101-104.
10. Accepting the donated eyes of prisoners cooled off and turned some against eye banking. In 1956, Townley wrote, "While tissue from the eyes of electrocuted persons is usable as donor material, little effort is made to obtain it because of the sensational (adverse) publicity attendant on securing the permission of the surviving family." Although the full meaning of his statement is not clear, newspaper articles criticized such practices, evidently seeming that it was taking advantage of prisoners. Ref: Paton, R.T.: "Eye-Bank Program," *AJO* 41: 419-424,1956.
11. Vail, Derrick: Foreword to Paton's book, *Keratoplasty*, The Blakiston Division, McGraw-Hill Co. New York, 1955. Also, Vail, D.: "The Eye Bank for Sight Restoration, Inc.," *Amer. J Ophthal*, 36:723, 1953.
12. See #6 above.

CHAPTER 14: HAPPINESS GETS COMPLICATED

Happiness is when what you think, what you say, and what you do are in harmony.
Mahatma Gandhi, 1869-1948

Throughout the 1940s and thereafter, American eye banks materialized in various urban centers, some becoming affiliated with hospitals. For example, within just a few years after the founding of the Eye-Bank for Sight Restoration, additional ones arose in Chicago, Boston, Buffalo, Rochester, and then in Colorado, Delaware, Iowa, North Carolina, Hawaii, Louisiana, and Texas. These were soon followed with other varieties of tissue banks, for organ transplants benefitted from the globalizing publicity of eye banking and enthusiastic journalists impressed by Americans endowing eyesight to blind recipients.

INSIGHT

Pledging was, of course, not necessary. Any death without an existing donor pledge (and more recently donor registration through state registries) was and remains a right of family decision, but a last-minute decision has always been more difficult, testing to the limit an immediate reflex of decency and devotion to a dear one's implicit trust. Most of the American eye surgeons became willing to take up a reminder of the Paton-Breckinridge crusade for donors and in 1948, Townley attended a meeting of the leading internationally known corneal transplant experts in Nantes, France. It was his first major meeting invitation, and he was very pleased to meet foreign colleagues from he had known by name and reputation.

That get-together was trumped in 1950, only six years after the founding of the Eye-Bank, when he was invited to present a paper at another meeting of the hierarchy of keratoplasty at the International Congress of Ophthalmology in London.[2] There he gave an eye bank presentation followed by many opportunities to engage in affable shop talk with more of the international keratoplasty VIPs.[3] Townley had earned the perk of reputation as "the eye bank doctor" which was an acceptable behind the back generic label. Indeed the harbinger role played by ophthalmology in tissue transplantation probably allowed Townley a much-appreciated nod among his welcoming peers in London. It was evident that eye surgeons everywhere foresaw the advantages of markedly increased transplantations made possible by the systematized eye banking process that was emerging from legal and religious hesitancies to become a common practice in the New World and Old World as well.

That Ophthalmology Congress was not only of scientific interest but it presented to American eyes some fascinating Old

HAPPINESS GETS COMPLICATED

World practices. One was the formal dress banquet that celebrated this eye convocation of unprecedented size with several thousand medical attendees, spouses, paraprofessional participants, political authorities and even the occasional royal visitor. Princess Margaret put in an appearance, along with the beautiful Sharman Douglas, daughter of the American ambassador to England. The Queen sent her best wishes to the crowd in one of the dinner addresses.

The leading eye doctors had among them their own touted royalty that included several famous corneal surgeons who during the meeting enjoyed ostentatious demonstrations of individualized surgical prowess in films. Even then, ophthalmologists and plastic surgeons were sometime over the top with graphic displays of their professional abilities. Ophthalmologists in general have been visually oriented and given to dramatic presentations, making a full-dress banquet an intellectual and visual reward exactly in tune with the accomplishments of their profession. All registrants could attend the banquet, providing that they had brought appropriate evening clothes as they had been forewarned well in advance.

The hosts and other UK influenced representatives such as those from India and Hong Kong had been nurtured on smart dress uniforms and elegant manners. They and the Brits arrived for the evening dressed to the nines. The more prevalent ordinary visitors had packed their best clothing to meet an acceptable standard of formality. Some of the most famous U.K. physicians and some from other countries wore neck ribbons with attached medallions and had miniature medals displaying whatever decoration they had won in war or in times of peace. An occasional riband or sash was worn diagonally across the chest, an award necklace bearing a large gold pendant was displayed just below a black bow tie.

INSIGHT

The banquet leaders were to sit at the long, straight head table as the evening's principals. They were uniformly suave, articulate, clubby and ever-so-at-home appearing. They, indeed, were very happy celebrants at a special evening. To characterize Townley's uncertain sense of belonging with this distinguished assemblage of very important international colleagues, the forthcoming banquet suggests a possible comparison. First, Townley was to be seated at a round table not far from those famous leaders. That was better than the more distant tables; but in rank and in contrast, he was more like one of the banquet's chief chefs invited to sit at a nearby table on the basis of his professional contribution but not to mix with the decorated leaders.

In fact, Townley did not have a single medal to wear. He simply wore the large registration badge with his name and country written on its card, as was true for all of the hundreds of ophthalmologists and their wives arriving for the banquet. But he made the embarrassingly awkward mistake of wearing that badge on his left lapel instead of on the right lapel where it belonged. There were no written instructions handed out with the badges, but everyone there was supposed to know that one wears only wartime or high achievement decorations on the left (over the heart) and definitely not to be substituted with the commercial badge pinned to his dinner jacket. It would not be polite to point out his error, thus he was soon to enjoy the dinner in ignorance of his gaucheness and with considerable delight from just being there. Helen would definitely get a postcard about the dinner.

The bedecked doctors were a match for their bejeweled spouses in their long evening dresses, all carefully coiffed and perfumed. There were some sniffy-clean exceptions, especially among

HAPPINESS GETS COMPLICATED

some of the older men such as those with a faint aroma of Cuban cigars or French cigarettes. Eye surgeons and their wives from the more eastern countries wore the formal dress of their nations, colorful, charming and exotic clothing.

Into this happy bedlam of a thousand or more Congress celebrants stepped Sir Stewart Duke-Elder, the president of the Congress. He was the reigning king of ophthalmology as well as ophthalmologist to the Queen. A Scot by direct inheritance, he was and deserved to be the toast of the medical Congress, not only for his presidency but especially for his extensive writing and organizational abilities that generally accorded him the unofficial designation of the world's leading ophthalmologist. He and Lady Duke-Elder, also an ophthalmologist and editor of his books and dissertations, were the stars who gave the evening its greatest luster.

Sir Stewart made his rounds, recognizing many, waving at others and occasionally spending some time in spur-of-the-moment chat. He was quite easy to spot in that morass of doctors, for he was wearing a red plaid kilt, dark jacket, shiny brogues, high socks, a white and black sporran at his waist, and most striking of all were several royal medallions hanging from a loose cloth neckerchief plus two rows of tiny medals on his left lapel--there must have been six or eight of them. He also wore a monocle as if it were his constant eyeglass but easily flipped off to be caught by its black cord if raising the right eyebrow higher than he might have wished led to a disconnect.

Duke-Elder was very clearly a pro at whatever he did. With his animated radiance and mischievous glances, there was a happy man with much to be proud of! There was the perfect British host for an occasion of this magnitude. Sir Stewart's harmless social habits were known *sub-rosa* and only in the context of a carry-over from Victorian times when in crowded rooms men often would surreptitiously pinch a lady's derrière as she stood in a group cheerfully chatting and listening to others on a topic, such as eye banking in the United States. As was the assumption of the pincher that evening, the targeted derrière almost certainly belonged to predictable ladies who would silently take the pinch with stoicism proportional to the esteem she had for the pincher, the smiling wanderer whose touch was known to her. Although as surely as she would not enjoy being pinched, she would know not to make an issue of it. Self-assured, fun loving Sir Stewart looked for all the world the champion that indeed he was.

After the luxuries of London, Townley and son spent a contrasting and grueling summer in sun baked Iran where they visited the majority of its cities and many of the towns in that largely desert and mountainous country that is almost three times the size of France. Traveling by car with a uniquely informed Iranian physician, Dr. Torab Mehra, as their guide, Townley spent most of the days examining and recording the causes and incidences of blindness and partial sight within each visited township. The predominant finding of rampant corneal blindness had been anticipated but not to the extent observed across the entire country. When Townley visited a city in southwest Iran, he had come to the epicenter of human eye destruction. It was Dezful, referred to in Iran as the "City of the Blind." There the predicament of the citizenry was overwhelming and iconic. Dezful was actually the City of the Corneal Blind, for trachoma's bacteria infested the eyelids of almost every citizen, leading to severely scarred corneas and profound loss of vision.

HAPPINESS GETS COMPLICATED

For the moderate to advanced cases there was no final alternative other than corneal transplantation. It was an eye disorder exceeding all others in each of the visited locations. Even the children were infected by that communicative disease, usually with irritable red eyes that today could be cured in the early stage with antibiotic eye drops alone. But in 1950, no such medication was known, and the advocated treatment with an electric needle was of no benefit. Townley was so aghast at the prevalence of blindness that he wrote a letter on July 26 to Mrs. Breckinridge that was passed on to Helen who kept it in her desk.

It was a moving letter about the blindness of Dezful and it also gave evidence of his dyslexic problem with spelling. Here are exact quotes as written: *...yesterday we saw the worste, the slums of this city...donkeyes, chickens, dogs and people all live together...there are literally many hundreds of cases for corneal transplantation. It is here where the worste eye diseases exist... David is getting a marvellous experience out of this trip...Sincerely,* (Townley)

What he saw that day was the visual devastation of an entire city in all stages of a progressive disease process. How fitting it was that this was the last major city of his visit to Iran. No place else in the world had a greater need for donor corneas for corneal transplantation. There would also be much demand for trained corneal surgeons whose operations would restore the lost vision to thousands upon thousands of unnecessarily blind sufferers. Sadly, that was only a theoretical possibility, for first there would have to be available donor corneas. It would be decades before adequate information regarding the cure of their blindness could be assimilated and acted upon.

INSIGHT

After weeks of documenting the causes of eye disorders in Iran, Townley was invited by the Shah to meet with him and discuss his findings and recommendations. The Patons had not brought the required morning coats and related formal clothing to wear in meeting with His Royal Highness. They had sent their dinner clothes home after the London banquet. Never mind, the Shah granted immunity from the clothing mandate and met with two travel-worn, rather disheveled Americans, the Shah wearing a rust-colored double-vested suit looking for all the world as informal as a subway commuter in Manhattan. He was very gracious and grateful in extending his thanks on behalf of the blind.

There was an American postscript to Townley's visit to Iran. When the Shah later came to the United States on several occasions in the 1950s, he stayed at the Waldorf Astoria Hotel in New York. He had various persistent eye complaints that led to perhaps ten or more office visits, which Townley gladly fit into his fully booked schedule. On one occasion it was Thanksgiving Day when the Shah had lunched with Eleanor Roosevelt in Hyde Park up the Hudson River, beyond Sing. His aide called Townley at home to request an eye exam for his monarch that would have to be provided the same afternoon upon the Shah's return to Manhattan.

As usual, and much to the displeasure of Helen, His Majesty was always accommodated no matter what the inconvenience. Townley beat him to the office and remained until the lights could be turned off in the evening. Both the examinations and resultant treatment were, by implication, gratis. At least, no payment was requested and nothing along that line of conversation was ever hinted either by the potentate or his aide — until one day the Shah must have had Divine Inspiration.

Very politely, his aide asked Townley what the Shah owed for services received. He had an expression of high expectation, a reward for a doctor's extended services, a gesture of friendship from a royal heavyweight of hefty eminence. Townley was not prepared for the question. He said he would have to give it some thought — punting until he could get his wife's thinking on the matter. Helen indeed had a valuable thought. She reminded Townley of Dr. Wilmer's alleged dealing with the King of Siam. Though Dr. Wilmer had not been the surgeon, he had seen that king on two occasions. Helen reminded her husband according to a historical tale that when the aide to the King of Siam asked for a bill, Dr. Wilmer answered with a dismissive sweep of his hand, saying in effect, "The king can do no wrong!" [3] In fact the king made his generous payment to the surgeon in New York, but the crux of the story was a generous gift from royalty resulting from a "no bill" message. That led Helen to advise Townley, "Just tell your Shah that the Shah can do no wrong!"

Townley found himself unable to be flippantly assertive. Back in his office, when the Shah returned for follow-up, Townley actually said to his aide, "There is no charge. Thank you for asking" or words to the effect. He went on to say that it was an honor to provide care to such a distinguished country's leader so concerned about blindness among his subjects. "No charge," he repeated to the emissary. That was indeed how he felt about the matter, but Helen had instigated a smidgen of yen. After all there had been many visits, many inconveniences. He let it stand as spoken.

Still, the Shah's henchman returned the following day with a gift "from His Royal Highness," handing Townley a cylindrical object about nine inches long and rather light in weight. An ancient scroll? The deed to a castle? Townley thanked him and later took it home

INSIGHT

without opening. There, with Helen watching with boundless curiosity, he unwrapped an 8½ x 11-inch signed black and white photo of the Shah in full military attire. The doctor then paid $15 to frame the photograph behind glass with a thin black frame. Today there are early foxing stains that show its age, Townley would not be pleased with that finding.

Three years after returning from Iran, 1953 was a year of distressing challenges in Townley's life and for his family. First, in May came the sudden death of his older daughter's husband in an airplane accident. Joan's husband, Bernard ("Bernie") Peyton, was only 25 years old and in his fourth year as a reporter for The New York Herald Tribune. His wife had not been in the aircraft at the time because she was pregnant with their third child.

Then came another life-altering event that was to have a profound effect upon Townley. By that year, Pam was a boarding school student who spent her long vacations at home with her parents. The Townley Patons' third child and second daughter was the parents' after-dinner cognac at the end of a delicious meal. An unexpected family addition, she proved to be a blessed game-changer for parents whose first two older children had flown the coop. The parents needed the re-play of cozy parenthood, which Pam provided. She was pretty, funny, light-hearted, playful and devoted to her siblings, her parents — and most particularly her father. If youthful parents are at times too busy to fully appreciate their children, by the time Pam was 15 her father was 53, her mother 50. Beyond any doubt, this

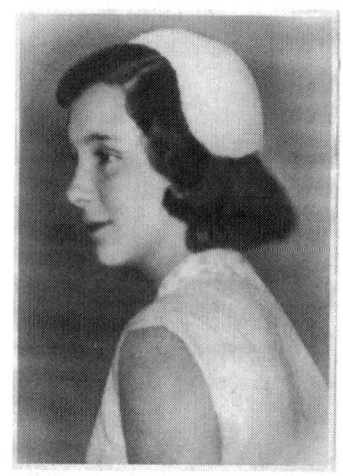

HAPPINESS GETS COMPLICATED

spunky, happy and loving child had become the doted-upon family princess.

In the same year as the other unforgettable events, Pam was visiting with a schoolmate at the summer camp of a friend's family in the Adirondacks. Pam and her pals were playing around in the woods not far from camp. When the group went back to camp, Pam was no longer with them. The children said they had no idea where she may have gone. They had been splashing in a woodland brook that led to a small waterfall. The search stopped there. She apparently had fallen down the falls, her head crushed against the stones at the bottom of a small pond at its base and was probably unconscious when she drowned.

A phone call was made to the Paton household in St. James. "Pamela has gone missing!" Townley was aghast, suspecting the worst. With his insistent son accompanying him, Townley drove frantically to catch a scheduled flight from LaGuardia to Troy, New York. He drove extremely fast with a white handkerchief tied to the car's aerial to indicate to highway police that he was on an emergency mission. Throughout the trip, Townley was very reserved, almost speechless but astonishingly stoic. Remarkably, the car was not stopped and they boarded the plane just moments before its departure.

At the Troy airport, as they de-planed, they were met by a male acquaintance on the tarmac. "I'm sorry to tell you, Townley, that Pam's body has been found and we must go straight to the funeral home for your identification of the body." So spoke the kindly but terse Albert C. ("Brother") Bostwick, a distant friend and summer neighbor of Pam's hosts.

INSIGHT

Father and son were driven to the funeral home and brought to Pam stretched out on a gurney with her heavily bruised pale skin, battered head and open eyes. Townley's face was an expressionless mask. He made the necessary official identification of her body.

"Would you like to..."

He interrupted, "No, thank you. We must return home."

Father and son traveled back to St. James again in almost dead silence. Helen was informed by telephone of Pam's confirmed death, and when Townley and his son returned home, daughter Joan had joined Helen and Helen's mother, Edith Meserve, in beginning a myriad of notifications and arrangements that this sudden death required. Where would Pam be taken? Where would the funeral be held? Who would officiate? Not that drunken minister! How could the funeral home be visited and what about her beautiful little body? Townley had almost nothing to say, and his son kept equally quiet and outside of the on-going preparations.

Pam's body was first taken to a funeral home in Manhattan. There were two viewings at specified times on two consecutive days before she was taken by hearse to a second funeral home in St. James. Townley would not enter the building in which she lay. The church funeral in St. James was short, with several familiar hymns but was mournful, melancholy and miserable, the service not the least bit enhanced by the ranting of the minister who spoke as if he had known her. *What did he know!* The burial in the family plot at Green Woods Cemetery in Brooklyn was perfunctory and abrupt. *Why? Why? Why?* Townley was mute.

HAPPINESS GETS COMPLICATED

Everyone went home, later to tell their own stories of a child they adored and a life filled with joy and family devotion. Talking it all over and over again seemed to be cathartic for Helen who wept inconsolably, mercilessly but also therapeutically. Not Townley. His stony sadness was as if a consuming sorrow had taken the air out of him.

Townley did not speak of Pam even with Helen, who wanted the relief of remembrances. The salve of recalling Pam's sprightliness, her humor and her sweetly expressed thoughts echoed in the minds and hearts of Helen and those of the other close family members. Townley would have nothing to do with their remembrances. When Pam's name came up in conversation, he excused himself and left the room. If he became moist-eyed it was not mentioned by anyone. Purposeful in whatever he did, he plunged into unimportant household repairs and gardening chores—anything to avoid those awful reminders of his precious child with whom he had a loving relationship that had now transformed his life into one of deep and silent mourning. He sought no counsel, nor was it offered to him.

A Johns Hopkins graduate at a small luncheon told Helen he had reminded Townley that Sir William Osler, when he was a professor at Oxford, had lost his only surviving child, a son at the front during World War I. That was true, and according to his friend and biographer, Dr. Harvey Cushing, Osler reportedly spoke often about Revere,[5] finding solace in pride-filled memories. Townley did not relate to that comparison, nor was he interested in hearing about other deaths. He could take care of himself. After all, he was a physician! His role was to heal others.

INSIGHT

For the last three decades of his life, Townley remained mute about Pam's loss. With his unwillingness or inability to come to grips with the death of his younger daughter, his life ever after became different from what it might have been. Superficially, however, to his friends, patients, colleagues and even family members he put on a happy face. He may well have felt some sense of guilt since blame is often a part of fatal accidents. Twisted logic as that may seem, it may have been part of the internalization of her death.

However, of all people in the world, Townley would seem to have been the most likely participant in furthering the reputation and the functioning of the Eye-Bank by the gift of his daughter's eyes. That was not to be. By not mentioning what surely was on his troubled mind, the passing of a few days after her death eliminated further possibility of eye donation. One could say, "See, he was human, not perfect — and a family man before all else." But that would be playing psychiatrist for an unapproachable Townley, the private mourner, the implacable Scot who was the most ardent of all eye-reclaiming proponents and for which his career would become widely known and long remembered. Meanwhile his life was otherwise contented and full of exercise and cheer, except for that one horrifying issue that even he would never fathom.

HAPPINESS GETS COMPLICATED

NOTES TO CHAPTER 14:

1. The surgeons in the photo are, left to right, Hermenegildo Arruga, Giambattista Bietti, Maurice Sourdille, Louis Paufique, Townley Paton, Louis Guillaumat, Adolphe Franceschetti, Jacques Mawas, Julio Moreono (representing Joaquin Barraquer), and Ramon Castroviejo.
2. The writer, substituting for Helen Paton, was Dr. Paton's guest and therefore well informed of the details described.
3. Today, corneal blindness in all of its forms remains the leading cause of curable blindness, but trachoma is generally well controlled in most countries. Keratoplasty and some form of eye banking will always be of prime importance in every nation.
4. Townley had friends in Princeton, NJ, by the name of Bogert who in 1971 wrote him asking for the true story due to a family bet as to whether Dr. Wilmer actually made that statement, operated on the king and received a huge check in thanks. Townley's letter of April 13, 1971 in answer to Mrs. Bogert includes this: "I happen to know all of the details as I was senior resident at the Wilmer Institute at the time that the State Department called to make an appointment for His Royal Highness. " He goes on to say that due to the animal laboratory located above the Wilmer O.R. the king was sent to Dr. John Wheeler. Townley continues, "When it came to paying the bill, the statement was sent to his [Dr. Wheeler's] secretary. The charge was not mentioned but merely the words that a King does no wrong. A check was returned to Dr. Wheeler for $60,000 which I understand he subsequently lost in the stock market." There goes one of the favorite Wilmer stories but it is about the same, merely took place in New York with a different surgeon.
5. Another Osler son had died in infancy.

CHAPTER 15: YEARS OF THANKSGIVING

Move onward, leading up the golden year.
"The Golden Year"
Alfred Lord Tennyson, 1809-1892

In the years thereafter, life for Townley returned to an apparent normal except for the secret sorrow of Pam's loss. She was with him always. The family arrived at that conclusion from the inference of his increased level of quietness at home and his departure when threatened by a mention of Pam. If he perceived this was a concern of his wife and children, it was his personal issue, only his. Whether or not he had insight regarding the undiminished intensity of his locked-up misery or of any awareness he might have that others felt his pain and would like to be helpful in his recovery will never be known.

A welcome distraction was a reinvigorated interest in tennis, and, as always, a sudden sparkle in his eyes would tip off another one of his bursts of gentle humor, often mischievous, never cynical. He once surprised his family by wearing a heavy brown wig he found in the children's costume trunk. Wearing that, he sat in his chair smoking a pipe and mimicking a schoolmarm teaching from a favorite bit of nonsense:

"When there are bats in your belfry that flut
When your comprenez-vous rope is cut
When there's nobody home in the top of your dome,
Your head's not a head it's a nut." [1]

YEARS OF THANKSGIVING

It was not Shakespearean but memorable just the same. His humor was often at his own expense. For instance, on Helen and Townley's 25th wedding anniversary, he arrived at dinner dressed in a white gown, a hat-like thing strapped to his head by a tied ribbon under his chin, a tiny parasol in his right hand and a very small handbag in his left hand which he presented to Helen amid gulping laughter from his amused and a bit embarrassed children. The handbag contained an envelope with a card that read: "I know I am the luckiest man alive so here is to the most beautiful girl in the world after 25 years of happiness." The gift was a mink jacket that was the ultimate woman's gift at a time well before activist and animal rights New Yorkers splashed paint on wearers of fur. The jacket was yet to be delivered, having been ordered too late for a timely presentation on their 25th anniversary. For a man with Scottish genes often working overtime, that was the ultimate expression of generosity. Helen was thrilled by his love and again by the jacket when it arrived. She wore it with joy on evenings out when she was, as ever, the light of his life and often the life of the party.

Helen for her part had given up tennis, which was about the only thing she did not do well enough to be competitive. For instance, although she was not formally trained as an interior decorator, she had a rare natural talent for its various components and most visitors could not fail to tell her how attractive she had made their house look with the furnishings and touches she so tastefully combined.

INSIGHT

Outdoors, she was a garden lover and became a member of the Southampton Garden Club, affiliated with the esteemed Garden Club of America. The GCA held a large annual meeting for its delegates from member clubs nationwide. It was not just the glorification of gardening and horticulture that explained its caché but also the prominent suburban matrons who came from the prime real estate of almost every state wearing their name tags, flowered silk dresses, hats, white gloves and sensible shoes. They met at a hotel to display their exhibits, members' floral arrangements that they had lugged from home for this sophisticated two-day encampment. Some of the women actually had flowers named for them. There were lectures, films, demonstrations and discussions and a black tie awards banquet. Mother Nature must have been very proud of her ladies diligent pursuit of garden perfection.

That year, Townley joined Helen as her chauffeur to the GCA meeting in Boston. Tired from the long drive that had originated in New York and ended at their hotel in Boston, the Patons were glad to have hotel reservations for two nights made well in advance. They were standing in line to register just ahead of an elderly couple. After registering and before leaving with a bellboy to be shown their room, Helen heard the woman tell the desk clerk her expectations, a room with a front view, preferably a sitting room as well and the bags can come up later. "We're exhausted from travel."

And then, lingering, Helen overheard the hotel clerk say, "I'm sorry, there are no more rooms available in the hotel." Helen thought she heard the woman called by name. She continued to listen unobserved.

"Well, you gave that couple a room just now."

"Yes, the doctor and his wife had a reservation. We do have other rooms but all are accounted for."

"That's ridiculous. We've come a long way and we are quite senior."

"I'm very sorry, Mrs. Pillsbury, please step aside for other registrants with reservations."

"This is outrageous. We will find a better hotel elsewhere." The annoyed woman's florid face spelled distress as she and her husband stormed off, probably to tell their friends how rudely they had been received at the best hotel in town.

When the Patons got to their room, Helen with a mischievous smile said something like, "Townley Dear, the time has come at last. For the first time in a very long while since that woman refused to let you examine her, we can have Pillsbury flour at home."

Indeed, it was a family epiphany, a due process; Helen's grudge in behalf of Townley was finally lifted. At last there would be an un-acknowledged pardon for an immaterial affront that got an unqualified forgiveness. Helen viewed the Paton hotel accommodation as a triumph of family fortitude. Her sense of justice may have been quixotic, but it was a final point of order. Helen's sacrificial defense of her husband had finally met its end—one might call it her own mini-version of homespun *aequanimitas*.

Home and happy, the Eye-Bank was running smoothly. Townley's surgery was never more active, his practice continuing to expand. He frequently spoke with Mrs. Breckinridge by phone or at the Eye-Bank. A change was brewing for American eye banking, now in haphazard proliferation. By 1955, some unqualified eye banks were springing up without adequate safety for the patients and for the convenience of the surgeons. Nothing could be more damaging to the eye banking crusade than a tarnished reputation.

Twenty-seven corneal surgeons representing 12 eye banks met under the auspices of the Council of the American Academy of Ophthalmology and Otolaryngology,[2] forming a Committee on Eye Banks with Townley Paton as chairman. He was to serve for fifteen years in that capacity as the eye banks' association became the American Association of Affiliated Eye Banks and later transformed into the Eye Bank Association of America to be governed by the Council of the American Academy's Board of Directors.

This evolutionary process was not without its critics and its growing pains. Evidence of Townley's role in the necessary remedial work of elevating eye banking to higher achievement came in a letter of thanks from Dr. Frank Newell as president of the AAO on November 18, 1975 wrote commending Paton's "remarkable contribution" to the success of the Committee on Eye Banks, and he added that the entire AAO Council was "impressed with the orderly way eye banks have developed in the United States with a high level of scientific excellence." Dr. Newell added that "each member of the Council felt indebted to you for your contribution" of leading the group and "providing the model, not only for eye banks, but also for temporal bone banks" which at the time was one of the early tissue banks to follow suit from the eye banks' precedence.

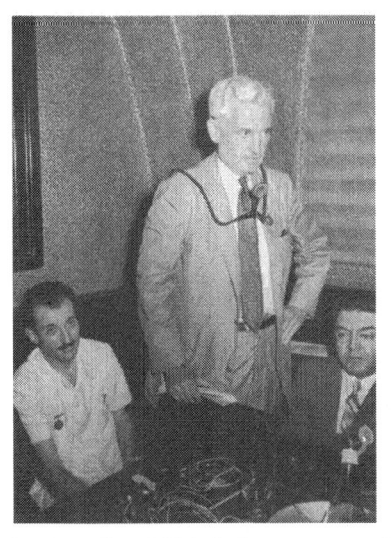

In the 1960s, the time had come for a centralized authority to assume the standardization and quality control of both services and skills. Eye banks became regulated by the U.S. Food and Drug Administration, licensed by each of the states' departments of health, and then accredited by the Eye Bank Association of America. Before long, the organization included most of the U.S. eye banks, a few in Canada and one in Puerto Rico. The EBAA began to offer senior technician certification and individualized assistance to banks seeking solutions for specific issues.

In 1961, the EBAA became the primary source of information about eye banking and the authority in the management of donor tissue, establishing a training program for increasingly sophisticated technical services. There was no legal precedent for obtaining donor tissue, euphemistically referred to as "anatomical gifts." And laws in most states required amendments to allow every individual to direct the manner in which his body should be disposed of after death.

Within a few years and with the participation of other medical organizations, some important legislative measures were achieved, the Medical Examiner/Justice of the Peace Law (first passed in Maryland in 1975); the driver's license laws that first were passed in the 1970s; and beginning in 1982, with numerous variations of tissue donation being sought, Routine Inquiry and Required Request

INSIGHT

Laws mandating that hospitals notify their patients' nearest of kin of the option to donate tissue or organs from the deceased.

By 1955, when Aida retired and eye banking had become a rock-solid social practice still maturing and spreading, she had become almost completely blind from the progressive glaucoma never fully held in check. What she made possible for countless blind people in her Eye-Bank work could not be balanced by comparable benefit to her lost vision. Six years earlier, when returning from work at the office, she fell into a poorly marked hole in the street that was under repair. Her left leg was badly fractured—and she was to walk with a pronounced limp for the rest of her life.

In her remaining years Aida lived with her devoted son and daughter at their homes near each other in Westchester County, New York. Aida died on May 26, 1962 at 80 years of age, two months shy of her next birthday. That was her actual age, the three years she had set aside were restored to her in death. Hers was an extraordinary record of contribution by commitment, deft fundraising insight, and personal sacrifice.

For Aida, an eye institute's establishment, health-care fundraising, indigent children's needs and eye banking were her callings and wherever she went she left human benefit in her wake. It would seem that she lived her life as that lone dirigible pilot, independent, daringly outspoken, charming and sharp minded. Aida was the added ingredient without whom one can only wonder if that first eye bank would have failed without her. Although her name is commonly associated with her Eye-Bank role in the 1940s and thereafter, any treatise that celebrates the first eye bank without recognition of Mrs. Breckenridge would be grievously uninformed.

Hawaii, aboard the S.S. *Lurline*

By the time of her death, Townley was ensconced in a new practice in Southampton, Long Island. At just 61, his move from Manhattan was earlier than one might have anticipated in view of his demand as an eye surgeon and his identity with the Eye-Bank. But he had become restless in the city. Helen figured he needed time to "learn to relax" and smell the roses. In fact, they bought a pleasant house with both rose and vegetable gardens to be looked after by the Patons themselves. They engaged a man-of-all-services, Donald Maran, to help with the heavy lifting and he became their "older son" as characterized by their younger son.

The governing board of Southampton's small community hospital was eager to have Townley join the medical staff as the first and at that time the only ophthalmologist in the area. Against his expectations, Townley became far busier than he had anticipated, and in a few years he took on two younger associates, Nathaniel R. Bronson MD and Richard G. Lennon MD. They also developed their own practices but were always willing to help in the "old man's" patient care when needed.

If it is correct that Townley played a role in their coming to Southampton, it would also be true that he was delighted by the abilities of his young colleagues and with the development of ophthalmology within a small town atmosphere with operating rooms of high caliber. Townley thrived on the closeness of these junior colleagues knowing for sure that his son had with considerable reluctance decided to remain in full-time academic medicine and would not be joining him in private practice. Townley never spoke of any disappointment his son's decision may have provoked, and no one would have expected him to protest on his own behalf. Townley was the inveterate family man, and he accepted everyone in the family as he was, not as he might wish them to be.

Once well established in Southampton, this energetic tennis competitor began hosting an annual medical meeting at the Southampton Hospital[3] with prominent corneal surgeons as instructors and three times their number of registrants who planned to specialize in corneal surgery, a total of usually fifty occupied chairs in a tiny conference building just right for the audio-visual needs and the quietness a conference room requires. Townley was the drawing card for the registrants and for the instructors as well. There was another ace in the hole for attendees who were also tennis enthusiasts. They were granted use of the superb grass courts at the private Meadow Club with the understanding that each player must be attired in all-white tennis clothing as required by club rules. Tennis on a fastidiously groomed, perfectly flat meadow was a pleasant throwback to the original lawn tennis that is to the tennis devotee like a Stradivarius is to a violinist. The annual summer Southampton Hospital cornea course was like none other.

(See After Note # 3)

INSIGHT

Many of the registrants would be hard pressed to say whether it was the meeting *per se* or the addition of tennis that made it so stimulating. The meetings were remarkable for the registrants' closeness to cornea "legends" they never dreamed they might meet, and the stars, the summer faculty, got just as much out of the inter-peer small-talk that at times gave rise to collaborative new ideas of considerable value. They too, sat in on all the talks their own contemporaries delivered and asked as many of the questions.

Townley's "eyeball and tennis ball" annual event was highly proclaimed within the royalty of keratoplasty experts. Sometimes, perhaps due to the allure of the lawn tennis, prominent but non-cornea ophthalmologists asked to attend and became participants, bringing their expertise to the tennis courts as well as the conference room. The high faculty-to-registrant ratio was a big part of the meetings' magic.

On the national scene, great-uncle Cornelius Agnew would have blown a gasket had he known the fate of the radical alteration in the AMA's Code of Ethics that he fought so hard to help establish at the turn of the 19th century: physicians were sealed off from communicating their views with the public in the interest of their profession that was damaged by doctors' exaggerations in self-promotion and by inaccurate assertions, sometimes deliberate lies. In 1976, a Federal Trade Commission's ruling, fortified by the Supreme Court, granted physicians (and lawyers) the right to advertise without limitation—as long as there was no risk to the public from misleading information. The FTC theorized that professional fees would be reduced if competitiveness were encouraged, andadvertising was the best way such competiton could be generated. That assumption was not borne out.

Soon, in many communities there were huge roadside billboards, four-color brochures for mailings, newspaper, radio, television and eventually Internet promotions of physicians' abilities and qualifications. Fees escalated by virtue of home-made "heroism." That 180-degree turnaround in respect to physician public relations and advertising makes it hard even to imagine the restrictions that Townley and colleagues faced in educating the public in the 1940s and '50s. Many level-headed social observers wish there could be a compromise somewhere between the professional restrictions of the mid-20th century and the limitless promotional preogatives of today.

For Townley's 75th birthday, on April 7, 1976, a reception was held at MEETH expressing the hospital board's gratefulness for the contributions he had made, with MEETH at the heart of the action. It was a rousing tribute that included for Townley an honorary board membership, the first in that hospital's history. MEETH was already well known for numerous "firsts" in eye surgery and in teaching and patient care. A vote of its medical staff to identify the most noted of those accomplishments since its founding in 1879 brought this statement: "The majority of the present members of the hospital staff believe that the most important contribution in the one hundred year history of the hospital and a real first was the establishment of the world-famous Eye-Bank for Sight Restoration, Inc. by R. Townley Paton and his various associates." Dr. Agnew, in 1869 the co-founder of MEETH, would surely have been happy to know that he probably had a gene or two in the game. As a surprise on that birthday Townley received over 50 letters conveying the numerous ways he had helped, influenced, or inspired the letter writers. There were three from contemporaries in his Johns Hopkins years who made a point of reminding Townley of Osler's *aequanimitas* in connection with his career (see Appendix I).

Among other kindly remarks were recognitions not usually featured in tributes of high praise. His modesty and self-deprecation were given the limelight. For example, Dr. A. E. Maumenee in discussing a paper by Paton, said the following: "I would like to state that Dr. Paton was unduly modest in giving you the history of corneal transplantation. He did not mention his great contributions to the eye bank movement in this country and abroad. I think we can truly say he is the father of the eye banks in this country, with the superb work he did with the New York Eye-Bank." That recognition had already become common parlance in introductions at medical affairs and in other both written and spoken ways, but coming from Dr. Maumenee made it even more special.

It was also remembered at that time at MEETH that Townley had been praised by a leading keratoplasty and eye banking authority, Dr. Herbert E. Kaufman, who went on to say that Dr. Paton "was incredibly knowledgeable, generous, and humble, and he provided extraordinary encouragement to us beginners in the field in which he was a master. It must be obvious at this point that in addition to being a devoted and excellent physician, he was a genuinely warm person who truly gave no thought to pride and position but cared only for his profession and his patients." Various agencies for the blind, ophthalmological organizations, and innumerable individuals high in professional esteem sent Townley Paton heartfelt praises especially upon his retirement.

In 1974, he had received an honorary degree, Doctor of Science, from Southampton College of Long Island University. Without intent to diminish this major thrill from receiving such an honor, it seems that somehow Townley had been otherwise passed over by academia, for this degree came from a small, private college in his home town. Never mind. For Townley, it represented the crowning compliment to everything that he had worked so hard to attain, for the country or maybe the world—and for his own sense of satisfaction. The full tribute read at the presentation listed the various ways in which he was exemplary with emphasis, of course, upon founding the first eye bank. It ended with this sentence: "Dr. R. Townley Paton's decades of practice as a physician have set a standard to be admired by the practitioners of all professions, one that is a source of great pride to those who have had the privilege of knowing him."

Townley's appreciation of the recognition he received was genuine and heart-felt. Helen wrote his gratitude better than he, sending letters of mutual appreciation to the college as if she too were

INSIGHT

an honoree—and in a special way she was. There is no question that Townley was all that she said of him then and throughout his life. Some might say that modesty is a guise for the mantle of greatness—that the true reward is its recognition. But Stewart and Townley as do'ers were more held to the challenging need for accomplishment than to its sustained celebration.

NOTES TO CHAPTER 15:

1. The source of this limerick is Anthony Henderson Euwer, first published in Collier's magazine in the early 1900s. See http://www.drzirm.org/ehistory.html.
2. There is a large photographic mural not far from the president's office wherein a group of the registrants are shown with Dr. Paton.
3. Annual photographs were taken, this one in 1977 at Southampton Hospital. These are names of some of the attendees. 1st row Left to Right: Dr. Richard C. Troutman, unrecognized instructor, Dr. Nathaniel Bronson, Dr. Herbert Kaufman, Dr. Claes H. Dohlman, Dr. R. Townley Paton, Dr. A. Edward

Maumanee, Dr. Max Fine, Dr. Lorenz E. Zimmerman. The second row includes Dr. Jorge Buxton, Dr. David Paton, and Dr. John Harry King, Just a head in the top row is Dr. Herbert M. Katzin. Apologies are extended to the others who are not recognized by this writer. (Other instructors in Townley's summer course in other years included Dr. Irving Leopold, Dr. Louis Girard, Dr. Stuart I. Brown, Dr. Delmar R. Caldwell, Dr. Daniel Albert, Dr. Ali Khodadoust, Dr. Arthur G. DeVoe, and Dr. Robert C. Welch.)

4. Rogers, B.O..: "Manhattan Eye, Ear and Throat Hospital: History and Contributions," *NY State J. of Med.*, p. 1561, Sept. 1976. This statement was made prior to the groundbreaking research and clinical studies performed by Charles Kelman at MEETH, for it was there he invented phacoemulsification, the microsurgical small-incision technique of cataract surgery that was to replace or serve as the model for other methods of cataract surgery worldwide.

CHAPTER 16: DENOUEMENT

Every man's life ends the same way. It is only the details of how he lived and how he died that distinguish one man from another. Ernest Hemingway, 1899-1961

Toward the end of the 1970s with Townley's active life deteriorating, his existence became more physically challenging with each ensuing month. It was impossible for Helen not to mention their beloved Pam, with Townley exiting the room as inauspiciously as possible, his mind obsessively fighting an overwhelming sadness that never quit. But the love constituting a long and wonderful marriage also never quit.

When Townley was almost 80, Helen became the family driver. One day she had been alone on a 30-mile round trip to Riverhead for household shopping and driving home she exceeded the speed limit. A police car came into pursuit. She stopped at the roadside. The highway policeman gruffly asked to see her license. She handed it to him with the apology, "I'm sorry I was going too fast."

That blatant admission made his job easier, "You should be more careful when you're driving on public highways. What was your hurry?"

"I was hurrying home to see my husband."

"Oh ... is he sick or in some other kind of trouble?"

"No, I just wanted to see him." This sounded to the cop like she had been away for considerable period of time.

"Well, when did you see him last?"

DENOUEMENT

"Before this errand. I finished and was heading home."

The officer was both chagrined and amused, "Just drive more carefully when you have another errand to do." He shook his head, tipped his hat and returned to his car. Helen drove on with a true story to tell Townley a few minutes later. He smiled but was not surprised. After more than fifty years of marriage, there are certain assumptions that need no amplification.

By then, his friends, colleagues and acquaintances who saw him realized that Townley's customary *joie de vivre* was sapping out. He had become less expressive, less responsive to favorite visitors. In keeping with his upbringing's customary reserve, Townley was still not seen to weep, but sometimes with emotion—good or bad—his signaling eyes were dulled, and that joined by an overcast glumness brought him close to tearful surrender.

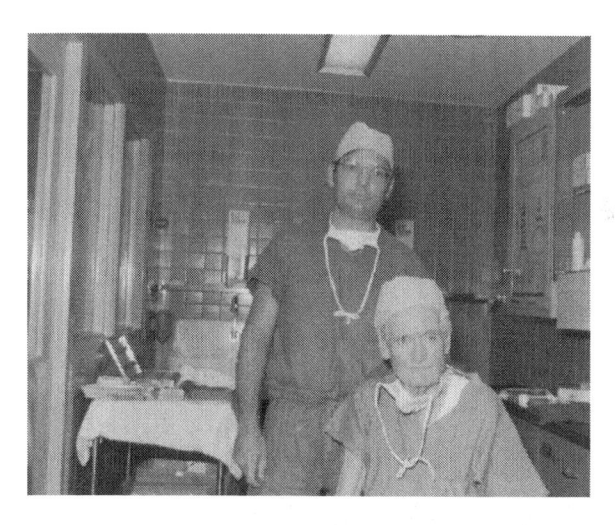

RTP at Southampton Hospital with Dr. Louis Pizzarello

The decline progressed. As Townley became more debilitated mentally and physically, Don Maran's learning curve became steeper.

INSIGHT

He served both as outside and inside man, driver, errand person, grass cutter, garden bug-sprayer, patch-up painter and even garbage disposer. Eventually he arrived early enough in the mornings to make the Patons' coffee and toast, even serving Helen breakfast in bed upon occasion. Don was her salvation from the quandary of her own limitations and the progression of her husband's decline.[1] Townley was becoming chair-fixed. The slow development of a tremor manifested only in his left arm had begun when he was still able to play tennis. It, too, worsened in his later months, but there were no other suggestions of Parkinson's Disease unless it added to an engulfing quietness slowly progressing.

Then, over his final weeks, Townley slid into a barely communicative and forgetful mood. This writer came from work abroad for a week's visit, then had to return to his job. Joan was often there, always just whom her parents greatly needed. Finally, within more weeks, shortness of breath and temperature elevation led to a diagnosis of pneumonia which Sir William Osler had referred to as "a dying man's friend."[2] Townley was admitted to Southampton Hospital. Surely knowing that death was near and with labored breathing cloaked in tiredness, he roused enough to say to a nurse helping him move from gurney to bed, "Don't forget. I'm giving my eyes."

On February 27, 1984, R. Townley Paton passed away, less than two months before his 83rd birthday. Helen was prepared for his death but it had an awful impact. He was "her Townley" and she was "his Helen." There is no measurement for sadness brought by the loss of a mate, but the truth seems to be that the better the marriage the greater strength of the survivor. At least that could apply to her admirable fortitude.

DENOUEMENT

Upon being notified of Townley's death, his office partner and loyal friend, Dr. Nathaniel R. Bronson, dutifully removed the eyes of this man who had been almost as close as a real father might be. Thus, the Father of Eye Banking had made his most resounding donation, the affirmation of the last forty years of dedication to its cause. Dr. Bronson would later comment that fulfilling Townley's longstanding request to the Eye-Bank was "the most emotionally challenging experience of my life," [3] testament to the fact that there are times when even surgery-hardened ophthalmologists cannot separate their hands from their head.

Shortly after his death, the EBAA honored Townley's memory by renaming its Society of Corneal Surgeons the Paton Society and using his name to identify its annual lectureship funded by endowment. His Eye-Bank for Sight Restoration had already named its highest award the R.T. Paton Lecture, to be awarded annually to the most outstanding corneal surgeon of the year.

Helen had become the senior survivor of the next Paton and Meserve generation. Both of Townley's siblings and her own two siblings had predeceased her. It was not a seniority to be envied, more like winning in the child's game ending with "and then there were none." Heavy-hearted, Helen and Joan busied themselves taking care of Townley's loose ends and answered letters of shared sympathy. As always, whenever Townley and Helen's family circle encountered difficult days, Joan was always there to help bear the burden and to share in the chores that come with every death. She was the strength that after the fact made others wonder how they could have coped without her help. When housecleaning, in the bookcases and cubbyholes of Townley's study, they discovered an astonishing scattered trove of full and empty whiskey samplers. He had been drinking secretly and haphazardly filing the evidence among his personal possessions. No one knew about those little bottles and no one knew about his clandestine boozing. It was as much a secret as was the cause of his inner turmoil — call it the Pam Predicament.

It was only two years and two months after Townley's death, on April 26, 1986, when Helen died — a sudden, painless but unnecessary death that came while dining with a husband and wife of her acquaintance at a now defunct Railroad Station Restaurant in the Southampton hamlet of Water Mill. During dinner, Helen lurched forward on the table. She was choking to death on a piece of chicken, but that was not discovered in time. She was 83. As with Townley, Helen's life was a great run, filled with family and love spread over eight decades, just one marriage for each of them.

Townley Paton and later Helen were buried in Brooklyn's old Green-Wood Cemetery, famous for being the site of the fierce Battle of Long Island fought against the English forces in August 1776 and for its thousands of headstones dating back to the same era that carries much of the history of New York in the names etched into granite and marble. That is also the burial place for Dr. C. R. Agnew and Dr. William S. Halsted.[4] Townley and Helen have simple headstones with their initials. Pam is on one side of her father, Helen on the other. Stewart and Margaret are buried nearby. There is space enough for Pam's two living siblings, but there is no telling what the future holds.

DENOUEMENT

Joan and her daughter Linda, an Episcopal minister are shown in the Brooklyn cemetery at the Townley Patons' gravesites.

This book has fulfilled its purpose in explaining the history of the first eye bank and how Townley Paton and Aida Breckinridge achieved that goal. Both of them have been studied critically and at this point only Townley's character has an open question regarding that astonishing inconsistency of not calling in the Eye-Bank upon Pam's death. Aida's character has seemed easier to plumb. There was no one like her, and her means of accomplishment were way ahead of her time. She would prefer "the noted Hopkins doctors' collaborator" to any less active name such as "intellectual administrator" or "money-sleuthing miracle maker," although she was these things too. Aida was indispensable to the Eye-Bank's existence, as Townley and Aida were professionally indispensable to each other. Indeed she spoke of Townley as its sole founder, but she had too much social awareness to suggest that the founding could not have been done without her. That would be the truth. By her inspiring mid-twentieth century example, she taught a great deal about how Big Money is raised, starting necessarily with small contributions, attracting mega-VIPs, flattering and cajoling them and never ceasing to stop pushing for higher contributions until the money was in the bank. She was accustomed to walking with the stars, relaxing with the gentlemen robbers, and having no hesitation in asking United States Presidents' First Ladies to join in the hunt.

The question asked at the start, "Who was Townley Paton?" now deserves its final consideration. The personality and character of Dr. Richard Townley Paton began with favorable genes soon evidenced to be mixed with others that carried what amounted to a familial dyslexia spectrum.[5] Those latter genes, this writer contends, became the determining lodestones of his life, starting in the school years and continuing throughout adulthood.

Dyslexia is known today as a common brain abnormality affecting as much as 20% of the population. For Townley it may have induced extra-beneficial imagination, ingenuity and creativity—as these attributes seem so frequently the compensation for a life-affecting but individually variable disorder. Those trouble-making genes must have caused Townley's somewhat hesitant speech, his preference for easily found words, and the acceptance that he was always to be a poor reader, bad speller and hopeless mathematician. Today, the few survivors who knew him (other than his two children) might take exception to naming his shortcomings because such might be viewed as a detraction from the memory of an outstanding man. To the contrary, he was the greater for how he dealt with various dyslexia's blockages that were balanced by an unfettered subtle charisma in a career well suited to his common touch.

DENOUEMENT

There were times when he required considerable leeway for the simplicity of what he expressed when noble speeches and persuasive exhortations might have been expected of a leader in pursuit of a major cause. That was not a means for Townley. He never was articulate. However, his attitude, enthusiasm and insight counterbalanced whatever he lacked in social facility. Corneal transplantation was his original fascination arising during his Wilmer training and, paradoxically, not encouraged by Dr. Wilmer. But it was a passion as inseparable from its supply-side need as the gas that fills the balloons for Fifth Avenue parades. By default, that need called for focus and resolution: eye banking was the answer, but until the public had adequate understanding it was a bugaboo of conflicting perspectives.

Not only did he have fine surgical finesse but a mindset fit to tolerate the sharp criticism of social reactionaries. He never regretted his chosen path. As recorded in the literature, "The story of keratoplasty is one of the most exciting and enthralling dramas in all ophthalmology, or for that matter, in the whole field of surgery." It is the "boldest fantasy," for "this operation ... has everything. There is the pathos of blindness, the nobility of sacrifice, the gruesomeness of death, the shuddering and reluctance of relatives of the donor corpse, the urgent transportation of the lonely cold eye by air" as was then commonly required, and hence "with sirens clearing the traffic" the donation reaches its intended destination. The distinguished author of this quotation, Dr. Derrick Vail, could have added "...and restoring vision when barely more than a decade ago, frequency of keratoplasty would have seemed almost impossible until awakening of man's caring for his fellow man."

Yet there was mystery in him that might never have been solved had this book not been undertaken. Internet research was gratified with a "eureka moment." Townley's bizarre behavior after Pam's death had been the only stumbling block to his full understanding. Why had he not given permission for the use of Pam's eyes for the need served by his Eye-Bank? Failing to request that act he had spent many years to promote made the founding father of eye banking seem weak in resolve. There had to be an explanation for his derelict neglect of what he had believed in unreservedly and what he envisioned as a permission that should be granted routinely throughout every modern community.

As unimportant as that omission may seem to others, it was a flash point of disconnect for his family and close others. More than three decades after his death, those who knew lived with fabricated excuses for the implied default of "not in my family but okay in yours." That could never have been what he believed should be done.

Then in the 1990s and thereafter, a previously unrecognized "psycho-neurological" entity (to coin a conveniently descriptive word) was reported in the medical literature that fit exactly with Townley's history of prolonged undiminished self-enforced denial that obscured the unbearable reality of Pam's death which was never to fade. It was an affliction that came on instantly when Townley was informed of her accidental demise like a veritable "brain blast" comparable to a localized stroke. That took place in some specialized regions of his brain, and although it served a protective role in screening his intolerable anguish in refusal of its reality, not his memory but his insight was destroyed.

Townley lost all sense of obligation to the management of Pam's body, her stay at a funeral home that he would not visit, and a funeral he may not have attended on the basis of disliking the church minister with a reputation for excessive drinking and carrying-on. Any excuse would be sufficient. It was not Helen's right to notify the Eye-Bank and she respected that. The diagnosis of Townley's disorder was initially named Complicated Grief Disorder. Later it has been called Persistent Complex Bereavement Disorder (PCBD) and nicknamed Complicated Grief. [6] It is a serious condition that perfectly explains the instantaneous onset of Townley's irreversible inability to withstand even mention of Pam due to the anguish it would otherwise generate. Unlike the sadness that affects everyone else who loses a close family member or special friend, Complicated Grief remains severe and unabated for many years, as it did for Townley—to the end of his life. If available, psychiatric management can be helpful, at least in some cases.

With that unusual syndrome, Townley's state of mind from the loss of Pam could at last be understood not as the usual depression from loss of a loved one but as another variety of illness closer to post-traumatic stress disorder (PTSD) that was formerly known as "shell shock." Ironically, that was one of Stewart Paton's most abiding interests. Townley had a sudden profound grief that he would neither discuss nor admit. Other cases also have histories of excessive drinking to dull down the sorrow of remembrance. Complicated Grief is not infrequently associated with an element of guilt-in Pam's case, her parents may have had a sense of responsibility for her visit with a family he and Helen did not know but who took vacations near the small waterfall where she died.

Another aggravating factor may have been his lurking dyslexia, always limiting Townley's communication, always curbing the articulation of his personal thoughts, and perhaps leaving him with a feeling of being too socially inexpressive to address the complexity of his mental predicament. A psychiatrist could certainly have helped, but he was a physician — need more be said? Those are people who can heal themselves. His resultant behavior thereafter was always to preserve that walled-off sorrow at any cost. He could not even think of eye banking for her when she died.

Aside from that finally comprehended and fortunately isolated segment of abnormal behavior, Townley was still an otherwise upbeat, inordinately genteel man. A gratifying life was very important to his wellbeing. He was similar to his father in lacking ostentation, boastfulness and self-promotion. He was not driven by academia nor in awe of it. What he published was straightforward and not stained by the big "I." His family considered him a fine-looking person who was energetically athletic, wonderfully otherwise "normal" and possessed with strong determination and endurance. Despite his excellent reputation both as a corneal surgeon and as founder of the Eye-Bank, he lacked the vanity and swagger that success brings to some. He was a man free of guile and envy with no hint of arrogance.

Typically, Townley accepted what came his way, asked few questions and sought no sympathy. It was not a question of nobleness but naturalness, and even though he was not churchy he lived the Golden Rule in relation to humanity in general. His most pleasing attribute may have been what was reflected in the genuine kindness of his eyes. As a family man, Townley was the devoted husband, the caring father—and everyone's friend with whom to confide, but not for this Scot to confide in return. Listing his characteristics one by one produces a series of favorable words. Considering them all together amounts to a man of quality and completeness. He was the father that everyone would wish for his own.

DENOUEMENT

Townley would surely have been amused by a current eye bank phrase, "Give New View From the Eyes of You." Who could say it more succinctly or more poetically tongue-tied than that? Envision Townley now at the peak of his career, filled with incandescent conviction, waving an Eye-Bank brochure and urging you to register your corneal pledge by Internet. He is smiling at you and offering to write his signature on any nearby piece of paper as if affirming his own pledge, adding sincerely he would sign hundreds of virtual corneal pledges if only it would bring as many actual pledges to eye banking.[7]

R. Townley Paton

Now you, too, are smiling full-faced from the appeal of his innocent hyperbole. And there you go, agreeing to fill out the pledge form, and he is looking at you with the gratitude of a true believer reflected in the reassuring squint of rheumy blue eyes.

INSIGHT

NOTES TO CHAPTER 16:

1. A complete surprise to him, Don Maran inherited the land of a former orchard in a nearby township, consisting of acreage that had become very valuable. In selling it, Don became an overnight multi-millionaire. His wife had died but with remarriage he acquired a young and spritely bride. On multiple occasions, Don took the royal suite on the Queen Mary back and forth to England, allegedly at the cost of $10,000 each way. Sitting at the captain's table, he was asked what he had done for a living (the captain imagining a Wall Street mogul in disguise). Don told the captain truthfully he had worked as a gardener and handy man for a Southampton doctor. His life had become a modern version of a bedtime story when the Good Fairy has smiled and waved her wand. Sadly, he died after only a few such wonderful years.
2. Cushing, H.: *The Life of Sir William Osler*. Oxford University Press, New York, 1940.
3. Dr. Bronson was later to say that even for him as an eye surgeon, removing the eyes of his mentor, his senior partner, and his good friend was the most onerous task to perform in his entire career.
4. The family's first ophthalmologist, Dr. Cornelius Rea Agnew, is buried nearby as is the great surgeon Dr. William Stewart Halsted.
5. In some ways, dyslexia is an insufficient name for a disability that reaches well beyond reading difficulty. The author is taking the liberty to refer to the "dyslexia spectrum" as a reminder that the word stands for a brain abnormality that has a range of impairments affecting some but not necessarily all of the following: reading, spelling, mathematics, and facility of expression.
6. Shear, M.K., Wang, Y., Skritskaya, N., Duan, N., Mauro, C., and Ghesquiere, "A Treatment of Complicated Grief in Elderly Persons: A Randomized Clinical Trial," *JAMA Psychiatry*. 2014; 71(11): 1287-1295. See also http://complicatedgrief.org/the-science-behind-our-work/cgt-research/#sthash.7OcIckBW.dpu.
7. Today, pledges are made by internet registration; go to eyedonation.org.

EPILOGUE: EYES OF THE WORLD

It is the mark of a truly intelligent person to be moved by statistics.
George Bernard Shaw, 1856-1950

The Paton-Breckinridge story is finished, but from the many iterations of the model they created come valuable enhancements as eye bank services keep pace with the increasing sophistication of the surgery. At least for the past decade, leading eye banks retrieve only the donor cornea with a quick and clean *in situ* procedure instead of removing the whole eye. This applies to approximately 98% of donor notifications. The semi-mechanical technique for this removal is quick, easy and without effect on the appearance of the eye from which the cornea was taken.[1] Moreover, eye bank technicians have easily mastered this method of cornea removal; therefore, neither the surgeon nor another physician is needed. The eye bank service is available at short notice any time of day or night.

Container holds cornea with scleral ring

INSIGHT

In this modern era of eye banking, use of the operating microscope and its micro-instrumentation has opened the door to a transformation of corneal surgery from good to great. It is like going from propeller aircrafts to jets. Most everything of importance about the jets required re-engineering to meet the new criteria for speed, safety and overall effectiveness. As for the pilot, the surgeon, too, had to master a new technology. Just as with the invention of the watch in the 17th century when miniaturization called for new tools and new skills for the watchmakers, so it was with ophthalmology's "revolutionary change" in adapting to the microscope.

Ophthalmic surgical microscopy began in Europe about a decade before the 1970s when it began to be popularized in America. Its initially slow adaptation with established ophthalmologists was due to their difficulty in re-learning familiar operations under elevated magnification with smaller instruments and initially unfamiliar hand positions. Due to the difficulty of readjusting his longstanding techniques with new instrumentation and newly limited positioning, In 1961, despite fine teaching by the superb corneal surgeon, Dr. Richard Troutman, Townley was never fully comfortable using the microscope throughout his surgeries. However, high-powered, three-dimensional, foot-pedal-adjusted operating microscopes by then were offering an enormous benefit in almost all forms of surgery, none more significant than its usefulness to ophthalmology. There was no choice to make, for the microscope led to new skills.

Previously impossible goals have become common-place as automated instrumentation was introduced. [2] For example, to evenly split the cornea which normally measures about half a millimeter in thickness, the desired thickness of a graft in the eye bank laboratory can be cut precisely with automated instrumentation. This technical service greatly facilitates and adds precision to the transplant procedure by preparing the graft in the eye bank laboratory before

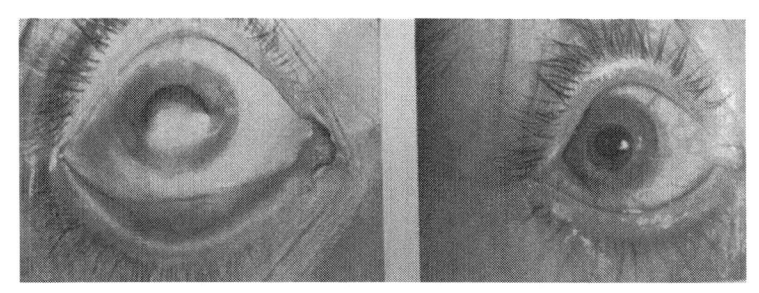

A cornea transplant by RTP

delivering it to the surgeon in the operating room. It is easy to understand why the incidence of keratoplasty has vastly increased with the new accomplishments afforded by laboratory and surgical microscopy.

By the 1980s, ophthalmologists from many nations joined the purpose of advocating and demonstrating corneal transplants by traveling under various auspices to wherever it was most needed. Countries as small as Singapore, Nepal and Colombia and as large as India, China and the Soviet Union were primary centers for microsurgical keratoplasty. Although it was also rapidly developing in England, Switzerland, France, Canada, Argentina and other nations, the technical "perfection" of microsurgical technique was best represented in the teaching films of Professor Joaquin Barraquer in Barcelona.[3]

Today, some of the most outstanding eye surgeons are to be found in some of the poorest countries–and many of those doctors have a place among the world's most inspiring people.[4] The outbreak of keratoplasty as a result of both the focus upon the availability of donor eye tissue and the more recent focus upon microsurgery has led to unlimited global demand for corneal transplantation.

For the visiting surgeon as teacher by "show and tell," the thrill of such participation was and will always remain an experience far more valuable than the personal cost of the time given to that work. It is truly a privilege of self-gratification conveniently disguised by the common assumption of the caring public that it is self-sacrificial heroism. It is and it isn't, depending on how it is viewed.

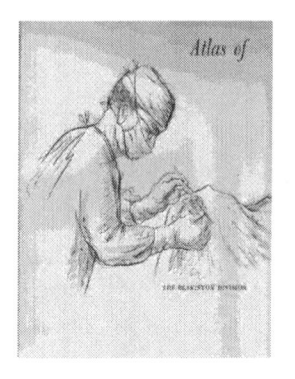

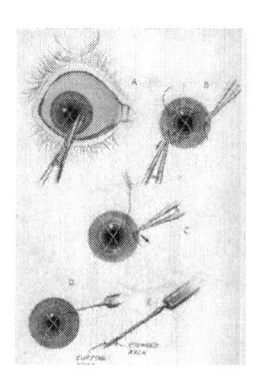

Illustrations from the Paton keratoplasty textbook

The microsurgical take-over within the medical profession has resulted in an entirely different but similarly profound "revolutionary" occurrence as the one related to new science requirements in Baltimore more than one hundred years ago, today commonly expressed as a "paradigm shift." It deserves to be said—with admission of author bias—that a corneal transplant operation which is a vitally critical step for the patient has become one of the most impressive, most delicate and most skillfully appealing surgical procedures of all surgeries performed on the human body.

The context of Townley's legacy may someday be perceived as larger than its "supply-side" augmentation for facilitating keratoplasty. His initiative of the 1940s and thereafter may eventually be understood as an iconic example of — to create a name — *participatory social science* for the advancement of public health. The eye bank pledge is a first step in fulfilling a public need and serving as an illustration of one's contribution to the public's welfare.[5]

Public health was closely related to Townley's father's lifelong interest in improving the focus and practices concerned with population requirements. In fact, as previously attested earlier in the book, Stewart was Dr. Welch's primary assistant in the conception and funding of what later became the Johns Hopkins Bloomberg School of Public Health. Stewart's interest lay at the junction of psychiatry and public mores. Townley's Eye-Bank for Sight Restoration on the other hand is at the junction of social science and the bond of eye banking with keratoplasty. Both are intrinsically related to overall focus upon the needs of public health.

Social science was taking shape in Stewart's lifetime and reached adolescence in Townley's. Today, social science includes an action-packed involvement of the public in various kinds of preventive care. It is where the proverbial rubber meets the road. For example, in 2013, a model goal of the World Health Organization was stated as the intent for citizens *to mutually support each other in performing all the functions of life to the maximum potential.*[6] The post-mortem fulfillment of a pledge for use of one's corneas by anonymous recipients is a public health process resulting from a commendable act, a classic example of "participatory socio-technical science.[7] As social science becomes more identified with Medicine and Public Health and in the current times of do-it-yourself health benefits, interchanges of significant benefit between individual citizens will become more common, possibly even a cultural norm.

Here is the point to be made: as the public's health becomes a more vital aspect of global health concerns, the roles of the world's individuals must gradually acquire more universal habits of self-involvement. The public's participation in health affairs is as fundamental to a thriving population as wind to a sail. The eye bank pledge thus symbolizes support for public performance of community needs.

Eye banking in general is not without significant cost. It is always a non-profit service starting with the donation of eyes (corneas) since no payment is ever made to anyone. Yet, the overall management of eye banking has increased markedly in expense. As society becomes pervaded by legal constraints and governmental controls, and as science adds layers of knowledge and caution to the process of handling donated tissue, the simple act of securing donor cornea material in a recipient eye has become a matter of some complexity, certainly as compared to when the first eye bank was founded. The ocular tissue processing cost would be much greater if the Eye-Bank for Sight Restoration lacked charitable support and a modest endowment. Each eye bank is a not-for-profit organization and determines its own processing fees based on their expenses in providing the tissue.

The Eye-Bank for Sight Restoration (EBSR) is a 501(c)(3) not-for-profit, nongovernmental (NGO) organization compliant with regulations set by the New York State Health Department and the

U.S. Food and Drug Administration. It meets the high accreditation standards established by the Eye Bank Association of America. Since 1981, its Board of Directors excludes practicing physicians but their input comes from a Medical Advisory Board and its Medical Director. As in the other states, New York has a registry for all potential donors, thus the "pledge" today consist of the registration of one's name with the state's registration of donor intent. Details can be found on the bank's web site. [8]

The role of establishing medical standards and providing technician education and certification lies with the EBAA. In 2014, that organization, headquartered in Washington, D.C., had a membership of 83 American eye banks that met its strict accreditation requirements. These banks reported a total of 76,431 corneal transplants of which 47,530 were performed in the United States. The demand for more donor corneas continues to skyrocket. Since the EBAA was founded in 1961, 1,600,000 corneal transplants have been performed. Mr. Kevin Corcoran, the president/CEO of the EBAA, ventures the guess that there are approximately 10,000,000 persons worldwide with severity of corneal blindness that will shorten their lives, add to the cost of their existence, prolong the misery of sightlessness and affect the affairs of their families until such time when corneal surgery becomes available to them.

The United States and other nations are generous in providing donor corneas abroad whenever the demand for corneas locally has been temporarily fulfilled. These exported corneas serve as catalysts for stimulating both keratoplasty and eye banking within developing countries where (as in the U.S. in the 1940s) the proof of corneal transplants' near-miracle outcomes "has to be seen to be believed," to turn an appropriate phrase.

Since Townley's death, there has been another advancement in corneal surgery that would be a mistake not to mention as an increasingly impressive achievement. A "keratoprosthesis" is a PMMA cornea replacement wedged into place within the patient's opaque cornea to provide a central window for vision to be provided as long as this prosthesis remains in place. It is only used when a cornea transplant *per se* would not be successful due to the damages the eye has undergone. For about half a century, various artificial cornea implants have been used for eyes badly damaged by injury or disease. Only in recent years has a keratoprosthesis been constructed that is likely to be retained and remain functional as a window to the world for numerous years but always dependent on sustained follow-up for tissue repairs or replacements as may be necessary to save the eye. [9]

More theoretical than demonstrably successful is the use of artificial substances for an entire corneal graft replacement. Recently, investigators both in the United States and in China are speaking enthusiastically about preliminary results of clinical trials using such artificial corneal grafts made of a bioengineered tissue replacement. Whether or not this will become a substitute for donor corneas remains to be determined by at least a generation of investigators pursuing clinical trials with resulting adjustments of the grafts' bioengineering. Perhaps it may indeed have valuable clinical usefulness.

Eye banking has a formidable global outreach. The most recent but still incomplete undertaking by the EBAA in league with the World Health Organization and various international agencies will be the Global Alliance of Eye Bank Associations (GAEBA) [10] that will offer internationally some of what the EBAA offers in the United

States and to a few other countries that came aboard quite a few years ago. To use the GAEBA wording, the Global Alliance "functions to provide peer and professional support, knowledge exchange, advocacy, surveillance, research and continual education opportunities to its members, thereby in line with local, national and internationally recommended Standards of Practice."

Summary of Eye Bank and Keratoplasty Information:

- Eye banking as "participatory social science" is a public health function worthy of wider recognition.
- In U.S. alone, approximately 1,000 ophthalmologists perform keratoplasty.
- 98% of U.S. keratoplasties are with donor cornea removal only, not the entire eye.
- Microsurgical keratoplasty technique is now universally performed.
- Small instrument automation yields precision in microns instead of millimeters.
- A variety of surgical techniques is used to provide for individualized keratoplasty needs.
- 2014: USA/Canada: 83 eye banks of the EBAA reported 47,500 transplants.
- 2014: Globally, almost 30,000 donor corneas were provided for grafts abroad.
- 1961 to 2014: Approximately 1.6 million transplants performed globally according to EBAA data
- Almost 180,000 cornea transplants are now performed globally per year (Dohlman).
- With otherwise healthy eyes, clear graft expectancy is in the 90th percentile.
- Today, an estimated 10,000,000 persons have surgically curable corneal blindness.

INSIGHT

- Boston's PMMA cornea implants (keratoprostheses) are now generally very effective.
- Artificial "tissue" is being tested as a substitute for corneal grafts in U.S., China, and elsewhere
- The forthcoming Global Alliance of Eye Banks will soon provide more global data and on-going cornea surgical news

How amazed and gratified Townley Paton would feel were he to know of the broadening and booming of eye banking in recent years. What he conceived and what he and the inimitable Aida Breckinridge made possible has been edified by the size and extent of the Eye-Bank for Sight Restoration's role as an enduring model of eye banking excellence.

At the end of a long story with glimpses of a promising future, perhaps whatever the reader has gleaned from this book will encourage another contributor to participate in the charity of eye banking for the gift of sight- — a benevolence hard to beat. If that message is expressed as convincingly as it deserves to be, it might persuade some calls to the nearest eye bank inquiring for ways one can be most useful to its work. By the purchase of this book the reader has already been helpful. As they say at the Eye-Bank, "See what your eyes can do for others."

EYES OF THE WORLD

NOTES TO THE EPILOGUE:

1. The Eye-Bank uses the 3e Moria microkeratome for this quick and easy process.
2. Keratoplasty requires further explanation for understanding of where its evolution is going. Traditionally, a full-thickness preparation of donor cornea is used to replace a full-thickness excision of the patient's cornea. This is referred to as penetrating keratoplasty (PK). There is also partial-thickness donor preparation to target only the diseased portion of the patient's cornea. These techniques are called lamellar keratoplasty (LK) and endothelial keratoplasty (EK). Major benefits of targeted transplantation include better preservation of the cornea's strength, blurred vision from corneal astigmatism is decreased, and transplant rejection is reduced. Over the last several years, the most exciting progress has been in EK tissue preparation. It is now possible to create progressively thinner tissue that is highly specific. Today, an eye bank's technical staff can prepare a form of donor tissue consisting of nothing more than a fine membrane to which is attached a delicate layer of endothelial cells; such a graft can then be applied to the inner surface of the cornea when its own endothelial cells have been compromised by acquired or genetic disorders common in our population. Such grafts with only the purpose of restoring the endothelial cells (EK) were not feasible before surgical microscopy. In recent years, when only the endothelial cell layer is dysfunctional (which is often the case), it is being replaced by a donor graft of endothelial cells introduced into the eye behind the cornea and held in place by an air bubble instead of sutures ~ the bubble pressing against the donor endothelium causes it to "stick" into place before the air is resorbed. Thus, the otherwise normal, but cloudy cornea regains its transparency when it has functioning endothelial cells, and in that surgery the eye itself has had less surgical manipulation and almost no suturing. Townley would have loved to know about that. He was among the first eye surgeons who had success with corneal transplants for endothelial disorders, but never by such greatly improved methodology as summarized above. [This note was prepared by Michelle K. Rhee MD, the current medical director of the Eye-Bank for Sight Restoration.]
3. See barraquer.com.
4. For example, look up online Dr. Sanduk Ruit of Tilganga Institute of Ophthalmology in Nepal, who is an outstanding example: Tilganga.org.
5. Aristotle in the 4th Century B.C. expressed such action more nobly by selecting the word *phronesis* for the "practical wisdom" of seeking the "common goodness" that leads to essential human participation as the driving force for applied **science.** He thereby anticipated the identification of social science, which was not to be

known as such until the end of the 19th Century as where the rubber meets the road. Rather than "road-rubbers," the crux of the do'ers' social identities might be given historic Greek sophistication with *phronesis phreaks*. That has a certain élan that road-rubbing misses. So much for ancient history.

6. WHO defines a healthy community: www.hria.org/community-health/healthy-communities.

7. Toward the end of the 20th century, Eric Lansdown Trist named the social roles dependent upon technical services sociotechnical *system*–that term perfectly identifies the basis of eye banking. But how can an advocate of social consciousness illustrate the need for numerous aspects of public participation for the common good? As the world becomes more crowded and as its people become more dependent upon each other in mutual support, eye banking (involving the most common kind of formed donor tissue and meeting the greatest global need for an ever-greater supply) epitomizes the understanding, the concern, and the willing act this form of human service requires. It is a multi-person collaboration as is this common form of social science involvement. It is the essence of a science-bound commitment every adult–regardless of gender, race, education, wealth or physical capabilities–is capable of pledging. Many more Americans would make that commitment once they understand the need and now the philosophy behind the act of the eye's cornea donation. Through educated understanding at almost all levels of society, eye banking can become the gold standard of social science's do-it-yourself collaboration. It has the need, the volume, the interdisciplinary team, the public participation and the compelling appeal of a curative scientific process of great importance to the individuals to be benefitted and, as shown by the data of the EBAA, to the nation's economy. Some comprehension of social science participations would help raise the public's grasp of eye banking's relevance.

8. www.eyedonation.org.

9. The best of these devices has been named the "K-Pro" and was designed in the 1960s by a noted and beloved surgeon-researcher and ophthalmology standard bearer, Sweden-born Bostonian ophthalmologist Professor Claes H. Dohlman, MD PhD, whose work takes place at Massachusetts Eye and Ear in Boston.

10. GAEBA will eventually become a source of helpful eye bank information with statistical backup. Its 2011 founding partners were the Eye Bank Associations of Asia, Europe, Australia, New Zealand, India, Pan America (that covers Central and South America), and North America (the EBAA).

APPENDIX I:

Letter Excerpts re Dr. Paton's Retirement from Practice, 1976

"Of all my teachers, and there are very many I hold in high regard, you alone stand out as the example of achievement, integrity and personal warmth on which I hope to have patterned myself."

Donald C. McFarlane, MD FRCS

"There were legal problems in the establishment of the Eye-Bank, and in dealing with those too...as with surgical and medical work ... you were a tower of strength. It still is amazing to me how many unexpected hurdles we found in our path, interposed by well-meaning public officials and based on well-meant provisions of law—such things as the statutory requirement that any part of the human body used for any medical or scientific purpose must be re-associated with the body from which it was taken and given decent burial. How well I remember how Mrs. Breckenridge made light of the objections interposed by the Board of Regents and the Banking Department and the Secretary of State's office and the Attorney General and Justices of the New York Supreme Court and a few others! She said that she would not take these legal objections too seriously—that we lawyers could not frighten her — that, after all, she had been married to one! Your tact in securing her complete (and very necessary and helpful) co-operation was just one of the many evidences of your competence in so many fields."

Edward E. Watts, Jr. Counsel

"Your leadership has been forceful, decisive and fair. Communication lines were always open and we learned in an atmosphere of warmth and good humor. Your innovative pioneering efforts were the stepping stones upon which we all climbed to ever more successful surgical skills. Our dreams of yesterday are today's realities, and for that humanity will be forever grateful."

Arnold I. Turtz, MD

"Aside from your many scientific contributions and your secure place in the history of ophthalmology, I wish to point out, as one who worked with you for many years at Manhattan, how, during your tenure, the Hospital became one of the greatest institutions in this country, if not in the world. Your ideas, enthusiasm, example, encouragement to others, and administrative talents, were the catalysts for the present high status, and those who have lived through this Hospital transition all know and appreciate it!"

Frederick H.J. Theodore, MD

"I am delighted (therefore) to have this chance to tell you what a privilege it is to have a friend and colleague of one who led the way in corneal surgery and, being an excellent teacher as well as surgeon, unselfishly and unstintingly shared his knowledge with the rest of us."

Harold B. Scheie, MD

"My admiration for your dedication to people, both personally and professionally, is enormous. Your knowledge and your wisdom benefitted me personally for a long time, and I know my own experience is multiplied a thousand-fold in this great city of ours."

Nelson A. Rockefeller, U.S. Vice President

APPENDIX I

"You are my "Number One" among the whole profession – and let me say promptly that your qualifications are not by any means restricted to medicine. Your professional achievements are known the world over, but a more limited group has had the luck to work closely with you, as I did during the period that you served as President of the Medical Board of "MEETH" while I was Chairman of the Lay Board. At countless meetings involving hospital problems, mergers, personnel and what-not, you always spoke for what was the best solution for the Hospital and nothing or anybody else counted."

Auguste Richard, MEETH Board

"Always, throughout those years your personal charm and gracious courtesy, your little chuckling laugh and constant good humor made you respected and loved by all your friends. Your professional achievements became legendary."

Otto B. Reimer

"However, for us who were privileged to train under your tutelage the gratitude is far more personal. You were always available to the lowest house officer, stimulated our curiosity and gently punctured our wildest ideas. You taught us never to give up on a discouraging case but also never do a procedure that would not really help a patient, to evaluate our results and learn from or failures. I hope the intellectual honesty that you taught my generation will be passed on by us to this generation."

William F. Regan, Jr. MD

INSIGHT

"For over 50 years, you-in our estimation of the personification of Sir William Osler's *Aequanimitas* - have been an important part of our lives not only because of the wisdom and skill you have demonstrated in the practice of your profession but also because of your and Helen's gift to us of your warm friendship. One of your very own special attributes has been that of always being as deeply concerned with the person behind the eye as you were with the technical aspect of the eye per se."

H.C. Potter, MEETH

"Since the first day (in 1948) I was sure that you were not only an ophthalmologist of high degree, but really a gentleman, a man of honor devoted to your patients (and) having always the intention of doing well, and also dedicated to have a life awarding as much time as possible for scientific research. You were one of the first pioneers of (keratoplasty) and ...the young colleagues doing these operations every day without difficulties, they must not forget the men like you who were the first to do the practice of this surgical adventure."

Louis Paufique, University of Lyon, France

"You are a man whom I consider a dear friend, a father-figure, a talented clinician, an excellent surgeon, a true gentleman and a humanitarian. You have given so much to your students and (our) patients' welfare. You have achieved true success because you have left your mark on society, having promoted its improvement."

Alfred E. Mamelok, MD

"From my talks with you, I realized quickly why you were so highly regarded and so deeply loved by everyone. Your fairness and consideration, your deep interest in all things, and your willingness to

APPENDIX I

go to great lengths to help your friends and patients endeared you to them and to me and gave me a broad foundation on which to base my own life. I can only say that you have provided me and many other individuals with guidance and inspiration through your exemplary gentleness, kindness, thoughtfulness, empathy, and great sensitivity to the needs of others."

Francis A. L'Esperance, Jr., MD

"Your modesty matched your outstanding abilities throughout your illustrious career at Manhattan."

Joseph Laval, MD

"We had a difficult case (to manage by the house staff). As resident, I might have done the surgery, but you said, "This may be a problem; let me do it and put my name down on the record." As a result of your taking the appropriate personal responsibility you avoided for me being drawn into the subsequent considerable litigation."

Michael Wiedman, MD

"Your scientific and organizational accomplishments are known widely and you have, of course, gained considerable recognition for them, but I believe only a privileged few of us have had the opportunity to know and enjoy you for yourself."

Lorenz E. Zimmerman, MD

[For my organization] You were among the very few who opened a door to me and extended your hand in friendship. There are no words to adequately convey the importance of that gesture and I hope I have justified your faith.

Mildred Weisenfeld, Fight For Sight, Inc.

"Over your full and incredibly productive life you had many students - but no one more eager to learn than I was ... to get an instant education to help David in making his dream of Orbis become reality. My ignorance was matched only by enthusiasm! Your caring and interest meant and means a great deal."

Betsy Trippe Wainwright (later DeVecchi)

APPENDIX II:

R. Townley Paton Selected Bibliography
(several duplications in separate journals)

<u>Eye Banking and Corneal Surgery Papers by R.T. Paton</u>

Paton, RT: "Sight Restoration Through Corneal Grafting," *Sight Saving Review* 15: 3-12, 1945.

Paton, RT: "Complications Encountered in Keratoplasty." *Am J Ophthal.* 30 (11):1436-9, 1947.

Paton, RT: "Technique and Complications of Keratoplasty". *Am J Ophthal.* 30 (10):1302, 1947.

Paton, RT: "Corneal Transplantation: Selection of Cases." *Trans Am Acad Ophthal. Otolaryngol.* 52: 312-6, 1948.

Paton, RT: "Corneal Transplantation: Selection of Cases.". *Am J Ophthal.* 31 (11):1365-9, 1948.

Paton, RT, McLean, JM, et al.: "Corneal Transplantation." *Am J Ophthal.* 31 (11):1365-99, 1948.

Paton, RT: "Symposium: Corneal Transplantation. 1. Selection of Cases." *Trans. Amer Acad. Ophthal. & Otolaryngol.* 52: 312-316, 1948.

Paton, RT: "Corneal Transplantation." *New Orleans Med and Surg J:* 01: 25-30, 1948.

Paton, RT "Corneal Transplantation: A Historical Review" in "International Symposium on Corneal Surgery," *Amer. J. Ophthal.* 33:3-6,1949.

Paton, RT : "Lamellar Transplantation." *Southern Med J.* 43: 939-940, 1950.

Paton, RT, McLean JM, et al : "Corneal Transplantation." *Arch Ophthal.* 43(1): 164-72, 1950.

Paton, RT: *Am J Ophthal.* 33 (3 Pt. 2):3-5, 1950.

Paton, RT: "Presentation of Cases." *Amer. J. Ophthal* 33, No. 3, Part 2, 63-65, 1950.

Paton, RT: "Corneal Transplantation: An Historical Review." *Am J. Ophthal.* 33: 3-5,1950.

Paton, RT: "Corneal Transplantation." *Guildcraft*, 1-6, 1951.

Paton, RT: "A Method of Preventing Retaining Sutures from Cutting Into Grafts." *Arch Opth* 8 (3):344-5, 1952.

Paton, RT: "Some Phases of Keratoplasty.".*Arch Ophth* 48(1): 116-8, 1952.

Paton, RT: ""Corneal Transplantation: A Review of 365 Operations." *Trans. Am Ophht. Soc.* 51: 581-688, 1953.

Paton, RT: "Corneal Transplantation: A Review of 365 Operations." *AMA Arch Ophth* 52: 871-916,1954.

Paton, RT: "Corneal Transplantation." *Arch Ophthal.* 52 (6): 871, 1954.

INSIGHT

Paton, RT: "Immune Biological Response in Corneal Transplantation." *Annals NY Academy of Sciences* 59: 462-465, 1955.

Paton, RT:" Recent Advances in Keratoplasty". *J Med Liban.* 8 (3-5):494-9, 1955.

Paton, RT: *Keratoplasty.* New York. Blakiston Division, McGraw-Hill, 280 pages, 1955.

Paton, RT:" Eye-Bank Program". *Amer J Ophth.* 41 (3): 419-24, 1956.

Paton, RT: Smith, B, Katzin, HM, and Stilwell, D: *Atlas of Eye Surgery.* Blakiston Division, McGraw-Hill, First Edition 248 pages, 1957.

Paton, RT: *Donor Material and the Law.* Rycroft, BW(editor). Corneal Grafts, Chap. 14, 216-230, Butterworth & Co. Ltd., London, 1955.

Paton, RT: "Complications and Pitfalls of Keratoplasty with a Note on Corneal Grafts for Fuchs Dystrophy," *Tans. Ophthl. Soc. U.K.*, 497-509,1958.

Paton, RT, Swartz, G: "Keratoplasty for Keratoconus". *AMA Arch Ophth.* 61 (3): 370-2, 1959.

Paton, RT, Swartz, G: *AMA Arch Ophth.* 61 (3): 366-91, 1959.

Keates, RH, Martinez, M, Paton, RT: "A Modified Technique for Mushroom Corneal Grafts with a New Instrument." *Am J Ophth.* 52: 239-41, 1961.

Paton RT, Martinez, M: "A Corneal Trephine with Built-In Optical Centering Device." *Am J Ophthal.* 49: 1031-2, May 1960.

Paton, RT: "Surgical Techniques and Instrumentation for Corneal Transplants". *Pac Med Surg* 73:231-6,1965.

Paton, RT: "Cataract Extraction After Keratoplasty." *Int Ophthalmol Clin.* 5: 95-7, 1965.

Paton, RT "Penetrating and Lamellar Grafting - Indications." The Cornea. World Congress. King, JH Jr. and McTigue, JW Editors. *Butterworths.* Washington, 525-529, 1965.

Paton, RT: "Why an Eye-Bank?" Blindness American Association of Workers for the Blind, Inc. Washington, D.C. *AAWB Annual.* 87-90, 1968.
Paton, RT : "History of Corneal Transplantation. Advances in Keratoplasty," *Internat. Ophthal. Clinics* 10:181-186, 1970.

Farge, EJ: "A History of the Eye Bank Association of America. Its Origins and Development, 1930-1991". Manuscript available at EBAA, 1001 Connecticut Ave., N.W., Suite 601, Washington, D.C.

Papers and Chapters About R.T. Paton

Paton D: "The Founder of the First Eye Bank: Richard Townley Paton." *J. Refractive and Corneal Surgery*, March 1991.

Paton D: "R. Townley Paton 1901-1984". Chap. VII. In *Corneal Transplantation: A History in Profiles.* Mannis, MJ and Mannis AA (edits), Hirschberg History of Ophthalmology. The Monographs. Vol 6:238-263, 1999. J.P. Wayenborgh, Belgium.

APPENDIX II

<u>Miscellaneous Papers by RT Paton</u>
Paton, RT: "A Metal Instrument Rack". *Arch Ophthal.* 7: 299, 1932.
Paton, RT: "The Clinical Significance of Choroidal Tubercles". *Ann. Int. Med.* 5: 997-999, 1932.
Wilmer, WH and Paton, RT: "Pantocain As a Local Anesthetic in Ophthalmology". *AJO* 16: 106-109, 1933.
Paton, RT: "Curved Cataract Knife and Its Advantages." *Arch. Ophthal.* 14: 108-109, 1935.
Paton, RT: "Device for Training of Children to Overcome Strabismus." *Arch. Ophthal.* 13: 636-638, 1935.
Paton, RT and Auchincloss, SS Jr.: "Moving Picture Fusion Training Apparatus." *AMA Trans. Section on Ophthalmology*, 1935.
Paton, RT: "Recurrent Retinal and Vitreous Hemorrhages in the Young – Eales' Disease." *Archives of Ophthal.* 20: 276-285, 1938.
Paton, RT: "Subconjunctival Injections of Neoprontosil in the Treatment of Ocular Infections," *AMA Arch Ophthal.* 22: 377-384, 1939.
Paton, RT and Montalvan, P: "Hemorragias Recidivantes de la Retina y del Vitreo en Joven Enfermedad deEales" (publication in which this appeared unknown to D. Paton), 1939.
Paton, RT: "Inter-Relationship of Ophthalmology and Systemic Disease," *Diseases of the Eye, Ear, Nose and Throat* 9:1-8, 1942.
Paton, RT and Abbott, HB: "A Headband Plate for Securing Lid Traction Sutures," *Trans. Amer. Acad Ophthal and Otolaryng* Jan-Feb. 1942.
Paton, RT: "Eye Ointment Dispenser," *Archives. Ophthal.* 39: 549-550, 1948.
Paton, RT: "Recent Advances in the Surgery of Retinal Detachment," *Medical Record and Annals* 44: May 1950.
Paton, RT and Katzin, HM: "A New Holder and Pins for Retinal Detachment Operation," *Amer. J. Ophthal.* 34, 1951.
Paton, RT: "Intracapsular Forceps," *Amer. J. Ophthal.* 38, 1954.
Paton, RT: "Ophthalmology" in *The Specialties in General Practice*, Chapter VII. W.B. Saunders Company, Philadelphia, 1961 (and prior editions).

INSIGHT

ACKNOWLEDGMENTS

<u>Eye-Bank Leaders:</u> The President and Chief Executive Officer of the Eye-Bank for Sight Restoration is Ms. Patricia Dahl. At her right hand stands Ms. Noël M. Mick, Director of Public Relations & Professional Education. Both women have been generously helpful from the book's concept to its finish, always available by telephone, always willing to provide abundant information about the past and present conduct of their primordial bank. Both have read an earlier proof of the manuscript and have found typos, errors of assertion, and the need for additions. For technical and current eye bank practices, further assistance has come from the multi-talented Dr. Michelle K. Rhee, Medical Director, and by Drs. Danielle Trief and David Ritterband, members of the Eye-Bank's Medical Advisory Board. In particular, they provided information for the Epilogue.

The Eye-Bank, a necessarily finance-sensitive organization, has provided some of the cost of producing this book, using the contributed Paton Family Fund. However, that investment in the recording of Townley's life is to be repaid, for every cent of income from book sales will go "in perpetuity" to the Eye-Bank. In the decade ahead perhaps a second edition by another writer will replace this one, but the same not-for-profit arrangement must apply. Fans of eye banking may wish to add their support by purchasing stacks of this book for shelf-fillers or doorstops--or they may prefer the more sensible alternative and send contributions directly to the EBSR at 120 Wall Street, NYC 10005 while imagining Townley Paton standing alongside, grinning in gratitude as the check is signed and the envelope sealed.

<u>EBAA:</u> The heralding poem by a former CEO of the Eye Bank Association of America, Patricia Aiken O'Neill, "Sights

ACKNOWLEDGMENTS

Unseen," seems the perfect warm-up for a book of memories. Patricia not only gave the use of that poem but volunteered editing assistance, resulting in the correction of several important misstatements and the addition of other modifications. Her role as former leader of the EBAA makes her poetic contribution all the more appropriate. She deserves and now gets big thanks.

Kevin Corcoran, the current President/CEO of the EBAA, kindly provided statistics for the Epilogue and had no specified changes to suggest because others beat him to the flaws of the first draft. Kevin has an important if not perpetually exciting organization to rule: the collaborative kingdom of eye banks.

<u>Paton Family:</u> David Townley Paton (who goes by Townley), Richard Townley Paton's grandson, first designed the book's cover and helped with the illustrations. He is a loving son with his own variant of the family give-and-take genetic anomaly that affects the minutiae in his life while also making him a remarkably versatile and creative digital man of business. He and his charming lawyer-realtor-agent wife, Shannon, and their two young daughters, Cricket (5) and Phoebe (2), are apples of this writer's eyes.

There are other in-laws to crow about equally. Remarkable wife, Diane's dear daughter, Lauren, and her hard-working husband, Brian Ivanhoe (a very capable but more traditional businessman), are the parents of an adolescent angel with long locks and lashes who would have been a great child movie star had she not grown up too fast to arrange for auditions. The Ivanhoes are horse people in southern upstate New York where they ride with hounds and horns. Their relationship to the book is one of style and sweep-teaching that one should never accept less than the possible, the writer's stubborn goal. Add then to those apples a stepdaughter, Garrison J. Franke,

INSIGHT

and her daughter, Daisy. These beautiful women are too sophisticated to give their ages. They live in France and are the advisers for the French words and phrases used on these pages.

The older daughter of Townley and Helen, Joan, lives in Maine near some of her brood. She is the Paton family's out-front bowsprit, leading in appearance, fastidious in manners, and almost infallible in memory. Joan and her four surviving children represent the true heart of the earth. She knows the inside story of almost all of the family's major "tree people" of interest in this book. Her help was supplemented by considerable correspondence with Cousin Noel B. Williams, formerly of Pass Christian, Mississippi, whose entire house with her detailed family genealogy compiled over many years was destroyed a few years ago in Hurricane Katrina. Noel is one of the two self-taught family genealogists identified on earlier pages.

Two others in the Paton clan who have been very helpful to this forgetful person are Rowena and Clifford Manuel of Shell, Wyoming. Row is the survivor of the four daughters of Bill and Rowena Paton, Bill being this nephew's favorite Marlboro-Paton cowboy highlighted early in this biography. Cliff and Row have been very helpful with information about their side of the family and with names and dates that needed to be resubmitted three times before being properly recorded. Row is dyslexic, as were her sisters and her father. She and Cliff are establishing a museum of relics from Wyoming dinosaurs that promises to put Shell high on the tourist map — arguably — as one of the most enthralling tourist attractions west of the Mississippi.

<u>An Inheritance:</u> The inheritance of a collection that belonged to Stewart Paton and later to Townley Paton, containing 70-some books plus an assortment of letters, photographs, notes, obituary

ACKNOWLEDGMENTS

reprints, newspaper clippings, diaries and framed citations, forms the basis for much of the 20th-century history in this volume. Numerous books are signed by their authors with names such as Osler, Welch, Barker, Cushing, Flexner, and Halsted. Other books in the collection are written about these and additional remarkable personages, detailing their career contributions. Most of this printed materials will be offered to the Johns Hopkins Alan Chesney Medical Archives, but books are not as wanted as they once were. Despite being cherished for many years, perhaps it is time for these to be auctioned for collectors, benefitting the Eye-Bank and/or the Wilmer Institute.

Aida Root Breckinridge's Family: The book's leading lady casually referred to in the biography as "Aida" has left very special relatives to help reconstitute her story. Consultations by letter, email and eye-to-eye chatting have provided otherwise important details that have been included in the manuscript. Aida's daughter-in-law, Daphne Skouras Root, is sharp as a tack and has strong family memories and has provided photographs and drawings eligible for use in this book. Daphne's son, Oren Root V, is Aida's grandson; he has been the primary family correspondent. Oren's sources of information have been supported by his sister, Dolores Root, and to some extent their cousin, Alva Bound, also collaborative. Without the Root family's assistance, much of the factual content of Aida's life would not have been available. They deserve the heartiest of thanks.

William Holland Wilmer MD's Family: As happens in the best of families, favorite ancestors are remembered by the gift of their names to favored progeny. So it is with William Holland Wilmer, Esq. of Baltimore, a busy lawyer and a kind helper with his grandfather's history. In fact, he shared Dr. Wilmer's unpublished biography that provided much confirmatory information about his

INSIGHT

grandfather as well as providing some interesting new details from the life of an historically important figure in the annals of ophthalmology. Much gratitude goes to him for such contribution.

<u>Stephanie Fleetwood:</u> Special thanks are extended to Stephanie Fleetwood, an authority on "Dr." Hippocrates and his era that began Medicine's evolution. She wrote an extended précis describing his relevance that appears in the After-Notes of Chapter 4. Thus, the reason for naming him the Father of Modern Medicine becomes evident as the ensuing history picks up his influences upon medical attitudes and mores. Stephanie deserves special recognition and gratitude for her authoritative and concisely written contribution to this book.

<u>Drs. Dohlman and Troutman:</u> Dr. Richard Troutman and Dr. Claes Dohlman are the only two major–major surviving "corneal" ophthalmologists who knew Townley Paton and kindly read this manuscript. (There are a few others, too, but they proved difficult to locate.) Claes and Dick have contributed greatly to the surgical successes of corneal surgery and have done much honor to the book with their kind comments.

<u>Drs. Stout and Wilhelmus and others at BCM:</u> Thanks are extended to those whose help was sought in a city very familiar to this writer. Dr. Timothy Stout (Chairman of the Department of Ophthalmology at Baylor College of Medicine in Houston, where this writer was a predecessor) was joined by Dr. Kirk Wilhelmus, Emeritus Professor; Dr. Douglas Koch, Dr. Bowes Hamill, and Dr. Richard Lewis, and Dr. John Gottsch (now a Wilmer professor) as available informers if and when needed. Tim, in particular, reviewed the assertions in the chapter on genetics and Kirk submitted characteristically illustrious comments that broadened the Epilogue.

ACKNOWLEDGMENTS

Dr. William Tasman: He is always very helpful. In particular, Bill knew about Dr. D. Hayes Agnew who is featured in his book. *The History of Wills Eye 1832-2012*, Valley Press, Inc., Bala Cynwyd, PA Sixth printing 2014. D. Hayes Agnew trained at Wills but still included a general surgical practice. He was a cousin of Dr. C. R. Agnew of New York.

Dr. Larry Schwab: A colleague more familiar with the eye needs of the developing world than anyone else known to this writer, Larry Schwab is unlike many who harden to the illnesses of the disadvantaged, their empathy wanes and those in need become statistics more than individuals. His books and his roles from teaching the care and prevention of eye disorders to his intense opposition to land mines constitute a mindset of noble and sincere commitment to his fellow man. Also a musician, he is a renaissance man in several regards and Larry has done honor to this book by offering suggestions, all of which were accepted.

The Johns Hopkins Alan Chesney Medical Archives: Much appreciation goes to Nancy McCall, Director of these archives and indeed the ideal person to lead a brilliant team dedicated to the preservation of an enormous amount of history otherwise difficult to discover or unavailable from other sources. What a gift that entity is to the preservation of what has gone before as an inspiration for what is still to come! And how fortunate it is to be directed by Ms. McCall.

Research Assistance: There is no secretary-assistant to thank, nor any other recording or compiling professional helper, and that is partly why this book has taken so long to complete-over two years. Help with chasing down references and looking up hard to find information came from Wayne Countryman. We were doing well with helpful input from him when illness required that he quit. Many medical papers and obituary reprints, newspaper clippings, old letters, photographs and personal letters in their envelopes have been used thanks to him.

Ophthalmologists' Input: Some of the story of Townley Paton has been previously published in a textbook both edited and written in part by Professor of Ophthalmology Mark Mannis and his son, Avi,[i] That valuable work consists of chapters dealing with the greats of corneal surgery. Most of the chapters are written by a selection of ophthalmologists with similar interests. The chapter about Townley was written by this writer, thus it has been poached in part with the permission of Professor Mannis. Avi was an important contributor to the authorship of that book as well as one of its compilers. He is now a senior vice-president of Hawaiian Airlines, an appointment level this writer would hope to emulate after comparable authorship were he not in the compulsory retirement category of top airlines.

This is the moment to mention that the Richard Townley Paton story has formerly been included without much detail in this writer's semi-autobiography, *Second Sight: Views From an Eye Doctor's Odyssey*, Create Space/Amazon, 2011, the "semi" referring to the fact that there was more life to follow when it was published, thus it is not recommended by this critic as worth the purchase price.

Finally as for the majority of writers today, thanks are also due for the sourcing and convenience of the vast and wonderful Internet, especially its priceless Wikipedia.

William F. Draper (1912-2003) is the artist who painted the book's cover painting which hangs in the Eye-Bank. His portraits include several American Presidents and national leaders of science, finance, military, and church. He is recipient of the Portrait Society of

ACKNOWLEDGMENTS

America's Gold Medal (1999) and examples of his work are easily found in the National Portrait Gallery in Washington.

<u>Brooke Hummer</u> is a very is a talented, accomplished and versatile professional photographer who took the photograph of the author shown on the back cover in her Chicago studio, snapping the shutter after throwing a scarf around his neck to spook him into smiling. She has a wrap-around technique that never fails. See for yourself on her website!

<u>Nancy Hardin</u> went over the manuscript from an axe to a nail clipper, chopping away overgrowths and finally pruning the minutiae. Her fast work was dogged by deadlines and mishaps with the manuscript. Working with a hoary writer is not a professional's dream, and she would have found a more sympathetic adjective. She is one of the finest editors and not responsible for any remaining deficiencies that may exist as this work is being rushed into print to meet an approaching deadline. Thank you, Nancy, most sincerely.

Along the way, corrective editing was also provided by numerous others, sometimes a chapter was helpfully abbreviated and in other instances dates were corrected or new names added. Some of these helpers have been mentioned but thanks are extended to those whose input is mistakenly overlooked at this last minute of finishing up.

<u>Photographs:</u> The following photographs were re-photographed by the author from medical books published by Professors Welch, Osler, Barker and Cushing in the early 1900s: The portrait of William S. Halsted; the up-close pictures of William Osler (and one with his son); and, a close-up of Clifford W. Beers. A close-up of Dr. Welch and another of him mounted on a small horse are

INSIGHT

all identified with the Johns Hopkins Medical Archives. *The Four Doctors* (a group portrait by John Singer Sargent, 1906, has been widely published.) The portrait itself is located in the Welch Medical Library where it still hangs today and is where this writer photographed it. The portrait photographs of William H. Wilmer and Professor Alan C. Woods were signed presentations to Dr. Townley Paton.

The early surgical photography setup of Professor Joaquin Barraquer operating in the 1940s was provided by Professor Barraquer and is published with his permission. A somewhat comparable photograph of Townley Paton operating was taken by a MEETH photographer, as was the photograph of Townley teaching in a clinic for ophthalmologists who were seeking to become keratoplasty surgeons. Both photographs have been published previously in hospital brochures and are published here with the encouragement of MEETH.

Several photographs and artists' renderings of Aida Root Breckinridge were provided with permission to publish by the Oren Root family.

The Southampton Hospital provided the group picture in Chapter 15. The before-and-after photos of an eye that received a corneal transplant were taken from Townley's textbook, "Keratoplasty," *The Blakiston Division, McGraw-Hill Book Company*, New York, 1955. Also from that source, the two drawings in the Epilogue are by Daisy Stillwell, medical illustrator. The photograph of a donor cornea prepared for surgery was provided by the Eye-Bank for Sight Restoration and used with the permission of its Executive Director and CEO, Ms Patricia Dahl.

ACKNOWLEDGMENTS

The photos showing the William Patons in Wyoming and Townley in Estes Park were provided by Rowena and Clifford Manuel of Shell, Wyoming. All other photographs were taken by family members, and used by permission.

Purveyor-in-Chief and Commanding Leader: The book was at risk of abandonment in early 2015 when a dear friend of this writer, Sheila Rogers, suggested that perhaps help could be found by Dennis Fabiszak, the highly acclaimed director of the East Hampton Library. Dennis, in turn, thought he might know of someone with enough heart and knowledge to salvage the book-writing of an historical nature. He contacted and may even have bribed Tom Clavin, a prolific and celebrated writer who at first expressed no interest in somebody else's book miseries. Then, unexplainably, he changed his mind, asking to have a look at what had been written.

The tide turned from dead low to a slow rise. Tom, in sheer kindness to a struggling lesser writer, decided he might be able to restore the energies of authorship with simple "buck-ups" plus curtailment of the writer's incessant detailing of details. Tom brought on board his good friend, Phil Keith, with a comparably earthy sense of how to negotiate the exasperating twists of a manuscript for publication. (It had been decided not even to try for publication by a mainstream publishing house because of the time that would require for a writer obsessively counting his years and because the income per book for the Eye-Bank would be higher from self-publication.) Hired, Tom and Phil were there when they were needed.

There was one fateful day when some of the book's guts were swept away while changing fonts. This resulted in the loss of references. No, there were neither identical file copies nor adequate notes helpful to the agonizing "surgical" replacement that gradually ensued. Tom suggested that it was fortunate new references and perhaps other thoughts might be better than the old ones — something like that. The manuscript dragged on in the technical tedium and in suboptimal satisfaction. On two occasions, estimated ETA's had to be deferred, the second in particular causing a highly deranging and embarrassing cancellation of its inauguration at the Wilmer Institute, resulting in a "writer's melancholia" and utterances filled with "bile and gas" only to be finally resolved upon the book's eventual arrival. Sometimes those medical diagnoses are needed to convey the agonies of literary process.

In the very last do-or-die days the book was "taken on" by Sheila Rogers, President of the Board of the East Hampton Library. Sheila became an instant benefactor, solving its publication issues, properly fixing the images, solving heading and page numbering problems and improving internal structuring — all in a two-day marathon. Again, only the use of the Mary Poppins metaphor (as used for Aida on page 212) is adequate description for Sheila's immediately inclusive role. She indeed must be credited with the book's final birthing.

The Lady Diane: She is this writer's young octogenarian wife, absolutely beautiful inside and out. In her career, she served three U.S. Presidents as the Executive Director of the President's Committee on the Arts and Humanities. With that snapshot of her background, it would be a correct guess that without her, this book would scarcely have left the brevity of a to-do list and later to survive a seemingly endless writer's amplification. Well before Sheila took on the terminal tasks, Diane was already pitching in relief. To help with the routines of copy editing, organizing and otherwise improving the

ACKNOWLEDGMENTS

text by judicious simplifications. Her basic approach was toward a better economy of words. For example, Diane in her executive capacity as advisor to Presidents might have suggested to President Lincoln upon writing his Gettysburg Address that he revise his talk with a concise opening sentence such as: *Eighty-seven years ago, our predecessors prioritized libertarian equality.* That abbreviated start is less than a third of the opening sentence that Lincoln squandered on a standing crowd of 15,000 people who were already weary and footloose from the verbose previous addresses.

Deep affection in the Paton family sometimes emerges in teasing, such as comments about Diane's succinct writing ability. She is one of the world's most capable and wonderful people who deserves more words but cloture is overdue. In this very serious and sensitive world, one only dares to hard-tease where the togetherness is strongest — with the one he loves the most.

INDEX

A

AAO 256
AAO Council 256
Aequanimitas 68, 85, 122, 136, 147, 164, 256, 264, 296
Agnew, Cornelius Rea 25, 26, 31, 38, 61, 62, 63, 64, 65, 67, 123, 137, 145, 147, 162, 184, 185, 194, 219, 225, 262, 264, 272, 280, 307
Agnew, D. Hyes MD 127, 307
Albert, Daniel, Dr. 146, 166, 221, 247, 267
Alienist 25, 71, 91, 106
Allen, John 30
Alton, L. 66
AMA .. 55, 61, 62, 63, 64, 65, 66, 67, 217, 226, 228, 217, 223, 262, 299, 300, 301
American Red Cross 226, 227, 226
Aphakic spectacles 156
Aristotle 125, 291
Armonk 184
Arruga, H, dr. 251
Asclepius 59, 66, 136
Astigmatism 291

B

Bacon, McNeil 187
Baker, Jean H. 103
Barker, Lewellys F. 26, 28, 31, 49, 77, 80, 81, 86, 95, 103, 117, 305
Barraquer, Joaquin Dr. .. 251, 283, 310
Bartlett, Donald 145
Batchelder, Nathaniel H. 110, 111

Beers, Clifford W 92, 93, 103, 310
Bernard, Peyton 246, 281
Bietti, G. Dr. 251
Blood banking 231
Bloomberg School of Public Health .... iii, 103, 285
Bogert, Edward 163
Brearley School 173, 174
Breckinridge, Aida 7, 9, 30 31, 126, 127, 128, 129, 130, 131, 132, 133, 134, 135, 138, 139, 140, 141, 142, 144, 145, 218, 219, 220, 221, 222, 223, 224, 225, 226, 232, 233, 234, 235, 258, 273, 290, 305
Brinkley, John R., Dr. 56, 57, 66
Bronson, Nathaniel R., Dr. 260, 266, 271, 280
Brown, Stewart I., Dr. 17, 66, 86, 267
Buckley School 174
Buxton, Jorge, Dr. 266

C

Caldwell, Delmar R., Dr. 267
Cambridge, UK .. 118, 119, 146, 169, 193
Cambridge Medical School .. 119, 170
Carrel, A. 86
Castroviejo, Ramon, Dr. 219, 220, 221, 230, 251
Cataract 155, 176, 300, 301
Chiropractic 53

INDEX

Clavin, Tom..................................311
Comfort, Nathaniel.................86, 103
Complicated Grief Disorder 277, 280
Corcoran, Kevin...................287, 303
Corneal transplant................14, 158, 223, 224, 228, 217, 226, 238, 284, 287, 288, 291........................
Council, AAO&O.................. 256
Curie, Pierre........................ 12
Cushing, Harvey William, Dr.......81, 82, 85, 86, 103, 116, 117, 249, 280, 305

D

Dahl, Patricia, Ms............................34
Darwin, Charles R. .... See
 Sir Francis 18, 52
Dawn Society 224, 225
DeVoe, Arthur G., Dr. 267
Dirigible..... 128, 129, 130, 132, 134, 258
Doctors Hospital, NYC 170
Dohlman, Claes H., Dr. 266, 289, 292, 306
Dohrn, Felix A..............................105
Dowbiggin, I.R..............................103
Doyle, Arthur Conan, Dr. 106
Draper, William P. 309
Duke-Elder, Sir Stewart 241
Dyslexia 117, 124, 230, 274, 277, 280

E

Earhart, Amelia............................129

EBAA .231, 257, 271, 287, 288, 289, 292, 300, 302, 303
Elitism in Medicine.................55
Elschnig, Anton, Dr............206, 213
Endothelium, cornea..............220
Endothelial keratoplasty.......291
Eugenics, epigenetics 86, 94-97
Euwer, Anthony H. 266
Eye-Bank 5, 8, 14, 15, 180, 222, 225, 231, 215, 217, 218, 220, 221, 222, 223, 225, 226, 228, 232, 234, 235, 236, 237, 238, 250, 256, 258, 259, 263, 264, 271, 273, 276, 277, 278, 279, 285, 286, 290, 291, 293, 300, 302, 305, 309
Eye-banking 8, 9, 10, 13, 15, 64, 87, 215, 222, 224, 226, 227, 230, 216, 222, 223, 224, 226, 233, 234, 235, 237, 238, 242, 251, 256, 257, 258, 264, 275, 278, 279, 282, 285, 286, 287, 290, 292, 302

F

Fabiszak, Dennis, ...311
Father of Eye Banking,
RT Paton...........................264, 270
Father of Gynecology,
Kelly.................................79
Father of Modern Medicine,
Osler 75
Father of Modern Surgery,
Halsted.. 77

315

Father of Neurosurgery,
Cushing 81
Father of Western Medicine,
Hippocrates...................................59
Farge, E.J.......................................231
Federal Trade Commission..........262
Fielding, Henry..............................87
Filatov, Vladimir P.Dr... 223, 231
Fine, Max., Dr..............................266
Fleetwood, Stephanie.......66, 306
Flexner, Abraham.....65, 82, 83, 85, 86, 98, 103, 144, 221, 305
Franceschetti, A.Dr.................251
Frissell, Toni.............................187

G

GAEBA................................288, 292
Garden Club of America.............254
Garfield, James A....................31, 126
Georgescu, P 31
Girard, Louis, Dr. 267
Glaucoma ... 139, 155, 159, 219, 258
Global Alliance of Eye Banks 290
Gonin, Jules................................156
Gracie Mansion, ...171
Green-Wood Cemetery........194, 272
Gruening, Earl, Dr.......................137
Guillaumat, L. 251

H

Hadeeth 231
Haggard, H.H 66
Halsey, Rosalie V. 22, 25, 26, 30, 31, 36, 70, 80, 81, 123
Halsted William S........26, 38, 77, 78, 79, 81, 156, 163, 272, 280, 305
Hanson, George...........................224

Hardin, Nancy..............................309
Harvard...116
Hemingway, Ernest......................268
Hippocrates..............59, 66, 152, 306
Hoffer, E...17
Hoffman, P. 144
Homberger, Julius, Dr..............54, 55
Hospital, Southampton................311
Homeopathy..................................53
Hoover, Herbert.................138, 141, 218, 221
Hummer, Brooke 309
Hurd, Henry Mills, Dr.............85, 93

I

Irving, Washington 7

J

James, William, Dr... 22, 23, 78, 106, 126, 224, 248
John Pierpont Morgan, Jr., ... 176
Johns Hopkins ..ii, iii, 26, 31, 33, 34, 50, 52, 62, 65, 67, 68, 69, 70, 71, 72, 73, 74, 75, 77, 78, 79, 81, 82, 83, 84, 85, 92, 93, 94, 95, 96, 98, 100, 101, 102, 103, 104, 105, 114, 116, 118, 119, 121, 122, 125, 126, 141, 142, 143, 144, 146, 148, 158, 161, 162, 164,169, 174, 218, 249, 264, 285, 305, 307
Johns Hopkins Chesney Medical Archives.................85, 305, 307
Johns Hopkins Medical School.. 114, 116, 118, 122, 146

INDEX

K

Katzin, Herbrt M., Dr..267, 300, 301

Kaufman, Herbert, Dr. 264, 266
Keith, Phil......................................312
Keller, Helen.................162, 195, 196
Kelly, Howard Atwood, Dr............79, 80, 114
Kelman, Charles, Dr......... 267
Keratoplasty.......... ..17, 87, 197, 219, 220, 222, 224, 227, 230, 222, 228, 236, 238, 251, 262, 264, 275, 283, 284, 285, 287, 289, 291, 296, 299, 300
Keratoprosthesis...................288, 289
Key, Francis Scott............................68
Khodadoust, Ali, Dr.....................267
King, John H., Dr...................154, 155, 245, 251, 266, 300
Kissam, Richard S., Dr........222, 223, 230
Knox, J.H.M....................................66
K-Pro..292
Kraepelin, Emil 43, 51

L

L'Esperance, Jr., Francis A.Dr. ...297
Lake Carnegie...............................107
Lamb, S.D.....................................103
Lamellar keratoplasty...................291
Latham, S.R....................................67
Laval, Joseph Dr. 297
Leeches...162
Lehr, Eleanor M. 216, 219
Lennon, Richard G., Dr. 260

Leopold, Irving, Dr. 267
Lindbergh, Charles 123, 133, 145, 150
Long Island University................. 265
Loomis, Academy....... 108, 109, 110, 112, 123
Lord Chesterfield 55
Lord Grey..................................... 139

M

Mainbocher......................... 181, 182
Mamelok, Alfred E. Dr. 296
Manhattan Eye, Ear and Throat Hospital, MEETH 6, 218, 230, 267
Manuel, Clifford & Rowen..........304
Maran, Donald.....................259, 280
Maumenee, A. E. Dr.....................17, 160, 163, 264
Manni, Mark Dr. & Ari 308
Mawas, J.......................................251
McCall, Nancy 307
McFarlane, Doanlad C. Dr 293
McKinley, William.............138, 151
McLean, John M., Dr........221, 222, 230, 299
Meadow Club, Southampton...261
MEETH 171, 219, 221, 222, 230, 215, 219, 222, 226, 235, 263, 264, 267, 295, 296
Mehra, Torab, Dr.......................242
Meserve, Edith............ 173, 180, 24
Meserve, Frederick H.........172, 173
Meserve, Helen (Paton).....115, 121, 172, 173, 180, 248, 271

Meyer, Adolf, Dr..............93, 94, 95, 98, 103
Mick, Noel................302
Milbank, Albert.......142, 221, 222
Moran, Gussie.................187, 269
Moreono, J.Dr. 251
Moria microkeratome............291
Morgan, John Pierpont Morgan, Jr 57, 150, 176, 177

N

Newell, Frank, Dr. 256

O

O'Neil, Patricia...................... 8, 302
Ophthalmic surgical microscopy .282
Ophthalmology 9, 31, 54, 64, 67, 114, 122, 137, 142, 143, 157, 162, 164, 217, 226, 238, 241, 260, 275, 282, 292, 294, 306
Ophthalmology Congress.............238
Ophthalmoscope 157
Osler, Edward Revere 76
Osler William, Dr., Sir 26, 31, 38, 65, 68, 70, 71, 72, 75, 76, 77, 80, 81, 84, 85, 86, 104, 105, 117, 136, 147, 249, 251, 264, 270, 280, 296, 305
Ossining Historical Society.......8, 235
Osteopathy..53

P

Paton, David Townley 303
Paton, Diane 304, 313
Paton, Pamela 149, 185, 247

Paton, F.Margaret. 25, 36, 42, 70, 94 25, 26, 28, 30, 31, 36, .37- 40-42, 48, 51,70, 73, 77, 79, 80, 83, 93-95, 97,103, 105, 106, 163, 190, 194, 239, 272,
Paton, Stewart 25, 35, 37, 38, 39, 41, 42, 43, 44, 45, 48, 49, 51, 65, 70, 71-77, 80, 83, 84, 85, 87, 88-116, 123, 137, 144, 171, 190-194, 217, 241, 266, 272, 277, 280, 285, 305
Paufique, L. Dr. 251, 296
Peri-ocular draping..................... 230
Phacoemulsification 267
Phipps, Henry 72, 93, 98, 103
Phipps Psychiatric Clinic 98
Pizzarello,. Dr. Louis 269
PMMA implants......................... 289
Potter, H. C................................. 296
Pope Pius XII........................228, 231
Powell, Pualus Pease, Adm..... 25, 43, 51, 145
Prajadhipok, King of Siam Rana VII 54, 155
Princeton Univ..... 25, 30, 31, 48, 51, 71, 73, 75, 92, 93, 107, 108, 109, 112, 113, 114, 116, 119, 123, 149, 162, 163, 169, 190, 251
Prisoners, donated eyes of........... 235
  see also Preface
Post traumatic stress.....................277
Potter, H. C. 296

R

Randolph, M.E Dr. 144, 145, 162
Reader's Digest.................... 225, 235
Regan, Jr., William F. Dr. 295
Reimer, Otto B........................... 295

INDEX

Revere, Paul 76
Rhee, Michelle K. Dr...........291, 302
Richard, Auguste 295
Ritterband, David Dr..................302
Roberts, A.....................................30
Rockefeller, Nelson A.............57, 74, 83, 94, 95, 142, 294
Roelker, Roberta..........................115
Rogers, B.O...........................230, 267
Rogers, Sheila..............................311
Roosevelt Field............................123
Roosevelt, Theodore.............94, 145, 197, 221
Root, Elihu..................................145
Root, Oren, Jr...............31, 126, 139, 140, 144, 145, 219, 305, 306
Rosen, G..............................67, 230
Ruit, Sanduk..............................291

S

Santos=Dumont, Alberto ...129, 131, 133, 144
Sargent, John Singer79, 86, 134, 310
Scheie, Harold B...........................294
Schwab, Larry Dr. 307
Scott, Eugene (Butch).............68, 187
Sculley, John, Jr............................187
Shah of Iran.................244, 245, 246
Sheppard and Enoch Pratt Hospital 71
Sigmund Freud, Dr..................51, 85
Sing Sing........................3, 1, 2, 4, 7, 225, 217, 235, 244

Smith, Frank R., Dr................49, 50, 163, 224, 225, 300
Snyder, C 66
Sommer, Alfred, Dr.......................iii
Sourdille, M. Dr..........................251
Southampton College..................265
Southampton Garden Club.........254
Southampton Hospital........260, 266, 269, 270
Spring Point, St. James................186, 188, 190, 194, 128, 186, 192, 196, 247, 248
St. Louis Post-Dispatch.................225
Starr, P..66
Staten Island, NY Advance..........231
Stavely, Anne.................................35
Stern, A.M...................................103
Sterne, Laurence..............................9
Stout, Timothy Dr.......................307

Surgical eye removals....................235

T

Taft, William Howard......... 138, 151
Tarkington, Booth 138, 151
Tasman, William Dr....................307
Theodore, Frederick H. J.Dr.......294
Tilney, Joan Paton.......122, 124, 174, 185, 246, 248, 270, 271, 304
Towneley Hall........................21, 30
Trachoma............................242, 251
Trephining..................................155
Trief, Danielle Dr. 302
Trist, E. L....................................292
Troutman, Richard C., Dr 266, 306

319

INSIGHT

Tucker, A. 85
Turtz, Arnold I. Dr. 294
Twain, Mark.....See Samuel Clemens

U

University of Maryland Hospital..158
University of Pennsylvania Medical School 84

V

Vail, Derrick, Dr. 232, 236, 275
Villa de Tunlay 30

W

Wainwright, Betsy Trippe (DeVecchi) 298
Warner, J.H 67
Washington, George...26, 53, 66, 70, 113, 114, 137, 138, 139, 140, 142, 160, 161, 163, 175, 231, 287, 300, 309
Watts, Jr., Edward E. 293
Weisenfeld, Mildred 298
Welch, William H. Dr. 41, 65, 70, 71, 72, 73, 74, 75, 76, 77, 78, 79, 83, 85, 93, 94, 95, 98, 142, 144, 145, 150, 160, 162, 267, 285, 305, 310

Wheeler, John M., Dr.154, 155, 163, 251
Wiedman, Michael Dr. 297
Wisesenfeld, Mildred....................298
Wilhelmus, Kirk Dr. 307
Williams, Noel.............................304
Wilder, Sampson V. S.......22, 23, 24, 25, 30
Williams, Noel B.............30, 81, 145, 162, 304
Wilmer, William H. , Dr........ii, 113, 114, 122, 124, 126, 135- 137, 138- 165, 169, 174, 177, 184, 221, 218, 222, 228, 245, 251, 275, 301, 305- 307
Wilson, Woodrow..........................75
Woods, Alan, C. Dr.............160, 310
Wordsworth, William....................68
Wright, Orville..............................144

Y

Yeats, William Butler.................. 215

Z

Zeitgeist 72, 166
Zimmerman, Lorenz E., Dr. 266, 297
Zirm, Eduard Dr. 206

INDEX

[i] Mannis, M.J. and Mannis, A.A.: *Corneal Transplantation: A History in Profiles*. J. P. Wayenborgh, Belgium, 1999.

Made in the USA
Charleston, SC
03 October 2016